MILLER CENTER SERIES ON THE AMERICAN PRESIDENCY

A Tale of
Two Agencies

A Tale
of Two
Agencies

A Comparative Analysis of
the General Accounting
Office and the Office of
Management and Budget

Frederick C. Mosher

LOUISIANA STATE
UNIVERSITY PRESS
BATON ROUGE AND LONDON

LIBRARY OF CONGRESS CATALOGING IN
PUBLICATION DATA

Mosher, Frederick C.
    A tale of two agencies.

    (Miller Center series on the American
presidency)
    Bibliography: p.
    Includes index.
    1. United States.   General Accounting
Office.   2. United States.   Office of Man-
agement and Budget.
I. Title.   II. Series.
HJ9802.M682   1983   353.0071   83-10634
ISBN 0-8071-1115-5

For those men and women who through their careers in public service contribute beyond measure to the safety and welfare of the people of America and the world

 The double ax (the labrys), one of
the distinctive artifacts of Minoan
civilization during the second and
third millennia before Christ, served
a variety of symbolic as well as dec-
orative purposes: protective, sexual,
mainly sacred. It may also have had
more practical uses such as in the
destruction of wild bulls or mytho-
logical purposes such as the opening
of the pregnant skull of Zeus to re-
lease the goddess Athena. In these
senses, the ax may not seem an appropriate logo for this book. Yet,
both of the governmental agencies
treated here grew from, and were attached to, a foundation of law and
ideals that was very nearly a secular
religion. And ax blades, like these
agencies, were intended to cut. The
representation shown here is of a
golden votive double ax uncovered
in the palace at Knossos, Crete, now
in the Museum of Fine Arts,
Boston.

Contents

Illustrations

Tables

Foreword

With this book, the Miller Center of Public Affairs at the University of Virginia continues a sponsored series of analytic works on the American presidency.

These works represent the scholarship of those whose research and writing have been encouraged by the center and who have participated as visiting scholars in the center's Program on the Presidency. Through this program, the center undertakes to contribute to the building of a new science of the presidency for our time. The focus is on the study of the organs and philosophies of central power and leadership in the American constitutional system; the underlying concern is how to reconcile the need for effective central leadership with the constitutional imperatives of limited government and divided but shared power—particularly under the twentieth-century conditions. Three main areas of inquiry are embraced in the center's presidency program. One is concerned with the nature and purposes of the presidency as an instrumentality of governance and of leadership in its larger institutional, political, cultural, and historical setting. A second area of inquiry concentrates on particular problems in which the presidency is deeply involved or which carry far-reaching implications for the conduct and organization of the office. A third area of inquiry concentrates on the study of individual presidencies to learn what lessons may be drawn from the past.

Frederick C. Mosher has been associated with the Miller Center since 1978 and has been White Burkett Miller Professor of Government and Foreign Affairs since 1980. He came to the University of Virginia following a distinguished career at the University of California at Berkeley and at Syracuse University. A prolific writer on problems of government and public administration in such classic works as *Democracy and the Public Service* and *The GAO: The Quest for Accountability in American Government*, Mosher also served as staff director of the Herter Committee on Foreign Affairs Personnel and associate director of the Division of Organization of the U.S. Department of State.

In the present volume, *A Tale of Two Agencies: A Comparative Analysis of the General Accounting Office and the Office of Management and Budget*, Professor Mosher examines the role of two different agencies that exercise administrative and financial control within the American political system. No other authority has undertaken a comparative analysis and evaluation of the two institutions of this scope and character. Dr. Mosher draws on a lifetime of scholarship and practical experience in a work that culminates his enormously productive intellectual journey. Not only does he sketch in the historical background of the two agencies, but he brings the story up to date through the first year of the Reagan administration. Mosher's demonstrated mastery of his subject does not preclude the play of imagination and wit as in such chapter and section titles as "The Born-Again General Accounting Office" and "Genesis and Exodus: The Budget and Accounting Act of 1921."

No one who has admired Professor Mosher as the doyen of American public administration scholars will be surprised to learn that as he approaches his seventieth birthday, he is hard at work on another crucial problem in American government: presidential transitions and their effect on foreign policymaking.

KENNETH W. THOMPSON, Director,
Miller Center of Public Affairs
JAMES STERLING YOUNG, Director
of the Program on the Presidency

Preface and
Acknowledgments

The idea of this study was planted during the latter 1970s when the author undertook an investigation of the history and current situation of the United States General Accounting Office (GAO). The result was published as *The GAO: The Quest for Accountability in American Government* (Boulder, Colorado: Westview Press, 1979). It seemed at the time that a review of the likenesses and differences in the development of that organization and of the Bureau of the Budget (BoB), later renamed the Office of Management and Budget (OMB), would provide an interesting and illuminating contribution to our understanding of the workings of government in this country. The two agencies were born at the same time, of the same philosophy of government and society, and with compatible, if not identical, goals. Their responsibilities and methods were, on the other hand, quite different, as were their leadership, the nature of their personnel, and their constituencies.

One of them, the Bureau of the Budget, was from its beginning a principal staff arm of the president, though in a rather narrow context; its scope was vastly increased after it reached adulthood at age eighteen. The other, the General Accounting Office, began as a virtually independent organization but after World War II became increasingly a staff arm for the Congress. The study of the two together provides insights about the modern evolution of both the presidency and the Congress and also about the complexities of the relations between the two. Students of organization will be interested in the ways in which the two agencies have responded to external influences, in the stresses and strains of their internal structures and cultures, and particularly in their contrasting modes of, and problems in, bringing about basic internal changes.

A pervasive problem of both these agencies, and indeed the underlying theme of this book, is the maintenance of continuity, expertise, and credibility on the one hand and of political responsiveness on the other: in short, the relating within the same organization of professionalism and politics without damage to either. Such coexistence must be a common problem in those public agencies that require much knowledge and skill and whose costs and outputs are of public concern and controversial. Indeed, it must be a pervasive problem of government in all the developed and developing countries of the world. In the two agencies considered in this study, it is particularly acute. Both have from their beginnings been staffed principally by career personnel

who expect to survive political and partisan shifts, and both have for at least
the last thirty years considered themselves, and been considered, professional. Yet, the work substance of each is the very stuff of politics—public
policies and programs, the receipt and allocation and application of public
moneys, the ethics of public officials. And each works for one of the two principal foci of American partisanship—the Congress and the presidency.

This book is roughly historical and chronological in its organization. But it
is not truly a history. It has long seemed to me that the understanding of our
present situation and problems requires some understanding of their roots and
stems, of how we got this way. I have therefore selected and emphasized from
the past what appeared to be key persons, key events, and key issues that
would shed light on the situation today and in the future. A full history would
be ten or a hundred times more inclusive.

Information for this study has been drawn from written materials, both primary and secondary; interviews with official participants and outsiders; and
meetings attended by the author as participant, consultant, or observer. For
the earlier years, fairly heavy reliance was placed upon original documents:
statutes, budgets, congressional hearings, records of meetings such as those
of the Business Organization of the Government, and reports of both GAO
and BoB. There have been a great many articles written about the budget
agency, somewhat fewer about GAO. Probably the best single introduction to
the Bureau of the Budget is the semiautobiographical account by its first director, Charles G. Dawes—*The First Year of the Budget of the United States*
(New York: Harper, 1923). Percival F. Brundage, a budget director during the
Eisenhower administration, wrote a book entitled *The Bureau of the Budget*
(New York: Praeger, 1970). The best recent book on the subject is Larry Berman's *The Office of Management and Budget and the Presidency, 1921–1979*
(Princeton: Princeton University Press, 1979).

For many years, the principal work about the GAO was Harvey C. Mansfield's *The Comptroller General: A Study in the Law and Practice of Financial Administration* (New Haven: Yale University Press, 1939). In the last few
years, there have been three other general books on that organization: the one
mentioned above by the present author; another in the same year by Joseph
Pois, *Watchdog on the Potomac: A Study of the Comptroller General of the
United States* (Washington, D.C.: University Press of America, 1979); and
most recently, *GAO 1966–1981: An Administrative History* (Washington,
D.C.: U.S. Government Printing Office, 1981) by Roger L. Sperry and
others. In addition, there has been a large amount of other material published
or issued relevant to both agencies as chapters in other books, case studies,
articles, monographs, dissertations, speeches, and oral histories. A highly se-

lected bibliography of these works, as well as of official documents concerning the agencies, is included at the end of this book.

During the course of my study of the GAO a few years ago, I interviewed most of the upper-level officials of that agency and a substantial number of employees and outsiders familiar with its work. I was privileged to attend a number of staff meetings of various kinds and was aided throughout by a panel, formed for the purpose, of knowledgeable persons from Congress, academia, and the business world. Since then, I have talked with a number of GAO officials with reference to the current book and have also participated in the semiannual meetings of its Educator Consultant Panel. My recent field-work has included a number of extensive interviews with current and former officials of the Bureau of the Budget and the Office of Management and Budget. As a consultant to the panel of the National Academy of Public Administration that prepared a report entitled *A Presidency for the 1980s*, I participated in all of its meetings and many meetings of its staff. These included testimony by, and a great deal of discussion with, OMB officials about their agency's role and problems. Indeed, several members of the panel had at one time directed or worked in that agency.

I am grateful to all of those who gave of their time, their knowledge, and their wisdom for this enterprise. And I am particularly indebted to several persons—scholars, practitioners, and in a few cases both—who read all or a major part of an earlier draft of the manuscript and criticized it with care and with candor. They have included James W. Fesler, Cowles Professor Emeritus, Yale University; Harry S. Havens, Assistant Comptroller General of GAO and former branch chief, Office of Management and Budget; Philip S. Hughes, former Assistant Comptroller General of GAO, former Deputy Director of the Budget, and presently Undersecretary, Smithsonian Institution; Roger W. Jones, former Deputy Director of the Budget and former Chairman, U.S. Civil Service Commission; Dale McOmber, former Assistant Director of the Budget for Budget Review; Thomas D. Morris, former Assistant Comptroller General of GAO and former Assistant Director of the Budget for Management and Organization; Elmer B. Staats, former Comptroller General of GAO and former Deputy Director of the Budget; Dwight Waldo, Professor Emeritus, Syracuse University; James S. Young, Director of the Presidency Program, Miller Center of Public Affairs, and Professor, University of Virginia; John D. Young, former division director and chairman of organizational self-study, Bureau of the Budget and Office of Management and Budget. The titles listed are intended to indicate only each man's proximity to, and knowledge of, the agencies discussed herein. All these men have held a variety of other positions, some more prestigious than those given here. Their comments have greatly enriched this book, and they have also helped me avoid at least some of my errors. I also owe a debt of thanks for the consistently helpful service of the public documents staff of Alderman Library at the University of Virginia.

My greatest obligation is to my colleague and graduate assistant, Max O. Stephenson, Jr., who has accompanied and helped me all the way down this tortuous path. It could not have been done without him.

This study has been sponsored and supported by the White Burkett Miller Center of Public Affairs at the University of Virginia. I, of course, bear full responsibility for its content.

Chronology

1789   The Treasury Act directs the secretary of the treasury both "to digest plans for the improvement and management of the revenue, and for the support of the public credit . . . and to prepare and report estimates of the public revenue, and the public expenditures"; Congress establishes the offices of comptroller, auditor, register, and treasurer and authorizes a system for issuing appropriations warrants and for federal accounting and auditing.

1800   Congress directs the secretary of the treasury to provide annually a report on finance, containing "estimates of the public revenues and public expenditures" and "plans for improving and increasing the revenues from time to time."

1809   Congress specifies that all proposed expenditures must be made for their stated purpose only and no other.

1817   Congress recentralizes all federal audit and claims functions in the Treasury Department.

1865   House transfers some responsibilities over appropriations from the Committee on Ways and Means to a new standing Committee on Appropriations.

1868   Congress declares acts of the comptroller "final and conclusive upon the executive branch of the government."

1877–1885   House transfers jurisdiction for appropriations from Appropriations Committee to legislative committees on rivers and harbors, agriculture, army, navy, post office, and others.

1894   The Dockery Act, enacted by Congress following the recommendations of the Dockery-Cockrell commission, provides for complete control of accounting and auditing functions by the comptroller of the treasury and for a revised federal financial system.

1905–1906   Antideficiency Acts require agency heads to control expenditures through apportionments.

1909   The Sundry Civil Appropriation Act makes the president responsible for recommending to Congress the means by which the annual expenditure estimates might be brought within estimated revenues.

1912   President Taft embraces the findings and recommendations of his Commission on Economy and Efficiency's report, *The Need for a National Budget*.

1916   The Bureau of Efficiency is established; both major political parties include calls for a national budget system in their platforms.

1919   Each house of Congress establishes a Select Committee on the Budget; the House committee holds extensive hearings on that subject.

1920   House integrates appropriations in a single committee; Congress passes
       a Budget Act creating a budget agency for the president and an accounting
       office independent of the executive branch; President Wilson vetoes it be-
       cause of constitutional objections.
1921   President Warren G. Harding signs the Budget and Accounting Act of
       1921 establishing an executive budget system, the Bureau of the Budget in
       the Treasury Department, and the General Accounting Office; he appoints
       Brigadier General Charles G. Dawes the first director of the Bureau of the
       Budget and J. Raymond McCarl as comptroller general; President Harding,
       by executive orders, authorizes the director of the budget to "assemble,
       revise, reduce or increase the estimates of the departments or establish-
       ments as submitted to the Bureau"; he establishes the Federal Coordinating
       Service and authorizes the Bureau of the Budget to review and clear pro-
       posed legislation.
1922   Senate integrates appropriations in a single committee.
1933   The Bureau of Efficiency and the Federal Coordinating Service are
       abolished; an executive order by President Roosevelt centralizes powers
       over apportionment in the Bureau of the Budget.
1937   The report of the President's Committee on Administrative Manage-
       ment is released.
1938   Daniel W. Bell, acting director of the Bureau of the Budget, proposes
       a realignment and expansion of bureau organization and activities.
1939   President Roosevelt appoints Harold D. Smith director of the budget;
       Smith implements Bell's proposal; Reorganization Plan No. 1 transfers the
       Bureau of the Budget to the newly created Executive Office of the Presi-
       dent; Executive Order 8248 specifies the functions of the bureau.
1940   Congressman Lindsay Warren is appointed comptroller general.
1942   GAO establishes War Contract Project Audit Section to provide site
       audits at the plants of war contractors.
1943   The Bureau of the Budget establishes the first of four field offices.
1945   The Government Corporation Control Act extends BoB review of
       budgets and GAO commercial audits to government corporations; Con-
       gress describes GAO as part of the legislative branch in the Reorganization
       Act of 1945.
1947   The Bureau of the Budget, GAO, and Treasury Department collabo-
       rate in forming a Joint Accounting Improvement Program (later called Joint
       Financial Management Improvement Program, JFMIP), and GAO forms
       an Accounting Systems Division.
1949   The first Hoover commission recommends performance budgets;
       GAO begins "comprehensive audits" for all departments and agencies of

the federal government and virtually abolishes the longtime functions of bookkeeping and voucher examination.

1950   Congress enacts the first major revision of the 1921 act, the Budget and Accounting Procedures Act of 1950, which provided for a performance budget, better administration of executive agencies, integration of statistical activities, and a continuous program for the improvement of accounting and financial reporting throughout the government. The act assigns primary responsibility for accounting and internal auditing to government agencies and for standard-setting and legislative monitoring to GAO.

1952–1953   Bureau of the Budget reorganizes to provide integrated divisions on a program basis; GAO establishes its first overseas office; BoB undergoes first transition from Democratic to Republican leadership; new administration abolishes its field offices.

1954   Following Lindsay Warren's resignation, President Eisenhower nominates Joseph Campbell to be comptroller general, the first certified public accountant to head the General Accounting Office.

1955   The second Hoover commission emphasizes accounting and costing to implement performance budget and strengthening of accounting function in Budget Bureau.

1965   The House Government Operations Subcommittee under Representative Chet Holifield holds hearings on GAO audits of defense contractors and issues a critical report.

1966   President Johnson names longtime Deputy Budget Bureau Director Elmer B. Staats to be comptroller general.

1967   President Johnson's Task Force on Government Organization, chaired by Ben Heineman, submits final report on reorganization of the Executive Office of the President, including the Bureau of the Budget; Congress requires GAO to make its first major program evaluation of the poverty program.

1970   On the basis of the final report of the Ash Council, Reorganization Plan No. 2 of 1970 establishes the Office of Management and Budget to succeed the Bureau of the Budget; the Legislative Reorganization Act of 1970 calls upon GAO to perform cost-benefit analyses of federal programs and OMB and GAO jointly to establish a standardized information and data-processing system for budgetary and fiscal information.

1971–1972   GAO organizes on a program basis roughly comparable to the 1952 BoB reorganization.

1974   Congress requires advice and consent of the Senate for future appointments to the offices of director and deputy director of OMB; Congressional Budget and Impoundment Control Act establishes the Congressional Budget Office, prescribes new congressional procedure for handling budget, and imposes greatly expanded duties upon both OMB and GAO; the Office of Federal Procurement Policy Act establishes a quasi-independent Office of Federal Procurement Policy (OFPP) within the Office of Management and Budget with a separate statutorily mandated assistant director responsible for its activities; President Nixon resigns.

1978   President Carter by executive order assigns the director of OMB responsibilities for management and oversight of the government-wide regulatory improvement program.

1980   The GAO Personnel Act permits GAO to establish a personnel system independent of the classified service overseen by the Office of Personnel Management; the Paperwork Reduction Act establishes a new unit, the Office of Information and Regulatory Affairs, in the Office of Management and Budget and strengthens the OMB role in reducing the paperwork burden imposed on the public by the federal government.

1981   Incoming Reagan administration appoints David Stockman director of OMB; he launches drastic budgetary cuts through use of Reconciliation Act of 1981; Comptroller General Staats completes his term in office and is succeeded by Charles Bowsher, a certified public accountant; President Reagan signs Executive Order No. 12291, which further strengthens OMB's role in regulation control and review.

A Tale of
Two Agencies

INTRODUCTION

The Agencies and Their Changing Milieu

This power over the purse may, in fact, be regarded as the most complete and effectual weapon with which any constitution can arm the immediate representatives of the people.

JAMES MADISON, 1778

Energy in the Executive is a leading character in the definition of good government.

ALEXANDER HAMILTON, 1778

On June 10, 1921, President Warrren G. Harding signed into law the Budget and Accounting Act (Public Law 67-13), which gave the nation an executive budget system and two new agencies, the Bureau of the Budget (BoB), and the General Accounting Office (GAO). The agencies were twins, born at the same time to the same parents (Congress and the president) following the same nine-year pregnancy. They were conceived in the same social milieu, and their purposes, as originally envisioned, were roughly consonant. But they were not identical twins, far from it. Most of the responsibilities of one (the GAO) were in fact very old before it was born, whereas the other (BoB) was truly a newcomer. Even ten years after their birth, the former was forty times the size of the latter, and it remains, after sixty years, about nine times as large. Their personalities came to differ as much as their sizes and other physical characteristics. And over the six decades of their growth and maturation, like a lot of other twins, the two were only in rather limited ways friendly and respectful toward each other.

The General Accounting Office was basically the product of a simple transfer of certain powers, responsibilities, and resources from an executive department (Treasury) to independent and congressional status. A few new responsibilities were added—such as the supervision of agency accounting systems—but the main GAO mission was a continuation of that given the Treasury Department by the First Congress of the Republic in 1789: to assure that the financial transactions of the United States government were proper, accurate, and legal.[1]

That mission was not greatly altered by the 1921 law; its executor simply became independent and partially legislative rather than executive, a situation that led to bitter controversy over the first half of GAO's history. In fact, its powers have not been greatly changed since 1921, but the original functions and the methods by which they are exercised have undergone two revolutions and are virtually unrecognizable today. GAO has become a large, pragmatic research organization, studying the organizations, policies, programs, operations, and effectiveness of the government and issuing reports and recommendations thereon.

From its beginning, the Bureau of the Budget, whose name was changed in 1970 to the Office of Management and Budget (OMB), has been one of the principal support agencies directly responsible to the president, usually the major one with a permanent staff and the only one, other than the White House staff, with generalized jurisdiction.[2] This was true even when it was officially and physically a part of the Department of the Treasury between 1921 and 1939. From its beginning it had responsibility for putting together, publishing, and supervising the *Budget of the United States* on behalf of the president. Almost from the start it was also concerned with the coordination and clearance of proposed legislation and agency comments and presidential action thereon. Since the late 1930s, it has been variously involved in questions of management and organization of the executive branch, but the nature and extent of such involvement have fluctuated and remain a major debating point. Many other functions have come and gone, and a few have returned. Perceptions of BoB/OMB have varied all the way from one of a simple budget-accounting agency with exclusive interest in numbers of dollars to another view that it is the general staff of the president, involved on his behalf in every major problem and policy of the executive branch.

The BoB/OMB has long—indeed from its very beginning—been regarded as one of the most powerful institutions in the federal government. The record of the General Accounting Office has been less consistent in this regard, and there is less agreement about it among observers today. But that it has had influence back to and before the New Deal and that its influence has been growing over the last twenty to twenty-five years can hardly be questioned. Its power is less immediate and less clear, particularly to officials within the ex-

1. See the Act to Establish the Treasury Department, Public Law 1-12, September 2, 1789.
2. In subsequent pages, BoB and OMB will be referred to by their single names when discussed in their separate time periods. When the organization is treated through time, it will be designated BoB/OMB.

ecutive branch. But it is one of the few major institutional tools of the Congress. And except for the unusual prominence of OMB and its director during the first year of the Reagan administration, its products—testimony, reports, recommendations—reach the media and the public far more frequently than do those of the OMB. Its indirect and long-range impact may be very great indeed, even if immeasurable.

There has been a considerable literature about BoB and OMB, mainly articles and brief studies, but rather few books. Until quite recently, there was little literature about the GAO, which publishes an enormous amount of literature, but not about itself.[3] It is interesting and also symptomatic that no one to my knowledge has undertaken to describe and analyze these two agencies, the twins, *together*: their histories within the temporal contexts of American society and its problems; their organizations and personnel; their relationships with the president and his executive office, with the Congress, with federal agencies both off- and on-budget, and with each other. Few scholars who have studied BoB/OMB have looked at the GAO, and vice versa. Very possibly, students of government have carried the separation of powers too far into their own research. Until about fifteen years ago, there was rather little interchange in personnel among the leaders of the two agencies, so that few could comment about their observations and experiences in both. This has been partly corrected recently, mainly by the movement of high officials of BoB/OMB into GAO, though seldom the reverse.[4] So we may before long benefit from their insights about the two agencies. In the meantime, I undertake in this study to summarize the parallel origins and development of the two and to offer some reflections on the influences that affected that development, their likenesses and differences, their problems, and most of all, their significance in the American system of government.

In some ways, and apart from the obvious differences between the presidency and the Congress, these agencies are the most striking yet enduring institutional expressions of the separation between the executive and legislative powers in the national government.[5] Both grew out of an issue as to presidential-congressional powers with respect to finances that has been fes-

3. For fuller, though still brief, discussion of the literature about both agencies, see the Preface and Acknowledgments.

4. Undoubtedly the most prominent example is Elmer B. Staats, who served as deputy director of BoB under four presidents (Truman to Johnson) and then as comptroller general during five presidencies or parts thereof (Johnson to Reagan). Others have included Harry Havens, Philip S. Hughes, and Thomas D. Morris, all of whom held high offices in BoB/OMB and later became assistant comptrollers general in GAO.

5. The Congressional Budget Office (CBO) might offer a similar contrasting posture relative to the OMB, but it is relatively young, and its experience is not yet as rich as that of the GAO.

tering ever since the Constitution was drafted in 1787 and that even then had precedents in British and colonial times. The Bureau of the Budget was set up as, and has always been regarded as, primarily a *presidential* agency. But not exclusively so. Although expected from the beginning to report directly to the president, it was originally a bureau in the Department of the Treasury. Even after it became a central element in the Executive Office of the President in 1939, its dependence on the president was not total; Congress continued to control its resources, to a varying extent its policies, and its powers and responsibilities. In 1973, when an irate Congress insisted that the director and deputy director of the OMB be appointed subject to confirmation by the Senate, that action further diminished the immediate dependence of the agency upon the president.

On the other hand, the General Accounting Office was conceived and established as primarily a congressional agency or at least as one outside the executive branch. It was given independent powers for which it accounts only to the deity and most of which it seldom exercises—at least in the last several decades. It is dependent on the Congress for its resources, powers, and responsibilities, though it has long had rather unusual freedom in planning and directing its work. It was not until 1945 that Congress in legislation declared that it was "part of the legislative branch."[6] Its head and his first assistant, the comptroller general and his deputy, are appointed by the president, subject to confirmation by the Senate. But unlike the director of OMB and virtually all other presidential appointments in the executive branch, they have long, fixed terms of fifteen years and are practically irremovable. None has ever been removed against his will. This means among other things that, once appointed, a comptroller general is unlikely to be subjected to official pressure from a president or others in his executive office. Some comptrollers general in the past have deliberately avoided contacts with high officials in the executive branch, and their contacts with presidents have been infrequent.

The contrasting conditions of their appointment and removal have led to astonishing differences between budget directors and comptrollers general in terms of lengths of service and continuity. In their first sixty years (from July 1, 1921) there were twenty-five directors of the budget, each with an average tenure of about two and a half years. In the same period, there were a total of five comptrollers general, each with an average tenure of about eleven years. Every incoming president of a different political party from his predecessor has almost immediately appointed a new budget director, and most of them have appointed one to three succeeding budget directors. Only President

6. Reorganization Act, Public Law 79-263, December 20, 1945.

Coolidge never appointed a new budget director. In this sixty-year span, only four of eleven presidents (not including President Reagan) had an opportunity to appoint even one comptroller general: Presidents Harding, Roosevelt (who appointed two), Eisenhower, and Johnson. The vast differences in length of tenure have had a major impact on the nature of the two agencies, their political postures, their adaptation to change, and their internal modes of operating.

These two agencies work primarily for two of the most political institutions in this nation or in any nation: the president and the Congress of the United States. There are many connotations to the word *political*—party, interest group, policy, ideology—and I refer to all of them. But the laurels of both agencies have rested for much of their histories on their neutrality, their objectivity, and their professional competence. Most of their staffs have from the beginning been career employees who could survive partisan or ideological changes without threat to their jobs. But the balance between neutrality and responsiveness to political change is a fragile one, requiring appropriate protective legislation and sensitive management at the top. For both agencies, though in different ways, this has been a recurring problem. It is a central theme of this study.

The Changing Context as They Grew

It requires no particular originality or insight to observe that the six decades since 1921 have witnessed tremendous changes in the world, in the society, and in government, and these changes have been paralleled or followed in these two agencies. Indeed, it is remarkable and a bit unfortunate that the titles of the comptroller general and his GAO remain as they were at the beginning for they are, and were then, misleading indicators of what they do. It took nearly half a century before BoB's name was changed to OMB, which some people today think is also a misnomer. In fact, the nature and the functions of GAO have been more completely transformed since 1921 than have those of BoB/OMB. The latter's responsibilities have always been tied to the budget and the processes utilized in its formulation and execution. Although different presidents have used the agency in different ways, it has always been close to the presidency and derives most of its influence and clout from that office.

Many of the most basic changes in these two agencies were responses, sometimes slow, to changes in the society and its values, in technology, in the role and responsibilities of American governments and particularly the federal government itself, in the economy, and in our international relations. In other words, the changes within the agencies often resulted from forces and conditions exogenous to them. To a considerable degree, therefore, their evolution offers parallels and some similarities. Both grew out of the same movements—scientific management and economy and efficiency, which from the turn of the century provided the driving forces of reform in many state and local governments. The drafting and passage of the 1921 act probably owed much to the financial experience and consequences of World War I. Financial mismanagement of the war was suspected. By earlier standards, federal expenditures and taxes were high, and the federal debt was enormous. These were the basic arguments for the Budget and Accounting Act of 1921; its rationale was thrift, efficiency, legality, and strict central control. The development and passage of this act are discussed in Chapter 1.

It would clearly not be feasible in a few sentences to describe the myriad changes since 1921 that have influenced federal operations generally or the activities of the two agencies here under consideration. But it may be useful to spotlight a few of them, some widely known, some less familiar. A first category has to do with the *dimensions* of federal operations. In the six decades from 1922, the first year in which the Budget and Accounting Act was fully operative, to 1981:

> the U.S. population, which the government is designed to serve, doubled (from 110 million to 225 million);
>
> the gross national product (GNP) multiplied by nearly 40 times (from $74 billion to $2,844 billion); a large part of this increase was due to decline in the value of the dollar; in terms of dollars of constant value, the increase was by about 7 times;
>
> the amount of federal outlays (unadjusted) grew from $3.8 billion to $663 billion, or by about 175 times; in dollars of constant value, the increase would have been by more than 35 times;
>
> the proportion of federal budget outlays to GNP grew from 5 to 23 percent.

The original practices of both the BoB and GAO were directed to details: in the case of BoB, to individual items (known as objects) with their numbers and prices, and in that of GAO, to individual transactions to be audited. For example, in 1947, GAO was called upon to audit over 40 million vouchers, 260 million postal money orders, and 770 thousand claims, and to reconcile 490 million checks. Were similar financial systems in place today, the comparable numbers would be beyond the imagination. The original central budgeting and auditing systems were doomed simply by scale.

One effect of the enormous growth in federal activity was to force a considerable degree of decentralization from the central agencies to the operating departments, their bureaus, and other units. One of the purposes of the original Bureau of the Budget was to centralize direction, review, and control of the budget in a single body, accountable to the president. The General Accounting Office inherited from the comptroller and the auditors of the Treasury Department one of the most highly centralized systems imaginable for reviewing, auditing, and settling financial transactions. However successful the centralizing effort was in the early years of BoB/OMB, the sheer dimensions of federal activity have necessitated that the great bulk of the work on the budget, on administrative management, and on other activities be performed in the operating agencies. Much the same is true of the auditing and program evaluation activities of the GAO. The work of both agencies must necessarily depend upon management by selection (of the unusual, the nonroutine), and their effectiveness depends in part upon the information and the wisdom with which they select the crucial and the exceptional.

A cluster of factors that have had enormous impact upon these two agencies include the tremendous enlargement of the *scope* and *variety* of federal undertakings and the *complexity* and *specialization* that have necessarily accompanied it. Scope can be described in many ways. The federal government is now involved in one or many respects with every person (including noncitizens), every institution and organization, and almost every activity in the country. Its assumption of responsibilities for the young, the aging, the poor, the handicapped, the sick, minorities, and a great many other groups of citizens during and since the 1930s now consumes nearly half of its financial outlays. It is heavily involved in fields and problems heretofore the exclusive province of states, local governments, schools, universities, industries, families—or not taken care of at all. These include energy, the environment, outer space, the resources of the oceans, abortion, the arts, civil rights, the aged and the children, pornography, drugs, alcohol, health care, housing, crime, and others almost without limit. The federal government has become the principal sponsor and supporter of research and development in most scientific fields. It is by far the biggest borrower and also the biggest lender in the nation. It is involved in a variety of relationships with every nation in the world, with most of the international organizations, and with all of the fifty states, the territories, the cities, the counties, and most of the school and other districts of the nation.

Many of these federal activities require a high degree of professional and scientific learning and experience, and cumulatively these specializations within the government comprehend almost every nook and cranny of human

knowledge today. The effectiveness with which a central agency such as BoB/
OMB can contribute to the planning, budgeting, and managing of activities in
such highly variegated and specialized fields without a vast assortment of its
own specialists is problematic. So is that of GAO in its effort to appraise management and evaluate results of federal programs against their costs. This
growing phenomenon of specialization raises questions not only as to the degree to which the central agencies should attempt to match the specializations
of federal agencies in their own staffing but also of the extent and depth to
which they should seek to penetrate the operations and appraise the results of
highly technical programs.

The growth in the scope of federal involvement has been complicated by
the growing realization of interdependence and interrelationships. No longer
are the convenient divisions of the past inviolable, the divisions between what
is foreign and what is purely national; what is federal and what is state or
local; what is public and what is private; what is legislative, what is executive, and what is judicial; what is defense and what is domestic; what is education and what is health or drugs or crime. The graying of these once familiar
boundaries has complicated the organization and operations of the government generally. It has particularly aggravated the difficulties of coordinating
related and overlapping programs, the appraisal of results against costs, and
the whole area of accountability—all central to the responsibilities of OMB
and GAO.

Another area of basic change for both of these agencies and indeed for the
entire federal establishment has been the virtual revolution in the *modes* and
means whereby the government carries out its programs. During and before
the 1920s, most of what the federal government was responsible for it did for
itself with its own personnel and facilities. The New Deal and later the Great
Society and subsequent programs relied heavily on nonfederal organizations—state and local governments, quasi-public organizations, universities
and other nonprofit organizations, and even private businesses—to carry out
operations presumably in the national interest and financed in whole or part
by federal funds. Furthermore, a large part of what the federal government
now does and buys in terms of services, equipment and supplies, research and
development, and even planning and policy-making is actually produced or
performed by individuals and organizations outside of itself. This is why, in
the last generation, roughly since the Korean War, though federal expenditures have grown, there has been little increase in direct federal employment.
At the present time more than one-half of all federal outlays consists of direct
payments to individuals and families for their support and for interest on the
national debt. About one-third consists of payments to state and local units for

grants-in-aid and payments to nongovernmental organizations, at home and abroad, in return for goods and services to be produced and provided by them for federal purposes. The remainder, about one-sixth of the total, is for services and other costs directly incurred for federal operations. Of this last category of federal operations, about two-thirds is for national defense. This means that only about 5 percent of the total federal budget goes to domestic operations that are carried out by the government itself. Indeed, the Reagan budget for 1983 showed only 4 percent for direct, nondefense federal operations.

The impact of this development upon the federal budget and financial management generally has been great. It means, among many other things, that a substantial part of the annual budget is beyond discretionary decision during the appropriation process because it is committed in law or contract in prior years.[7] It means, too, that when the government plans, projects, and budgets its programs and outlays, it is dealing in large part with operations and with things that will be performed and produced by nonfederal agencies, public and private, foreign and domestic; that is, by organizations and individuals beyond the immediate hierarchical control of the federal government itself. Budgeting today is largely a matter of predicting what others, outside the government, are entitled to receive from, or do in behalf of, federal programs. Furthermore, there are a good many potentially leaky straws twixt the cup and the lip. This introduces new complications to the problems of appraising program effectiveness against costs, or in other words to the problems of accountability in its broadest sense. How far is it appropriate and permissible for a federal agency to audit or investigate the affairs of foreign governments, international organizations, state and local governments, private businesses, universities, and even individuals to ascertain whether they have used their federal funds legally and efficiently in pursuit of federally mandated purposes?

Another important change in the modes and means of operations has been the increasing reliance for carrying out national goals upon tools that have no impact or very slight impact upon budgetary outlays. Among these are the increasing numbers of off-budget government and mixed ownership enter-

7. Such outlays have somewhat misleadingly been described as "uncontrollable" in recent budgets; they are now believed to comprehend three-quarters of the federal budget. But there are degrees of uncontrollability and there are differentials in time. Some items that are not controllable in the current or in the next (budget) year may be controllable in years following. Most federal outlays must be sanctioned in appropriations bills and authorized in separate and prior substantive legislation, much of which precludes any real discretion in the appropriations process. In 1981, the Reagan administration, with the assent of majorities in Congress, showed that some items theretofore considered uncontrollable could in fact be changed through the reconciliation process. Whether this experience will prove unique remains to be seen.

prises such as the Postal Service, AMTRAK, CONRAIL, COMSAT, and the Corporation for Public Broadcasting. Another device is the use of credits, deductions, and exemptions of various kinds from federal taxes, now commonly known as tax expenditures, for the purpose of carrying out federal policies. Another is the guaranteeing of loans to encourage or support housing, trade, energy, railroads, agriculture, education, community development, small business, ailing cities (such as New York), and ailing corporations (such as Lockheed and Chrysler). Finally, mention should be made of the recently exploding use of regulations to carry out federal policy in both private and public realms of activity. The cost to the government of regulation of others is relatively minor, but its costs to the economy as a whole, though immeasurable, are certainly substantial.

A final type of change to be mentioned here has been the development of *technology*, which has virtually revolutionized the processes of financial management. In 1921, a great deal of the work of building and executing budgets and of auditing of vouchers and accounts was done by pencil on paper, augmented here and there by typewriters and telephones. Adding machines, punch-card systems, computers were still in the future. Today, most of the spadework of financial management is computerized, individual vouchers are seldom seen by auditors, accounts are consolidated and retained in memory banks, funds are electronically transferred, and alternative programs and their costs are programmed and calculated on machines. Such developments, whose invention was largely extrinsic to these two agencies themselves, have made budgeting, accounting, and auditing infinitely more complex. But in light of the growth in dimensions and scope and ramifications of federal undertakings, they have made them possible. The jobs could not be done with the tools that were available in 1921.

Their Stages of Development

In response to these tremendous changes of federal dimensions, scope, modes of operating, and technology, the two agencies changed, but probably at a somewhat slower pace than the changes that were going on around them. In general, GAO's pace of change was slower than that of BoB/OMB, at least until quite recently. Thus, their changes, though roughly parallel in nature, were not coterminous. Over the sixty-year period, GAO went through three fairly definable phases; BoB/OMB, three or possibly four.

The first phase for both agencies, which is described in Chapter 2 below, was generally but not totally consonant with the letter and intent of the 1921 law as perceived by the legislators who had passed it. The emphases during this phase were upon economy, efficiency, compliance with law, and strict central control. Both agencies stressed detail, and neither was much concerned during the first decade with public policy or management.

The top leadership of both institutions became distressed, sometimes heatedly, with the Roosevelt New Deal policies. This led in the case of BoB to a complete change in the leadership and in the nature of its work in the 1930s. The leadership of GAO likewise changed in 1939 and again in 1940, but World War II postponed an immediate transformation in its operations until after the war. The Great Depression, the multitude of New Deal programs, and finally World War II made the original routines of budgeting and auditing impracticable if not impossible. Furthermore, there had developed over those years a new and much broadened concept of administration that went well beyond the counting and control of dollars. This view was best set forth in the famous 1937 report of President Roosevelt's Committee on Administrative Management, better known as the "Brownlow report."[8] The Committee envisioned the Bureau of the Budget as the major agent of the president in bringing about better management of the executive branch, and this responsibility was written into BoB's charter in 1939. Later, at the close of World War II, the GAO began moving away from detailed voucher-checking into professional auditing of agency accounts and agency accounting systems. And still later it began what it called "comprehensive auditing" (another misnomer), which encompassed, on a selective basis, financial management generally and even nonfinancial aspects of management. These developments in BoB and GAO are discussed in Chapter 3 below.

In the period since about 1950, the parallels between the two agencies, to the extent that they existed at all, are less easy to identify. Both agencies were influenced during the 1950s by the first Hoover commission's call for development of a performance budget with emphasis upon classification of activities, work measurement, and lump-sum appropriations. Both were later influenced by the second Hoover commission and its stress on accrual and cost accounting, and both were affected by the introduction of the so-called planning-programming-budgeting system (PPBS), which was introduced in the Defense Department in 1961 and then extended to the rest of the executive branch in 1965. Ultimately, PPBS probably had more impact upon the GAO than upon BoB/OMB because of the attention it directed to the analysis of policies and programs and their results, which became the main course of

8. The three-man committee was chaired by Louis Brownlow and also included Charles E. Merriam and Luther H. Gulick.

GAO's fare during the 1970s. Indeed, this shift in emphasis constituted the second transformation of the GAO.

During all of this thirty-year period, the vicissitudes of presidents and Congresses and the relations between them had profound, but quite dissimilar, influences upon the two agencies. Probably the most important legislative event was the Congressional Budget and Impoundment Control Act of 1974. It was one of several manifestations of the resurgence of Congress in national power, which affected the two agencies in divergent ways. It was but one of a number of forces and events that drove the OMB in the direction of political responsiveness to presidential influence. But, if anything, it probably strengthened GAO's resolve to maintain political neutrality.

In the light of the widely different developments of BoB/OMB and GAO in the three decades after 1950, they are here treated in separate chapters. Chapter 4 deals with BoB/OMB; Chapter 5, with GAO. The closing chapter endeavors to synthesize these two and indeed the earlier parts of the book, to show how the two agencies have related to each other, how they compare and contrast, and how they fit into America's divided scheme of government. Almost the entire book to that point deals with the first sixty years following the effective date of the Budget and Accounting Act of 1921, and most of it concerns the period up to the inauguration of President Reagan in 1981. I have added two epilogues. The first treats the first fifteen months of the Reagan budget experience. Rather little can yet be said about the GAO because the new comptroller general, Charles A. Bowsher, did not assume his office until the fall of 1981, shortly before these lines were written. Epilogue II is a brief evocation of the nostalgia of past and present employees of GAO, BoB, and OMB. In the middle of the book is an Interlude concerning the buildings that have housed the two agencies from their beginnings.

CHAPTER I

Genesis and Exodus

The Budget and Accounting
Act of 1921

The Act was passed with almost
masterly inattention to draftsman-
ship. Nearly every ambiguity of jurisdiction under existing law was
retained, and some additional ones
were created.

HARVEY C. MANSFIELD, 1939

This Act is probably the greatest
landmark of our administrative history except for the Constitution
itself.

HERBERT EMMERICH, 1961

Over the centuries the financing of governments has vied with religion, eth-
nicity, and territory as a principal object of civil contention, disruption, and
war. Indeed, the American Revolution itself was provoked, though not entirely caused, by disagreement over finances, particularly taxation. The management of our public finances has been a source of continuing difficulty and
argument ever since. From the British and to a lesser extent the French, we
inherited a few very broad principles: that taxes and borrowing should only
be authorized after approval by representatives of (some of) the people; that
the same requirement should apply to expenditures authorized by appropriations; that financial transactions should be audited by individuals independent
of those who made them. In the case of France, the "people" consisted of
the three great estates—clergy, nobility, and bourgeoisie—until 1789, when
the French Revolution upset the whole arrangement. Our British heritage includes a few words like *appropriation, accounting, audit,* and *comptroller*.
We also inherited some continuing and often heated tensions: between the executive (the Crown in Britain, the royal governors in the colonies) and the
legislature (the Parliament in Britain and the colonial legislatures), and between the central government and the territorial subdivisions (the Crown and
Parliament in Britain versus the colonial governments in America). The former issue underlies the continuing contests between the president and Congress in this country; the latter, those about state versus national powers.

The decision in Philadelphia in 1787 to adopt a system of separated and shared powers complicated matters.[1] Most of the Founding Fathers feared and suspected executive power, perhaps especially in matters financial. On the other hand, experience during and following the revolution did not encourage reliance upon a legislative body to plan, allocate, and audit revenues and expenditures. The Continental Congress had experimented with three different types of treasury boards, a variety of committees, a single-headed superintendent of finance, and a division among a comptroller, a treasurer, a register, and a number of auditors. Nothing worked very well. The drafters of the Constitution were firm and emphatic in giving Congress power to lay taxes, borrow money, and make appropriations. But the Constitution was silent on who should initiate financial plans and proposals, who should manage the finances, who should keep the accounts, and who should audit transactions and when they should do it—before or after they were made or both. Near the close of the convention, the draft constitution contained a provision empowering Congress "to appoint a Treasurer by ballot." On the convention's last day, this provision was stricken by a vote of eight states to three.

This lacuna was among the first problems confronted by the First Congress of the United States in 1789. At the outset, the new Congress considered bills to create three departments—Foreign Affairs (later the same year changed to State), War, and Treasury. Although both State and War were given some domestic duties, they were treated differently from Treasury because the Constitution recognized special presidential responsibilities in foreign affairs and national defense, whereas all the basic financial powers specifically enumerated were allotted to Congress. Thus, on the question of the removal power of officers appointed by the president with the advice and consent of the Senate, both houses after lengthy debate agreed to language implicitly recognizing presidential authority to remove without advice and consent. But on the secretary of the treasury, the Senate split evenly, and the question was finally settled by the deciding vote of the vice-president in favor of presidential removal. A proposal that the Treasury Department be headed by a three-member board was debated and rejected.

The Act to Establish the Treasury Department was distinctly different from those setting up the State and War departments in a variety of respects, most of which reflected a congressional intent that the Treasury be partly if not principally responsible directly to the Congress rather than the president. The

1. This account of the proceedings of the Constitutional Convention is summarized from James Hart, *The American Presidency in Action, 1789: A Study in Constitutional History* (New York, 1948), 215–16.

Treasury was labeled simply a "department"; the other two were "executive departments." The secretary of the treasury was "head of the department"; the heads of the other two were "principal officers." Each of the latter two was directed to "perform and execute such duties as shall from time to time be enjoined on or entrusted to him by the President of the United States." But aside from the provisions for appointment and replacement, the Treasury Act makes no mention of the president. Instead, the secretary of the treasury is called upon to prepare a variety of reports, plans, and estimates on financial matters for submission to the Congress—without any reference to the president. The only mention of subordinate officers in the State and War departments was the requirement that each have a chief clerk. In contrast, the Treasury Act included the titles and duties of several subordinate officers—a comptroller, an auditor, a treasurer, and a register—all to be appointed by the president with senatorial confirmation. Clearly, the Treasury Department was originally conceived to stand somewhere between the president and the Congress, probably closer to the latter than to the former. It was a halfway house. And the Treasury Act of 1789 was the real genesis of what would later become an agency of the legislature, the GAO.

Alexander Hamilton, the first secretary of the treasury, who was also reputed to be principal author of the Treasury Act, had taken a different position in one of the Federalist papers he had drafted two years earlier in advocacy of adoption of the Constitution.

> The actual conduct of foreign negotiations, *the preparatory plans of finance, the application and disbursement of the public money in conformity to the general appropriations of the legislature*, the arrangement of the army and navy, the directions of the operations of war—these and other matters of a like nature, constitute what seems to be most properly understood by the administration of government. The persons, therefore, to whose immediate management these different matters are committed ought to be considered as the assistants or deputies to derive their offices from his [the president's] appointment, at least from his nomination, and ought to be subject to his superintendence. (Emphasis added.)[2]

But in fact, neither Hamilton nor most of his successors until 1921 encouraged much presidential involvement in financial affairs, with respect either to estimates and appropriations or to accounting, auditing, and financial management generally. The Treasury dealt with the departments and agencies on one hand and with committees of the Congress on the other. Presidents occasionally intervened but not in any systematic way.

2. Clinton Rossiter (ed.), *The Federalist Papers* (New York, 1961), No. 72, pp. 435–36.

Evolution of the Federal Financial System

The underpinning of the federal financial system was provided in the Treasury
Act of 1789, and the superstructure was set in place by the first treasury secretary, Alexander Hamilton. Although there have obviously been a great many
changes, many of the original practices continued until and even after 1921,
and a few vestiges survive to this day.

The original act required the secretary of the treasury to "prepare and report estimates of the public revenue, and the public expenditures," and this
soon evolved into the practice of an annual call to the departments and agencies to submit their estimates to the Treasury, which would put them together
and send them to the appropriate committees of the Congress.[3] Both Secretary
Hamilton and his successor under President Jefferson, Albert Gallatin, undertook to review and reduce or change some of the estimates—that is, to serve
as a true budget director or minister of finance. But neither was successful in
implanting such a procedure. The departments did not want Treasury med-
dling with their estimates; not did the Congress. Insofar as there was a budget
at all, it was a congressional budget. In its main features, this practice survived until 1921. The role of the president was normally nil; that of Treasury
was strictly routine—calling for, receiving, and consolidating estimates from
the spending agencies into a book of estimates. Indeed, for a large part of the
nineteenth century, this function was delegated to the register of the treasury,
a patronage appointee. Furthermore, the heads of the departments and agencies by and large were no better staffed or inclined to review and modify the
estimates of their constituent bureaus than was the president. Most of the estimates in the nineteenth and early twentieth centuries were products of the bureaus, untarnished by secretarial, presidential, or Treasury review. They
might as well have gone directly from the bureaus to the congressional committees; in fact, many of them did.

With respect to general financial management, accounting, and auditing,
the Treasury Act provided a system and officers largely modeled on practices
first invented and later abandoned under the Articles of Confederation. The
system was slow, cumbersome, but safe since a number of different officers,
independent of each other, were involved in almost every action. On the basis
of appropriations—and later, some receipts that were not appropriated—the
treasury secretary issued warrants to the agencies and the treasurer to spend
and receive moneys. The warrants had to be countersigned by the comptroller,

3. Treasury Act, Public Law 1-12, September 2, 1789, sec. 2. More specific directions were
provided by Congress in a later act, Public Law 6-58, May 10, 1800.

recorded by the register, and passed on to the treasurer as authority for payments. On the basis of the warrants, officers in the agencies would authorize expenditures (and receipts) and would transmit to the auditor in the Treasury Department statements of their accounts. The auditor would examine them, make adjustments or disallowances as appropriate, and certify the balances to the comptroller for settlement. The treasurer would then disburse the funds. Hamilton, as the first secretary of the treasury, almost immediately modified the system, particularly for obligations incurred abroad or far from the capital city. He issued warrants that were essentially advances for such payments so that disbursements could actually be made by the agencies prior to review and settlement in the Treasury Department. For these expenditures, the auditor's and comptroller's review became essentially a post- rather than a preaudit. This practice became prevalent for the great bulk of expenditures during the nineteenth century. It was made possible by the designation and bonding of disbursing officers in the various agencies, with authority to make payments.

The comptroller under the first Treasury Act was essentially the great-granddaddy of the comptroller general, head of the GAO, though the office underwent a variety of permutations between 1789 and 1921. Most of the powers bestowed upon it in the original act still pertain. The comptroller general can still countersign warrants, superintend the adjustment of accounts, review accounts, disallow payments, and initiate prosecution for delinquencies. The comptroller's duties, even at the outset, were recognized to be partly legislative, partly executive, partly judicial, and consideration was given to providing the office a fixed term, not dependent on the pleasure of the president. This proposal was rejected, and all the Treasury accounting officers, as they were collectively called, remained removable by the president until 1921.

The financial system as envisaged, apart from the process leading up to appropriations, was highly centralized in the Treasury, and its focus from the beginning was the comptroller. The secretary of the treasury had a wide range of other responsibilities and interests. During Washington's first term, partly because of antipathies to Hamilton, Congress empowered the secretary of war to issue warrants and to authorize the treasurer to disburse funds without reference to the Treasury's auditor and comptroller. Later a similar arrangement was provided for the Navy Department and, in substantial part, for the Post Office. These aberrations were, however, corrected within twenty-five years, and thereafter the system with few exceptions remained highly centralized in Washington and in the Treasury and, later, in the GAO until the close of World War II.

However well or poorly the financial system worked in normal times, it was not equal to the pressures, the speed, and the turmoil of war. Almost every significant war in American history occasioned long arrearages and near chaos in governmental finance. And most of the basic changes—usually labeled reforms—followed major wars.

The American Revolution and the unhappy experiences with the Continental Congress and the Congress of the Confederation certainly contributed to the Constitution and the Treasury Act.

Following the War of 1812, Congress passed an act in 1817 that recentralized in Treasury the powers previously granted the War, Navy, and Post Office departments, and set up a second comptroller to handle the war and navy accounts, and four additional auditors, each responsible for the accounts of one or more departments; later a sixth auditor was established to audit the Post Office, and the commissioner of the customs became in effect a third comptroller with respect to customs revenues.

In 1868, after the Civil War, Congress enacted a statute declaring that the balances of accounts, after certification by the comptroller, "shall be taken and considered as final and conclusive upon the executive branch of the government, and be subject to revision only by Congress or the proper courts."

The Budget and Accounting Act of 1921 quite clearly followed on the difficulties of World War I, at least in major part.

World War II and its aftermath contributed to the Budget and Accounting Procedures Act of 1950 as well as to a number of other statutes in the late 1940s and early 1950s.

The Vietnam War added some stimulus to the reform movement in Congress that culminated in the Congressional Budget and Impoundment Control Act of 1974.[4]

Yet, one of the most important pieces of legislation on federal finances was not immediately provoked by any war—the Dockery Act of 1894.[5] It was one of a number of products of a joint congressional group, the Dockery-Cockrell commission, set up to study and make recommendations on the business practices of the various departments, with emphasis on financial management. The Dockery Act provided the first basic changes in the Treasury's financial system since the act of 1817, and most of the powers and practices it instituted

4. Public Law 14-45, March 3, 1817; Public Law 40-36, March 30, 1868; Public Law 81-784, September 12, 1950; Public Law 93-344, July 12, 1974.
5. Public Law 53-174, July 31, 1894.

were transferred without change to the GAO in 1921 and remain there today. It combined the duties of the three comptrollers into one comptroller of the treasury, as in the first Treasury Act. He was directed to "provide a uniform construction of the appropriation laws, conclusive upon all the departments; to render advance opinions on the legality of payments on request"; and to prescribe "the forms of keeping and rendering all public accounts" except postal accounts. He was placed in an appellate capacity with regard to questions raised by claimants, departments, and auditors. He was thus relieved of re-reviewing all accounts after they had been examined by the auditors. The six auditors were retained, but their jurisdictions were changed and their responsibilities augmented. These changes, plus a large number of technical and procedural modifications, essentially defined the system of federal control of finances until 1921. In summary, the system (not including the development of estimates and appropriations) was:

highly centralized

concerned almost exclusively with legality, accuracy, and regularity, with little attention to wisdom, effectiveness, and efficiency

detailed to the last penny

duplicative, with financial transactions reviewed by at least three different officers—the administrative officer in the agency, a disbursing officer, and a Treasury auditor

dictatorial in that decisions by the comptroller of the Treasury were final upon officers in the executive branch

routine, clerical, and unprofessional, for almost none of the comptrollers, auditors, or their staffs had training or experience in accounting

largely independent of either Congress or the president, who didn't much care or, if they did, couldn't do much

and slow

Economy, Efficiency, and the Budget

The movement that led to the Budget and Accounting Act of 1921, however, had little to do with the financial management practices of the Treasury Department, and the act itself made few changes in those practices, though it radically changed their organizational situs. It was a product of the drive for what is now called an executive budget system, which was itself fueled by a growing demand for economy and efficiency in government. The reasons and arguments for it were many. In the first place, with increasing urbanization and growing public services, government at all levels was costing more, even before World War I, when federal costs spiraled to unprecedented heights. During most of the nineteenth century, except in wartime, the federal government had rocked along with a comfortably balanced budget or a surplus, mainly on the strength of customs duties that were largely invisible to the public. But in some of the early years of the twentieth century, surpluses changed to deficits as customs revenues declined in relation to expenditures. In February, 1913, just before the inauguration of President Wilson, the Sixteenth Amendment to the Constitution, authorizing the income tax, was ratified—barely in time for World War I. That tax is of course highly visible and somewhat painful.

There was widespread suspicion of corruption, waste, extravagance, and inefficiency, particularly in local units where most governmental activity occurred. At the federal level there was growing criticism in the late nineteenth and early twentieth centuries of the pork barrel, whereby individual congressmen were able to get appropriations for federal projects in their states and districts. Much of this alleged chicanery was blamed on legislatures and on government by political machines.

Scandals and general disaffection gave rise to a variety of reform movements—for civil service, the short ballot, initiative and referendum, and other changes. For present purposes, the key reform effort concerned public organization and administration generally. It was initially led by the New York Bureau of Municipal Research, founded in 1906, by comparable bureaus later established in other cities, and by the Institute for Government Research, which was established in 1916 and subsequently became the Brookings Institution. In every case, a central theme of administrative reform was an integrated and comprehensive budget to be prepared under the direction of the chief executive, whether he be city manager, mayor, governor, or president, and to be reviewed, modified, and passed in appropriations by the legislative body. The budget movement, like many other administrative reforms, started in the cities and moved up to the states in the first two decades of this century. The federal government was a latecomer.

Among the more scholarly reformers, the principal arguments for a budget system were the now familiar ones: rationality in decision-making, focused responsibility, integrated and professional management, comprehensiveness and accuracy of information on which to base judgments, openness of government to press and public, more effective legislative participation, and efficiency of operations.[6] But to the politicians and the general public, the argument was single and simple—economy in government, to which efficiency and legality would contribute. It was proclaimed that a budget system would lower the costs of government or at least keep them from rising as quickly; it would thus keep taxes down, prevent deficits, and lower public debt. Economy was the great banner of the budget crusaders, and it was so effective that it became almost blasphemy by 1920 to oppose a budget system.

The Budget and Accounting Act was an innovation of major proportions. There was very little precedent for it; indeed, most of the nation's experience had been moving in an opposite direction. The word *budget* itself was practically unknown, at least in its governmental connotation. Its derivation is interesting. It is the anglicized version of the French *bougette*, which meant a small package or bag. Its usage in connection with finances originated in England in the seventeenth century, when it came to connote the proposed taxes and expenditures of the Crown, contained in the briefcase brought before the Parliament by the chancellor of the exchequer. Hence the expression "open the budget," meaning open the bag containing the financial plan. It is possible that the word was used in colonial America, but the only reference to it I have seen from the eighteenth century occurs in the journal of William Maclay, a senator from Pennsylvania in the First Congress. He wrote on January 15, 1790, "This day the 'budget', as it is called, was opened in the House of Representatives." Maclay, a dedicated anti-Federalist, was irate at Hamilton's plan, apparently contained in the budget, to redeem the depreciated paper money of the old Congress. "It [the budget] had occasioned many serious faces. I feel so struck of an heap, I can make no remark on the matter." [7] Current politicians, practitioners, and observers of budgeting may also be amused that etymologists trace the word to the same Latin sources as the current words *bulge* and *budge*.

6. In testimony before the House Select Committee on the Budget, W. F. Willoughby, a prominent reform-oriented scholar, emphasized the importance of the accountability arising from establishment of an executive budget: "In the first place, starting at the beginning, the fundamental principle at issue is that of establishing definite responsibility upon some officer of the Government for the formulation of a budget; that is, a general financial and work program. It seems to me that there can be no doubt that that responsibility must necessarily be placed upon the President." U.S. Congress, House, Select Committee on the Budget, *Hearings on the Establishment of a National Budget System*, 66th Cong., 1st Sess., 78–79. For a highly critical but sophisticated examination of the executive budget idea see Edward A. Fitzpatrick, *Budget Making in a Democracy: A New View of the Budget* (New York, 1918), ix, 292. See also Charles Wallace Collins, *The National Budget System and American Finance* (New York, 1917), 104–20.

7. Edgar S. Maclay (ed.), *Journal of William Maclay, United States Senator from Pennsylvania: 1789–1791* (New York, 1890), 177.

Neither the word nor the idea of budgeting had much if any expression in this country during the nineteenth century. As Frederick A. Cleveland wrote in 1915: "Taken as a whole it may be said that until within the last few years the 'budget idea,' as the term is here used, has had no evolution whatever in the United States. Our citizenship, our legislators, and our constitution makers have until recently been as innocent of such an idea as an unborn babe."[8] An executive budget system had been tried in New York City as early as 1908, spurred by the New York Bureau of Municipal Research, and in a few other cities. The National Municipal League, a citizens' reform organization, included an executive budget in its model city charter in 1916, and later, in 1921, wrote similar provisions into its model state constitution. Between 1909 and 1921 a number of states, including Illinois, Maryland, Massachusetts, New York, Oregon, and Wisconsin had considered such budgets as parts of general reorganizations, and several, notably Illinois, Maryland, and Massachusetts, had adopted executive budget systems. In fact, the first two of the thirty-seven witnesses who testified before the House Select Committee on the Budget in 1919 were Governor Frank O. Lowden of Illinois and his director of finance. Most of the states and cities had provided for an auditor independent of the executive branch and elected by the people or selected by the legislature.

In addition to the states and cities, the Congress was informed of budget systems used abroad. It was noted repeatedly in the congressional hearings and floor debates that preceded passage of the Budget Act that the United States was the only major nation in the Western world without a budget system. There was much discussion and apparently also a good deal of misunderstanding about the British system, the role of the Ministry of the Treasury and of the comptroller and auditor general, both of which were for a variety of reasons rather inapt models for the United States. In 1917, the newly established Institute for Government Research, under the direction of W. F. Willoughby, published a series of five books on budgeting in the United States and abroad, including one comprehensive history of the development of the budget in European states and separate volumes on the British and Canadian budgets.[9]

As a matter of law, presidents and secretaries of the treasury could have

8. This passage appears in Cleveland's article "Evolution of the Budget Idea in the United States," in an issue of the *Annals of the American Academy of Political and Social Science* wholly devoted to "public budgets," (LXII [November, 1915]), 21.

9. See, for example, René Stourm, *The Budget* (New York, 1917); H. G. Villard and W. W. Willoughby, *The Canadian Budget System* (New York, 1922); William F. Willoughby, W. W. Willoughby, and Samuel McCune Lindsay, *The System of Financial Administration in Great Britain* (New York, 1922).

interjected their views on expenditures and revenues at the beginning. After Hamilton and Gallatin, they rarely did so, because of lack of interest, lack of confidence that their views would make any impression on the appropriate committees of Congress, or later because they were inhibited by laws from doing so. In an act of May 10, 1800, Congress directed the secretary of the treasury to "digest, prepare and lay before Congress . . . a report on the subject of finance, containing estimates of public revenue and public expenditures." [10] More than a century later, on the day of President Taft's inauguration, Congress in effect asked the president, in the event estimated appropriations exceeded estimated revenues, to recommend "such measures as he may judge necessary" and also recommend "how in his judgment the estimated appropriations could with least injury to the public service be reduced so as to bring the appropriations within the estimated revenues." [11] Of course, the president had no qualified staff to help him with such a task, and Congress offered none.

To my knowledge, none of Taft's predecessors had ever asked for such a staff. Indeed, viewed from the perspective of 1983 or even of 1940, the reluctance of presidents to become involved in financial and even general administrative questions during the nineteenth century is surprising. Most of the financial and other administrative legislation originated in Congress or in bureaus of executive agencies without reference to the president. Between the Civil War and 1900, four different study groups, the last being the Dockery-Cockrell commission, studied finances and the details of administration in the executive branch. All were set up by, and reported to, the Congress, and all were composed exclusively of congressmen. President Theodore Roosevelt broke the pattern when he named members of the Keep commission, which was chaired by Assistant Secretary of the Treasury Charles H. Keep and consisted entirely of federal administrators at the second level—assistant secretaries and bureau chiefs. Congress originally paid no attention to its recommendations, which were many and far-reaching and most of which were ultimately adopted. [12] But the commission was the first real expression by a president, except in wartime, of interest and responsibility for the conduct of business within the government. Curiously, the Keep commission made no recommendation for a budget.

10. Public Law 6-58, May 10, 1800.
11. Public Law 60-328, March 4, 1909.
12. Among its recommendations were position classification, salary standardization, a retirement system, an official gazette (now the *Federal Register*), the coordination of federal statistical activities, units within the departments for continuing analysis of administrative systems and methods, a central purchasing and supply agency, and lump-sum appropriations.

Meanwhile, Congress had so fragmented itself that no one in the entire body was in a position to look at estimated expenditures as a whole, to weigh priorities among different programs, or to consider expenditures in relation to revenues. In 1789 the House had established a Ways and Means Committee and the Senate, a Finance Committee, to consider both appropriation and revenue proposals. At the close of the Civil War, appropriations were removed from both of those committees and lodged in separate committees for appropriations. A few years later, the appropriating power over several activities was removed from the appropriations committees and lodged in other standing committees—a condition that continued until 1920.[13] Furthermore, during the nineteenth century, appropriations were divided among a number of different bills—as many as fourteen. It is interesting in nostalgic retrospect that the first appropriation bill for the entire government under the Constitution was one paragraph long and consisted of four items.

There may have been some discussion of a national budget in the late nineteenth and early twentieth centuries.[14] But basic credit for initiating the idea should probably go to President William Howard Taft. Unlike virtually all the presidents before him, Taft busied himself soon after his inauguration with superintendence of the preparation of estimates in the departments. Thus, in his annual report for 1910 Taft's secretary of the treasury, Franklin McVeagh, stated: "I wish to call attention, as I did last year, to the exceeding care on the part of the heads of departments with which these estimates have been compiled, under the immediate attention of the President. There could scarcely be more scrutiny given to the work of the estimates than was given last year and has been given this year by the President and the members of his Cabinet." [15] But Taft's more lasting contribution grew out of his establishment—with congressional authorization and funds—of the Commission on Economy and

13. Appropriations removed from control of the appropriations committees included many of the largest and most important departments and functions. For example, in the House, they included agriculture, foreign affairs, Indian affairs, military affairs, naval affairs, post office and post roads, and rivers and harbors.

14. For example, one scholar has credited James A. Garfield with proposing a national budget in the 1870s, when he was chairman of the House appropriations committee and before he became president. See Don K. Price's testimony of March 5 and 9, 1973, in U.S. Congress, House, Committee on Government Operations, Subcommittee on Legislative and Military Operations, *Hearings Concerning Confirmation of the Director and Deputy Director, Office of Management and Budget*, 93rd Cong., 1st Sess., 134. Garfield's comments in an article in 1879 are suggestive. See Garfield, "National Appropriations and Misappropriations," *North American Review*, CXXVIII (June, 1879), 572-87.

15. U.S. Department of the Treasury, *Annual Report of the Secretary of the Treasury on the State of the Finances for the Fiscal Year Ended June 30, 1910* (1911), 1.

Efficiency in 1910. It must have been clear from the beginning that Taft's main interest in such a commission was to obtain authoritative recommendations and publicity for a national budget system. Before it was formed, the president authorized a preliminary inquiry that focused on the need for a budget. And Taft named as chairman of the commission Frederick A. Cleveland of the New York Bureau of Municipal Research, perhaps the preeminent exponent of the executive budget at the time. Other appointees were also known to be sympathetic with the idea.[16] The first item on the commission's agenda was a national budget, and though its twenty reports ranged widely over the administrative spectrum, the one entitled *The Need for a National Budget*, published in 1912 and almost six hundred pages long, won the most attention.[17] President Taft pressed on. With the help of the commission, he prepared a budget for 1914 along the lines it had recommended. Congress, by this time controlled by the Democrats, ordered the departments and agencies to submit their estimates in the customary form and no other. Taft then ordered that they be submitted in both forms, but the committees ignored the new style of estimates and worked with the traditional format.

President Woodrow Wilson, though sympathetic with the executive budget doctrine, did not pick up Taft's crusade, partly, it may be supposed, because he had other and higher program priorities, and partly perhaps because it was a Republican initiative. Neither did the Democratic Congress. In 1916 and again in 1920, both parties included calls for a budget system in their platforms, but the Democrats in 1916 indicated that the first step should be reorganization of the appropriation committees in the Congress. Soon thereafter, of course, the country became involved in World War I and talk of permanent financial reform quieted. There was little further attention to the subject until the closing months of the conflict. But the war, with its tremendous expenditures and debt, magnified the enthusiasm among the public and particularly in the Congress for any measures that promised reduction of alleged governmental extravagance and taxes, and this was exactly what the supporters of a budget system offered.

16. The other members included Harvey S. Chase, a certified public accountant; Frank J. Goodnow, political scientist; W. W. Warwick, a federal judge, who would later become comptroller of the treasury; and W. F. Willoughby, then assistant director of the census, who would later become the first director of the Institute for Government Research. M. O. Chase, auditor of the Post Office, later became a member.

17. U.S. Congress, House, Economy and Efficiency Commission, *The Need for a National Budget: Message from President of the United States Transmitting Report* (House Document 854), 62nd Cong., 2nd Sess. The summary section is reprinted in Frederick C. Mosher (ed.), *Basic Documents of American Public Administration, 1776–1950* (New York, 1976), 76–82.

The Budget and Accounting Act of 1921: History and Content

The drive for budgetary reform as it developed during the first two decades of the twentieth century had three basic elements. First was the initiation and recommendation of the budget, including both revenues and expenditures, by the chief executive or an agent immediately responsible to him. This was the early central theme, pressed by President Taft, Secretary of the Treasury Franklin McVeagh, the Commission on Economy and Efficiency, and the bulk of the proponents of budgetary reform. The second was the reorganization of both houses of Congress so that all appropriations (and, some hoped, all revenues) would be considered together by the same committees. A few went further, arguing that this was all that was needed. The third element was an audit of financial transactions of the executive branch by an agency whose primary responsibility was to Congress. This idea was a latecomer, added probably to gain congressional support as a counterbalance to the granting of powers and staff to the president for initiating the budget. It was not included in the recommendation of the Taft commission and was barely mentioned in much of the literature that followed it. But it was a major feature of the principal budget bills introduced in Congress. Most of the witnesses who testified before the special committees on a budget system said virtually nothing about it, though they favored the executive budget. But it received a lot of attention from the senators and representatives in their floor arguments and in committee reports.

The first and third of these elements would require legislation. The second could be accomplished by separate resolution of each house of Congress. In fact, the consolidation of the appropriations in a single committee was accomplished in the House of Representatives in 1920, a year before the Budget and Accounting Act became law. The Senate took the same step in 1922.[18] Neither house seriously considered combining the appropriations with the revenue committees (Ways and Means in the House, Finance in the Senate). The objectives of these congressional reorganizations were the seasoned consideration of appropriations for differing programs against each other and against probable revenues. For a variety of reasons to be discussed in later chapters, these objectives were apparently not fully realized. But the reconsolidation of appropriations powers of several committees over the objections of the mem-

18. Final House consideration of Resolution 324 to amend the rules of that body to create a single appropriations committee occurred on June 1, 1920. The measure passed by a comfortable 200–117 margin after vigorous debate. See *Congressional Record*, 66th Cong., 2nd Sess., 8108–21. Senate adoption of a similar resolution came on March 6, 1922, by a roll-call vote of 63–14. See *Congressional Record*, 67th Cong., 2nd Sess., 3418–32.

bers of those committees and of the agencies and interest groups involved was still a considerable achievement.

The first serious consideration of budget legislation following Taft's effort was conducted by a special committee of the Democratic caucus of the House of Representatives in 1915 and 1916. It apparently reached no conclusions and issued no report. There were also proposed resolutions, speeches, and some discussion of budget reform in 1917, without result. In the spring of 1918, Congressman Medill McCormick, an Illinois Republican, introduced a comprehensive "Plan for a National Budget" that included a number of bills and resolutions and a rationale for them.[19] McCormick, who originated some of the reforms of Governor Lowden's administration in his native state of Illinois, modeled his proposals upon the Illinois system and also, to some extent, upon the British model.[20] In some respects, such as restricting congressional power to increase or add to items in the executive budget or removing all of the operating bureaus from the Treasury Department, his proposals went far beyond what the Congress would then, or ever, accept. The proposals went nowhere in 1918. But in the elections of that year, the Republicans won control of both houses of Congress, and McCormick moved from the House to the Senate. The Republicans were by now heavily committed to budget reform.

On July 14, 1919, the Senate created a Select Committee on the Budget and made McCormick its chairman—presumably for his interest and expertise, since he was a freshman senator. Two weeks later, on July 31, the House established its own Select Committee on the Budget and named as its chairman Congressman James W. Good, a Republican from Iowa who was also chairman of the Appropriations Committee. Thenceforth the leaders of the budget reform movement in Congress were Good for the House, McCormick for the Senate. The principal advocate outside the Congress was unquestionably W. F. Willoughby, former member of the Taft commission and director of the Institute for Government Research. The major bill considered by the House,

19. *House Documents*, 65th Cong., 2nd Sess., No. 1006.

20. They would have given the secretary of the treasury authority to examine and modify departmental estimates and to submit them to the president for his review, approval, and transmittal to the Congress; created a budget committee in the House to receive, examine, and recommend a single budget bill (but it could not increase any item or add any new ones except by a two-thirds vote); created an auditor general and assistant auditor general to be appointed by a committee of leaders of the House to take over the Treasury Department's audit responsibilities and report annually to the House; stipulated that the audit be limited to questions of legality, authority, and accuracy—not policy or efficiency; provided that the House establish a committee on departmental accounts to receive and examine the reports of the auditor general and to make recommendations to the House for transmittal to the executive branch; and freed the Treasury Department of its operating functions by transferring units such as the Secret Service, Public Health Service, and others to other agencies.

H.R. 9783, was introduced by Good and probably drafted in large part by Willoughby. The Senate response was a rewritten bill, also largely drafted by Willoughby on the request of McCormick. Willoughby testified at great length before the House Select Committee on the Budget. As a matter of fact, some members of the House expressed disdain of the theoretic and unrealistic views of academics who had testified before the committee, including particularly Willoughby.[21]

The House committee held two weeks of hearings on the Good bill in September and October, 1919, These attracted much attention, partly because of the fame of some of the thirty-seven witnesses, such as former President Taft, Secretary of the Treasury Carter Glass, Assistant Secretary of the Navy Franklin D. Roosevelt, and Governor Lowden of Illinois. The majority of the witnesses, however, were representatives of civic and professional groups and research organizations. They were virtually unanimous on the need for a national budget system, and most presumed that preparation of a budget would be under the direction of the president. Relatively few paid much attention to the question of an independent audit, but most of those who did (not including Secretary Glass) thought it should be moved out of the Treasury Department.

Subsequently, the Good bill was submitted to the House, and following a vigorous two-day debate, was passed on October 21, 1919, by a majority of 285 for, 3 against, and 143 not voting. There must have been strong public and constituency pressure against opposing it. Several of the congressmen who expressed strong opposition to giving the president such—or any—influence on the budget voted for the bill. Even the former Speaker of the House, Joseph G. Cannon, who had just written a vituperative article against any kind of executive budget, voted in favor.[22] The Good bill called upon the president to receive the departmental estimates, have them examined, modify them according to his judgment, and send a comprehensive budget to the Congress. For this purpose it set up a Bureau of the Budget in his office, headed by a director and assistant director appointed by the president without confirmation. It transferred the powers, personnel, and facilities of the comptroller of the Treasury and the Treasury auditors to an accounting department that would be headed by a comptroller general and assistant comptroller general,

21. See, for example, the remarks of Representative Thomas Sutler Williams of Illinois during House debate of the 1919 budget measure. After declaring his conviction that several college professors who had recently testified before the Select Committee on the Budget had shown themselves to be "absolutely ignorant . . . of the practical operations of the Government," he paraphrased a predecessor's statement that "a treatise by a college professor on how to run the government was about as valuable as a dissertation by a soured old maid on how to rear children." *Congressional Record*, 66th Cong., 1st Sess., 7201–7202.

22. Joseph G. Cannon, "The National Budget," *Harper's*, CXXXIX (October, 1919), 617–28.

both of whom would be appointed by the president with the advice and consent of the Senate and who could serve indefinitely or until retirement age of seventy on good behavior. Presumably the president could remove them if their behavior was bad.

On December 2, 1919, President Wilson sent a belated annual message (his seventh) to the Congress. It was delayed because he had spent much of the spring at the peace conference in France and much of the summer on a speaking tour in behalf of ratification of the Versailles Treaty and American membership in the League of Nations and had suffered a physical breakdown in September. In the first substantive sentence of his message, he declared, "I hope that Congress will bring to a conclusion at this session legislation looking to the establishment of a budget system." He went on to outline what in his opinion such a system should include: preparation of the budget by a single executive (the president) on the basis of "one single comprehensive plan of expenditure properly related to the nation's income"; a single appropriation committee in each house to consider all appropriation bills; and assurance that the money would be spent "wisely, economically and effectively" by providing for "highly trained auditors with permanent tenure in the Treasury Department . . . authorized and empowered to examine into and make report upon the methods employed and the results obtained by the executive departments." [23] He would presumably have opposed establishment of a comptroller general beyond presidential control.

At about the same time, Senator McCormick published a magazine article that took vigorous exception to the House budget bill: "The bill written by Professor Willoughby, and which bears the name of Congressman Good, is not a budget bill. It does not create a budget system. It postpones the day when a true budget system may be established." [24] Apparently, his main objection was that it divided responsibility between the office of the president and the secretary of the treasury, thus providing the budget bureau with powers already conferred on the secretary of the treasury and making of the president a finance minister. McCormick wrote that with the assistance of Secretary of the Treasury Glass and former congressman John J. Fitzgerald, he had prepared a bill that would put budget preparation where he thought it properly belonged but that omitted reference to the postaudit pending codification of the laws relating to auditing. It does not appear that this McCormick bill was ever introduced. Instead, his Select Committee on the Budget, during Decem-

23. Albert Shaw (ed.), *The Messages and Papers of Woodrow Wilson* (2 vols.; New York, 1924), II, 1138–39. Robert I. Vexler (ed.), *Woodrow Wilson: 1856–1924* (Dobbs Ferry, N.Y., 1969), 106–107.

24. The article was reproduced in the *Congressional Record*, 66th Cong., 2nd Sess., 619–21.

ber and January, met and held hearings under the heading of the House bill (H.R. 9783), asked (of all people) Willoughby to rewrite it, and entered the new version as an amendment to the House bill. The three major changes from the House bill were to place the budget unit under the secretary of the treasury, to reduce the tenure of the comptroller general to a fixed term of seven years, and to give the new auditing agency powers to prescribe and supervise agency accounting methods and to control all accounting activities of the government. The title of the accounting department was changed to General Accounting Office to emphasize that it was not one of the executive departments. The Senate version was in more detail than the original House bill and made a number of minor changes.[25] The rewritten version of H.R. 9783 passed the Senate on May 1, 1920, barely in time to satisfy Wilson's hope of passage of the bill during the current session.

The House refused to accept the bill as rewritten, so there was a conference in which the differences were compromised, mostly, it would appear, in favor of the Senate version. The conference bill made the president responsible for the budget and provided him a Bureau of the Budget, the director of which would be the secretary of the treasury. It accepted the bulk of the Senate's provisions about the control of accounting. The comptroller general and assistant comptroller general would be appointed by the president with the consent of the Senate and would enjoy terms of fifteen years. They could be removed involuntarily only by impeachment or concurrent resolution of both houses of Congress, which does not require presidential signature. The conference report was accepted without a record vote in both houses and went to the president on June 2, 1920.

To the apparent surprise of the members of Congress, President Wilson vetoed the measure two days after he received it and one day before the scheduled adjournment of Congress. His message declared: "I do this with the greatest regret. I am in entire sympathy with the object of this bill and would gladly approve it" except that, in his opinion, the provisions for removal of the comptroller general and assistant comptroller general were unconstitutional.[26] The president contended: "The effect of this [provision] is to prevent

25. Willoughby wrote to the trustees of the Institute for Government that the Senate committee "permitted him practically to rewrite the bill with the result that . . . in some respects it is a superior bill to the House bill." This is somewhat surprising since Willoughby was adamant that the Budget Bureau should be in the office of the president, not in the Treasury Department.

26. Current and former directors and staff of BoB/OMB might be given some pause to reflect that, had not Wilson objected to the provisions for the removal of the comptroller general, the director of the budget would have been the secretary of the treasury and might still be. The Wilson veto message may be found in *House Documents*, 66th Cong., 2nd Sess., No. 805. Quotations in the text appear on page 1 of the message.

the removal of these officers for any cause except either by impeachment or a concurrent resolution of Congress. It has, I think, always been the accepted construction of the Constitution that the power to appoint officers of this kind carries with it, as an incident, the power to remove. I am convinced that the Congress is without Constitutional power to limit the appointing power and its incident, the power of removal derived from the Constitution."

Wilson's argument harked back to the congressional debates about the removal power in 1789. Interestingly, seven years later the president's power to remove an executive "officer of the United States" without Senate consent was upheld in the case of *Myers* v. *United States*, but that rule was modified later in the case of regulatory commissioners in *Humphrey's Executor* v. *United States*. The constitutional rationale against the presidential power to remove was (and is) that the comptroller general as conceived would exercise judicial and legislative as well as executive powers. The real reason that most members of Congress opposed Wilson was that they wanted the comptroller general outside and independent of presidential influence. During the debates, Congressman Good had quoted President Cleveland, who, when his comptroller of the treasury had told him he could not spend moneys for a certain purpose, quipped, "I must have that fund, and if I can not change the opinion of my comptroller, I can change my comptroller." [27] Actually, to the date of this writing, the presidential power, or denial thereof, to remove a comptroller general has not been tested in the courts.

The House was unable to override the president's veto, and a frantic later attempt to push a modified bill through the Senate failed for want of time. So the 1920 effort failed. But that fall the Republicans won sweeping victories in both the presidential and congressional elections, and the new president, Warren G. Harding, proved less of a stickler on constitutional prerogatives than Wilson. Both parties had again included budget legislation in their platforms, and Congress went about the business of framing new bills again. There was further debate in both houses, a conference, and further compromises. Three of these were of some significance. First, the Congress was authorized to remove the comptroller general or his assistant by *joint* (rather than concurrent) resolution, which does require the signature of the president. It does not appear that this change would have satisfied Wilson's constitutional objection. Second, the Bureau of the Budget would be located in the Treasury Department but would be directly responsible to the president and would be headed by a director and assistant director appointed by the president without Senate confirmation. Third was an amendment introduced at the end of House debate

27. *Congressional Record*, 67th Cong., 1st Sess., 982.

by Massachussetts Republican Robert Luce intended to broaden the scope of GAO's work beyond legality and propriety to comprehend efficiency and effectiveness. The original legislation had authorized the comptroller general to investigate "all matters related to the receipt and expenditure of public funds"; Luce's amendment expanded this objective to comprehend "receipt, expenditure, and application," a change that would add legal strength to the broadened programs of GAO undertaken many years later.[28]

So modified, the budget and accounting bill passed both houses of Congress in late May and was signed, without any further question, by President Harding on June 10, 1921. That act, though considerably modified over the following sixty years, remains the basic charter of the OMB and the GAO. It was *genesis* for BoB; the American national government had never had anything remotely resembling this agency. For GAO, it was *exodus* from the executive branch to independent status, qualified by tenuous connections with the Congress and the president.

Concluding Observations

Probably at no time since their founding has the connection, in the abstract, between GAO and BoB/OMB been so close and so clear as it was in the period leading up to passage of the Budget and Accounting Act. They were seen as parts of the same system of public financing with the same goal—economy. That system was a somewhat imperfect representation of the executive budget doctrine. According to some purists, the act did not create a truly executive budget since it did not limit the authority of the legislative branch in the making of appropriations, which might have been accomplished through a prohibition against congressional raising of appropriations or adding new ones, or through a presidential item veto. Such provisions had been included in some of the state budget systems. However, the proponents of the Budget and Accounting Act insisted: "The plan outlined does provide for an Executive initiation of the budget, but the President's responsibility ends when he has prepared the budget and transmitted it to Congress. To that extent, and to that extent alone does the plan provide for an Executive budget, but the proposed law does not change in the slightest degree the duty of Congress to make the minutest examination of the budget and to adopt the budget only to the extent that it is found to be economical."[29] Observers up to and including

28. *Congressional Record*, 67th Cong., 1st Sess., 1090.
29. *House Reports*, 65th Cong., 1st Sess., No. 14, pp. 6–7.

TABLE 1

The Budget Process: Ideal Model Compared to Pre-1921 and
Post-1921 Practices

BUDGET STEP	RESPONSIBLE BRANCHES OR UNITS		
	Ideal Model	*Practice (Pre-1921)*	*Practice (Post-1921)*
Preparation	Executive	Spending agencies	Spending agencies, under direction of, and with revisions by, the president, helped by BoB/OMB
Appropriation	Legislature	Congress through several committees	Congress through single appropriations committees of each house
Execution and control	Executive	Spending agencies and Treasury Department	Spending agencies, BoB/OMB, and GAO
Postaudit (Accountability)	Legislature or independently elected officials	Treasury Department	GAO

1983 might wish to enshrine the first sentence above in the "famous first words" department.

Modelers of executive budget systems divide the whole process into four steps. These are depicted in Table 1 with comparative presentations of the process before and after the act of 1921.[30]

The basic flaw of the 1921 act, according to many students, was its confusion of the third and fourth steps noted in the table. During the debates on the budget and accounting bill, proponents repeatedly complained that, whereas the Congress would pass the appropriations, it had no means of knowing whether, how, or with what effect the money would be utilized. They visualized the GAO as the closing arc of the budgetary loop since it would report back to Congress what had happened to its appropriations. But this would not occur for at least two reasons. First, Congress set up no internal counterpart to the British Committee on Public Accounts to receive, consider, and act on

30. For an early version of this model see Stourm, *The Budget*, 52ff. The post-1921 column would be much changed and more complicated following the changes in direction of GAO after World War II and the Congressional Budget Act of 1974.

the reports of its comptroller general. (The Congress already had a considerable number of expenditure committees, most of which actually did little or nothing.) But the American comptroller general was in no position to make such reports anyway. Insofar as he was rendering advance decisions and making preaudits on some transactions, his postaudits were meaningless. And insofar as he was himself settling all accounts, there was no point in reporting them to Congress; they had already been decided and settled. Furthermore, in settling agency accounts, deciding upon claims for and against the agencies, and prescribing agency accounting systems, he was involving himself in executive business, thus dividing and confusing responsibility for performance. In short, the mixture of current controls with postaudit accountability was an indigestible combination, both in theory and in practice. Many years later, W. F. Willoughby, the principal intellectual author and proponent of the Budget and Accounting Act, criticized its "failure to distinguish between these essentially different functions [audit and control]. . . . The most striking example of where this faulty procedure has been followed is presented by the national government, which, in creating its General Accounting Office . . . has vested the performance of these two functions in the hands of the same officer—a procedure which has given rise to much trouble in operating a system which otherwise has great merit." [31]

In retrospect, it appears that the mistake about the GAO resulted mainly from a failure on the part of the framers of the Budget and Accounting Act to carefully review and fully understand the responsibilities of the auditors and comptroller of the treasury, some of which were plainly incompatible with an independent postaudit. The simple transfer of the powers and personnel of those offices perhaps made the drafting and passage of the bill easier but made little sense in terms of realizing the concept of an executive budget system.

It is perfectly possible that the two seemingly contradictory statements quoted at the opening of this chapter are both correct. Mansfield was addressing Title 3 of the act having to do with the GAO; Emmerich was thinking of Title 2, which established the budget system and the Bureau of the Budget. As Dwight Waldo has suggested, government organization is an elephantine problem. [32]

---

31. W. F. Willoughby, *The Government of Modern States* (Rev. ed.; New York, 1936), 487.
32. Dwight Waldo, "Organization Theory: An Elephantine Problem," *Public Administration Review*, XXI (Autumn, 1961), 210–25.

CHAPTER 2

Economy, Compliance, and Detail

I am for economy. After that I am
for more economy.

PRESIDENT CALVIN COOLIDGE, 1924

The Bureau of the Budget and the General Accounting Office launched their careers in mid-1921 on courses that were in some ways parallel, in others perpendicular, to each other. The character of the two organizations, which would persist for many years, was essentially set by their first heads—General Charles G. Dawes, the first director of the budget, and J. Raymond McCarl, the first comptroller general. Both were Republican politicians appointed by President Warren G. Harding; both were trained in law and had practiced that profession in Nebraska; both were strong-willed men who enjoyed the exercise of power and sought to enlarge their measure of it; both were dedicated to economy, efficiency, and integrity in government; and both allegedly had, or would later have, aspirations for higher political office (the presidency).

General Dawes and the Bureau of the Budget

There the likenesses end. Dawes was a whirlwind. After several years of law practice in Lincoln, Nebraska, he moved to Chicago and went into the banking business, which provided his basic home and occupation for the rest of a long, active, and wealthy life. As a young man he became involved in Republican politics. A leading supporter of President McKinley, he was considered for a cabinet position in 1897 and was appointed comptroller of the currency, an assignment that in those days had much power and autonomy and that he preferred to a cabinet post. He remained sporadically active in the Republican party until the United States entered World War I, when he enlisted as an officer in the Army Corps of Engineers. After his regiment arrived in France, his old and dear friend John J. Pershing, commander in chief of the American Expeditionary Force, detached him from the engineers and put him in charge of United States purchasing of supplies in Europe. In this capacity, he gained international fame in the fields of finance and logistics. After his election in 1920, President-elect Harding asked Dawes to accept his first cabinet appointment as secretary of the treasury. Dawes refused but indicated he would be interested in becoming the president's assistant for the budget, who was in certain respects above the cabinet, or director of the budget if the budget bill passed. This, he thought, would provide a much better opportunity to bring about real economy and efficiency in the national government. Harding then appointed Andrew Mellon to the treasury position but later turned to Dawes for the budget post a few days after signing the Budget and Accounting Act.

Dawes accepted the job for one year only, but for a man of such energy and drive, one year was quite enough. On June 22, 1921, the day after he accepted, he left Chicago for Washington and met soon after his arrival with the president. Pursuant to Dawes's request, Harding issued a statement on June 27 to the effect that his new budget director would prepare a new and lower budget for the fiscal year ending June 30, 1922, though the appropriations for that year had already passed. The deadline for the new budget was July 30, 1921. On June 28, Dawes met with the cabinet in the president's office. On June 29, the president, at Dawes's instigation, convened a meeting on the budget of all the department and agency heads, their first assistants, the chief clerks, and the chiefs and assistant chiefs of all bureaus and offices, more than 1,200 persons in all.[1] The president gave a speech on the budget and economy and then introduced Dawes, who set forth his principles and objectives for the budget. Two days later, on July 1, the president, again at Dawes's request, addressed all the new department and agency budget officers (positions required by the Budget and Accounting Act, section 214), stressing the importance of their assignments and his strong support of the new budget director. On that same day, Dawes issued the first budget regulations to the departments and agencies, prescribing the handling of the new estimates applicable to the fiscal year that began that day. In addition, work was started almost immediately to produce the first full-scale budget for fiscal year 1923, which had to be submitted to Congress by the first Monday in December. During that first summer and fall, he organized a variety of interagency coordinating boards on government business matters, and by the end of June, 1922, when he departed, the Budget Bureau had issued no less than seventy circulars on the budget and other business matters of the government.

Dawes's accomplishments in that single year seem the more remarkable since they were achieved with what now seems a minuscule staff (not exceeding at the maximum twenty-five professionals) hastily assembled and working in an area in which there was no precedent or experience. He relied principally upon officers he knew and had supervised in the army and navy during

---

1. This was the first meeting of what came to be known as the Business Organization of the Government.

his tour with the AEF in Europe, augmented by a handful of businessmen, mainly employed on a "dollar-a-year" basis (a category of employees that we would now call "without compensation"). Most of his top assistants had experience in military logistics or finance. This military tradition in the Bureau of the Budget survived for many years. Dawes's successor was General Herbert M. Lord, formerly chief finance officer of the army, who served until after the departure of President Coolidge in 1929. Lord's successor, who served through Hoover's presidency, was Colonel J. Clawson Roop, who had been assistant director of the budget under Dawes.

In at least the early years, the Bureau of the Budget seems to have been imbued with the same kind of dedication and enthusiasm as the army in the field. Its enemy was not Germany but extravagance and waste; the goal not Wilson's Fourteen Points but economy and efficiency, mainly economy. The emphasis upon economy permeated the Harding administration and the whole budget system even more than it had the earlier discussions about the Budget and Accounting Act in the Congress. In his first remarks before the officers of the executive branch (the meeting of June 29, 1921), President Harding announced: "The present administration of the Federal Government is committed to a period of economy and efficiency in government. . . . There is not a menace in the world to-day like that of growing public indebtedness and mounting public expenditures." In introducing General Dawes as director of the budget, he said that "every resolution, every commitment, every determination of the administration is to join with you and have you join with us in inaugurating the new efficiency and economy of administration in these United States."[2] The president and his successors, Coolidge and Hoover, reemphasized the importance of economy and efficiency repeatedly over the following decade (as indeed did Franklin D. Roosevelt at the beginning of his presidency). And the budget system, including its key organization, the BoB, was seen as the principal tool for saving money. Dawes and his colleagues in the bureau echoed the sentiment in word and deed over and over again. In his budget message for 1923, Harding indicated considerable pride in the reductions in "ordinary" expenditures from 4.1 to 2.1 billion dollars between 1921 and 1923, or by nearly 50 percent.[3]

Dawes was responsible for establishing two categories of extracurricular institutions, both for the purpose of preaching the gospel and for extending

2. U.S. President, *Addresses of the President of the United States and the Director of the Bureau of the Budget at the First Annual Meeting of the Business Organization of the Government* (1921), 1.

3. Ordinary expenditures are all those except payments on principal of the public debt and to retirement funds.

the practice of economy and efficiency in the government. The first was called the Business Organization of the Government, which was actually a convocation of all the top officials in the executive branch twice each year to listen to and applaud pep talks by the president and the director of the budget about economy and efficiency—their importance and benefits, examples of achievements during the preceding half year, and also examples of extravagance and waste. The first of these, as mentioned above, was held on June 29, 1921. The audience included not only the budget and financial officers but also the heads, deputies, and assistants of all the departments, agencies, bureaus, and offices—a total of between one thousand and two thousand persons whose attendance was, at least implicitly, compulsory. Presidents Harding and Coolidge faithfully appeared and spoke along with the budget directors, and the proceedings were regularly published. Indeed, the eighth meeting, on January 26, 1925, was broadcast over the radio with a program of music by the United States Marine Band. President Hoover, who as secretary of commerce had listened to these semiannual exhortations over the course of eight years, was apparently rather bored with them. They disappeared from the executive branch agenda in 1929, never to be revived.

The second institution inaugurated by Dawes came to be known as the Federal Coordinating Service, initially created by a budget circular and given presidential sanction by an executive order.[4] It consisted of a series of interdepartmental boards, each composed of appropriate official representatives of the major departments and agencies, to plan and coordinate activities in areas of common concern, such as surplus property, purchasing, statistics, and others. In addition, coordinating offices were established in each of the nine military corps areas in the continental United States. The system was modeled on that of the American Expeditionary Force in France. In fact, Dawes enlisted the advice and assistance of General Pershing in setting it up. Each of the boards and each of the areas in the field was headed by a coordinator—in almost every case a military officer—with assistants borrowed or detailed by participating agencies but also mostly military. The coordinators were appointed by the president on the budget director's advice, and the budget direc-

4. See Budget Circular No. 15 (July 27, 1921) and Executive Order No. 3578 (November 8, 1921). The material that follows concerning the Coordinating Service and the regional business associations is based upon James W. Fesler's paper "Executive Management and the Federal Field Service," prepared for the President's Committee on Administrative Management, *Report of the Committee with Studies of Administrative Management in the Federal Government* (1937), 273–94, and Fritz Morstein Marx, "The Bureau of the Budget: Its Evolution and Present Role," *American Political Science Review*, XXXIX (August, 1945), 672–74.

tor oversaw the entire operation through a chief coordinator, also appointed by the president. All the coordinators and their staffs were financed by their home employing agencies.

The Federal Coordinating Service operated as a kind of extension of the Bureau of the Budget in both Washington and the field. Its full-time staff, by the end of the Hoover presidency, consisted of eighty-three persons and was thus two and a half times larger than that of the bureau's staff of thirty-three. Although there were additions and subtractions in the boards and their functional responsibilities during the dozen years of their existence, they generally covered a substantial portion of the support activities of the federal government.[5] But as these agencies aged, like the bureau itself, they were increasingly routinized, and enthusiasm waned. Soon after his inauguration, President Franklin D. Roosevelt abolished the Coordinating Service entirely (by Executive Order No. 6166, issued June 10, 1933), though the activities of some of its boards continued in other forms.

The rather elaborate structure of the Coordinating Service was augmented, beginning in the early 1920s, by the establishment of regional business associations on the initiative of the regional coordinators and more or less paralleling the Business Organization of the Government in Washington. These consisted of representatives of all the federal agencies operating in a county or cluster of counties, who met together periodically, discussed common problems, elected officers, and formed committees in different fields of common interest, such as personnel, real estate, supply, and traffic. Like the Coordinating Service, they confined their activities to nuts and bolts problems of administrative support and did not venture to coordinate policies and programs. The principal value of the regional business associations was to encourage discussion of common problems among officers of different agencies in the same areas. They flourished for several years, their number reaching almost three hundred at its peak in 1930. But thereafter, it was downhill all the way. When the Coordinating Service disappeared, leadership was transferred to the Treasury Department's Procurement Division. The New Deal agencies did not join, and the movement gradually evaporated.

On at least one occasion, Dawes expressed the view that economy was not the only purpose of the BoB. In his report to the president on the budget for 1923, issued on December 5, 1921, he wrote:

5. There were separate boards for purchasing, specifications, contracts and adjustments, real estate, hospitalization, traffic, motor transport in the District of Columbia, forest protection, patents, printing, a standard stock catalog, and simplified office procedures, among others. Morstein Marx, "The Bureau of the Budget," 475.

There is a tendency on the part of many to assume that the Bureau of the Budget is established primarily for the sake of reducing expenses. The Bureau of the Budget is designed, through its facilities for securing information, to be in a position to give impartial advice to the President and to Congress in all matters regarding the proper business functioning of government. Because at the time of the establishment of the Budget bureau there was a great necessity existing for the reduction of governmental expenses, and since under the old decentralized system of governmental business great extravagance existed, the activities of the bureau which became most prominent were those where it acted as an agent for the imposition of Executive pressure in forcing down expenditures where not in contravention of congressional mandate and efficiency. This is but one function of the Budget bureau.

It must be as willing to advise an increase in appropriations where the same is clearly in the interest of governmental efficiency and true economy as it is to advise reductions in expenses, which at the present time are so necessary. It is only by this method, under which it gives an impartial business judgment as to the necessity for expenditures and the functioning of government, that it can, in the long run, maintain its proper influence with the Executive and with Congress and justify its existence.[6]

There is little evidence that this somewhat broader view of BoB's role had much impact upon the behavior of its own personnel. Their budget-cutting, economizing image and self-perception persisted for many years—even down to the present day—like those of most of the subcommittees of the House Appropriations Committee.

Dawes left many other marks on BoB almost as important as his stress on economy. In the meeting of June 29, 1921, he set forth four principles of the budget system that he said "must be so firmly established . . . that they will never hereafter be questioned in this administration or in any other." He further asserted that "these principles which are laid down now must be those which shall exist for all time."

1. The Budget bureau must be impartial, impersonal and nonpolitical.
2. The Director of the Budget in the matter of governmental business administration has no responsibility under the law save for the administration of his own bureau. He is simply an adviser of the President and Congress in the matter of correcting business administration.
3. The Director of the Budget, in gathering information for the use of the President, acts for the President, and his calls upon the chiefs of bureaus

6. U.S. Bureau of the Budget, *Report of the Director of the Bureau of the Budget to the President of the United States* (December 5, 1921), xxi–xxii.

and other administrative officers for purposes of consultation or information take precedence over the Cabinet head of a department, or any head of
an independent organization.

4. The Budget representative in each department, being appointed by the
   Cabinet head, will present to the Director of the Budget the views of the
   Cabinet head upon the wisdom of conclusions drawn by the Director of the
   Budget, for the use of the Chief Executive and Congress; but, as in the
   case of bureau chiefs and other officers, the call of the Director of the
   Budget for their presence and advice takes precedence over the Cabinet
   head.[7]

Dawes felt very strongly about these principles. He frequently referred to one
or more of them, and they were issued as Budget Circular No. 1. To this day
many of the crucial issues of the OMB concern their interpretation and application, especially the first one demanding political neutrality. In addition to
them, Dawes had a number of other convictions about how the budget system
should work in the federal government, some underlying and some deriving
from these principles. In the first place, he was convinced that policy and substantive operations could and should be separated from business organization
and administration—a separation roughly if not exactly comparable to the dichotomy between policy and administration, so familiar for the last hundred
years to students of public administration. He contended that he and his bureau, like the budget officers in the agencies, should have no part in making
policy or in carrying out the governmental functions themselves. These were
the proper responsibility of the Congress, the president, and the heads of departments, agencies, and bureaus.

On the other hand, the director of the budget and his colleagues were very
heavily involved in the business side of the government. Dawes did not define
business very specifically but used the term generally in connection with those
support activities essential to carrying out the goals of the organizations: the
budget itself, accounting, and other elements of financial management; purchasing; supply; property and equipment; real estate; transportation; records;
printing; and others. (He did not include personnel, perhaps out of conviction,
perhaps because he did not wish to tangle with the Civil Service Commission.) There were certain significant connotations to his stress on the business
organization of government. One was that government was in fact a very big
business; it could and should be run according to business principles. For example, he averred that, in installing a budget system, "the President is simply

7. Charles G. Dawes, *The First Year of the Budget of the United States* (New York, 1923),
8–9.

putting into effect . . . a condition which exists in any business corporation." [8]
He deplored the absence of standards and standardization in accounting, purchase specifications, contracting, printing, and financial and other procedures. He contended that the government and every major agency should have
a balance sheet and strove to establish one for the Post Office Department as
an example.

A second connotation of business organization was that the president,
as head of the executive branch, is the business manager of the government.
In this capacity, he uses the Bureau of the Budget as his business agent. Thus,
on business matters and for the information of the president, the bureau's demands and requirements take precedence over the heads of departments and
agencies. "So far as the business organization of the government is concerned, a Cabinet officer cannot be considered in any other light than as an
administrative vice-president subject to the call of the president of the corporation or his authorized representative in matters of business administration
only." [9] The "authorized representative" in this case was of course the director
of the budget or his designated subordinate.

Dawes claimed, or feigned, humility for himself and his bureau. At the second semiannual meeting of the Business Organization of the Government in
February, 1922, he said: "The President, advised by the Cabinet, and Congress determine the great questions of policy. As for us, we are men down in
the stokehole of the ship of state, and we are concerned simply with the economical handling of fuel. . . . I want to say here again that the Budget bureau
keeps humble, and if it ever becomes obsessed with the idea that it has any
work except to save money and improve efficiency in routine business it will
cease to be useful in the hands of the President." [10]

However much Dawes did or did not affect the course of government other
than in reducing its expenditures, he certainly provided precedents and machinery that would enable his successors in subsequent decades to exercise
tremendous influence. Partly this was through his relations with the president.
Apparently, they met and corresponded frequently. Clearly, Dawes com-
manded the tremendous respect of President Harding, who backed him on almost every major proposal and controversy. Harding is reported to have told

8. *Ibid.*, 9. On this same theme see *Report of the Director of the Bureau of the Budget* (December 5, 1921), xi–xiii.

9. See Dawes's memorandum to the president of July 11, 1921, reprinted in Dawes, *The First
Year of the Budget*, 27.

10. U.S. President, *Addresses of the President of the United States and the Director of the
Bureau of the Budget at the Second Semiannual Meeting of the Business Organization of the
Government* (1922), 13.

Dawes before his inauguration that he wanted to serve only one term in the presidency and that he would "like to see you nominated and elected President in 1924." In addition, Charles Curtis, like Dawes later a vice-president himself, reports Harding as saying three years later, a month before his death, that "Charley Dawes is the man who is going to succeed me." Dawes, for his part, was almost euphoric about the president: "It is a pleasure and honor to work under a great President such as this nation has at present. No one can associate with him without being profoundly impressed with his great sincerity and loftiness of purpose—his absolute honesty of thought and action, his kindness and his ability. This is his work, not mine, except as an agent carrying out express directions." [11] Similar remarks are scattered through his notes, and he wrote on a number of occasions that he was trying to establish precedents for future presidents who would be less interested and able in administrative matters than Harding.

In a variety of ways that would have lasting effects—to the present day in many cases—President Harding enhanced the role and the influence of the director of the Budget.

> He supported the director's insistence that cabinet officers and others come to the cabinet room at the White House on matters related to the budget or "ordinary business" when asked by the director.

> He authorized the director to convene two or more cabinet members on his own initiative in the White House cabinet room.

> He gave his authorization that the director's calls on chiefs of bureaus and offices for information or consultation should take precedence over heads of departments and agencies.

> He authorized the director of the budget to sign directives to the departments with the caption "by direction of the President" when "in ordinary business administration and coordination, an exercise of his authority is needed."

> He authorized the issuance of a directive (Budget Circular No. 49, December 19, 1921) requiring all agency requests or recommendations from the departments for legislation that might later affect appropriations to be referred to the president through the director of the budget to ascertain whether it should be approved by the president and was in accord with his financial program. It also required that the

11. Bascom N. Timmons, *Portrait of an American: Charles G. Dawes* (New York, 1953), 202; Dawes, *The First Year of the Budget*, 30.

president's approval be conveyed with the recommendation. The same procedure would apply to departmental advice asked by the Congress concerning proposed legislation.

He authorized the Bureau of the Budget, under the director's supervision and subject to the review and determination of the president, to "assemble, revise, reduce or increase the estimates of the departments or establishments as submitted to the Bureau. The Director of the Budget shall determine the plan as to the contents, order and arrangement of the estimates." [12]

Dawes recognized from the outset the complete dependence of his office and his bureau upon the president—and their complete independence of anybody else. This dependent posture of BoB with respect to the president would be enhanced if the president was also made dependent upon the bureau. Such a relationship of interdependence was encouraged from the first by the high personal esteem in which the president and his budget director held each other. This esteem was expressed many times publicly. It was strengthened by the president's adoption of economy and efficiency as the foremost objective and issue of his administration and by his and Dawes's repeated announcements that the bureau was the principal engineer of that program.

On one matter of the greatest significance—the lack of involvement of the budget agency and system in matters of policy—Dawes very probably either had his tongue in his cheek or was using a very curious definition of policy. It is hard to imagine how an agency could reduce expenditures by 30 to 50 percent, how it could advise the president on all proposed budget estimates and on all legislation that might later affect appropriations, or how it could coordinate many basic activities of different departments, without becoming concerned with policy. Dawes in fact belied his own professed innocence of policy in the instructions he issued to the investigators on his own staff. After the usual opening gambit about economy and efficiency, he wrote, "His [the investigator's] investigations should cover not only questions of economy and efficiency which may present themselves as the result of his study of the administrative policies already in effect, but should extend to that of the policy itself, with a view to advising the Director of the Bureau of the Budget, for the information of the President, as to whether limitations should be put upon existing policy and what, if any, new policies should be recommended." Later in the same memorandum, he was even more explicit. He said the work of investigators fell into two categories. The first related to economy and efficiency. The second related "to policy; that is to say, whether certain projects

12. *Ibid.*, 29, 139, 21, 161–63; Executive Order No. 3350 (September 21, 1921).

should be undertaken, whether others should be curtailed or expanded, and whether certain old projects should not be discontinued altogether." [13] But a declaration that the Bureau of the Budget was involved in determining public policy would no doubt have been waving a red flag before two bulls—the leaders in the executive branch and in the Congress. And these areas remain sensitive today.

One other field of activity was conspicuously and deliberately neglected by Dawes—and by his successors for the next seventeen years. This was organization and management. For most of the nation's history, work in this field had been considered the special province of the Congress, and proponents of the Budget and Accounting Act had considered the responsibility placed upon the Bureau of the Budget by section 209 of that act particularly significant.

> The Bureau, when directed by the President, shall make a detailed study of the departments and establishments for the purpose of enabling the President to determine what changes (with a view of securing greater economy and efficiency in the conduct of the public service) should be made in 1) the existing organization, activities, and methods of business of such departments or establishments, 2) the appropriations therefor, 3) the assignment of particular activities to particular services, or 4) the regrouping of services. The results of such study shall be embodied in a report or reports to the President, who may transmit to Congress such report or reports or any part thereof with his recommendations on the matters covered thereby. [14]

When Dawes arrived in Washington, he found already operating a congressional Joint Committee on the Reorganization of the Administrative Branch of the Government. Its chairman was in fact a presidential designee, Walter F. Brown. To avoid confusion, overlap, and conflict, Dawes, Brown, and the president agreed that the investigations toward reorganization should be left with the congressional committee and that the BoB should stay out of that field, at least at the outset. It may be noted parenthetically that when the joint committee reported its recommendations to Congress, it included some of the most far-reaching reorganization proposals in the nation's history: consolidation of the Departments of War and Navy into a Department of National Defense; establishment of a Department of Education and Welfare; removal of all nonfiscal functions from the Treasury; and others. [15] Congress apparently paid scant attention to them.

Dawes also found another going agency in the field of organization and

13. Dawes, *The First Year of the Budget*, 191, 192.
14. Public Law 67-13, June 10, 1921, sec. 209.
15. U.S. Congress, Joint Committee on the Reorganization of the Administrative Branch of the Government, *Reorganization of the Executive Departments* (1923).

management on his arrival in Washington—the Bureau of Efficiency. It, too, was headed by a man named Brown, in this case, Herbert D. Brown, its long-time chief. That bureau was the first permanent organization in the executive branch dedicated to administrative problems. Following upon, but apparently not based upon, the Taft Commission on Economy and Efficiency, Congress had in 1912 required the Civil Service Commission to establish a system of efficiency ratings for federal employees. The following year it extended this responsibility by ordering the commission to "investigate and report to the President, with its recommendations, as to the administrative needs of the service relating to personnel in the several departments and independent establishments in the District of Columbia, and report to Congress details of expenditures and of progress of work hereunder." Within two weeks, the commission established a Division of Efficiency, which promptly postponed the establishment of an efficiency ratings system and directed its attention to the "administrative needs of the service," such as "eliminating useless red tape and duplication of work, simplifying methods wherever possible, and introducing labor-saving machines and devices." In 1915, Congress made the director of the division a presidential appointee and the following year removed it from the Civil Service Commission, making it an independent agency reporting to the president with the same powers and duties previously conferred on the division.[16] For the following seventeen years, the Bureau of Efficiency was the nearest approach the government had to a management consulting unit. It retained its special responsibilities for developing and superintending efficiency ratings systems and later acquired such other functions as assisting in the development and installation of a position classification system, providing actuarial counsel with respect to retirement systems, and keeping up to date a government-wide index of agencies and activities. It also was given statutory responsibility for investigating the administration of the District of Columbia.

The Budget and Accounting Act of 1921 made no mention of the Bureau of Efficiency, even though there was a clear overlap of its functions with those intended for the Bureau of the Budget, which BoB largely ignored for its first eighteen years, and a potential overlap with the functions of the General Accounting Office. In fact, many of the investigations by the Bureau of Efficiency—the lion's share of its work—were initiated on request of Congress or its committees and dealt with subjects very comparable to those of GAO today. Most of the others were invited by the agencies themselves. During its

16. Public Law 62-299, August 23, 1912; Public Law 62-427, March 4, 1913; U.S. Civil Service Commission, *Annual Report*, 1914, p. 13; Public Law 63-290, March 4, 1915; Public Law 64-26, February 28, 1916.

early years, the studies of the Bureau of Efficiency were broad-gauged and quite general. For example, in its *Annual Report* for 1919–1920, it listed studies in four categories.

>   organization—general inconsistencies; reorganizations in the State and Treasury departments, reorganization of statistical work

>   personnel—inequity and inadequacy of salaries, examining methods in the Civil Service Commission, reclassifications and salary standardization

>   accounting—accounting systems in the State and Treasury departments, the Indian Service, and the Pan American Union

>   business methods—passports in the State Department, the Patent Office, the Bureau of Foreign and Domestic Commerce, and payroll methods generally

The importance and scope of its projects seemed to decline in its later years. An increasing proportion of its effort was directed to the District of Columbia government, to actuarial problems of the retirement funds, simplification of routine reports, improvement of currency papers, and the like.

There is not much evidence that any president paid much attention to the reports of the Bureau of Efficiency, though it was about as presidential an agency as existed at the time. In December, 1932, President Hoover, in his package of reorganization proposals, recommended that the bureau's powers and duties be transferred to the Bureau of the Budget, but this proposal, along with all the others, was turned down by a Democratic Congress. The day before the inauguration of President Franklin D. Roosevelt, the Bureau of Efficiency was abolished in an appropriation act, on the presumed grounds that the functions would be performed by the BoB.[17] Its records and files were moved to that bureau, but its functions were not picked up for several years. The federal government's first experiment with a permanent central management staff was thus abruptly terminated.

J. Raymond McCarl and the First GAO

Had President Wilson not vetoed the first budget and accounting bill in 1920, the first comptroller general would probably have been W. W. Warwick, Wilson's comptroller of the treasury, who had had a hand in drafting the GAO

17. The Treasury–Post Office Appropriation Act for 1934, Public Law 72-428, March 3, 1933.

section of the bill. (Rumor had it that Warwick suggested the fifteen-year term for the office, since he was then fifty-five years old and the regular federal retirement age was seventy.) But a Republican president with the consent of a Republican Senate was unlikely to reward a long-standing Democrat with a fifteen-year post. J. Raymond McCarl had been a young and active Republican and a practicing lawyer in McCook, Nebraska, before he came to Washington as secretary to that outspoken progressive who would later be banished from the Republican party, Senator George W. Norris. Norris, who labeled himself accurately in the title of his autobiography, *A Fighting Liberal*, was perhaps most famous as the father of the Tennessee Valley Authority, which would later become the *bête noire* of his former assistant, Comptroller General McCarl. McCarl left Norris in 1918 to become executive secretary of the National Republican Congressional Committee, a position he held for nearly three years. It is reported that McCarl advised President Harding for and against a number of potential candidates for comptroller general, but Harding, acting partly on the advice of some members of Congress, selected him for the post.[18] In a variety of ways he was comparable to many of his predecessor treasury comptrollers—a lawyer, a not very prominent (and therefore not very threatening) politician of the president's own party, with associations and friends in Congress. And like most of those predecessors, he brought with him little knowledge or experience of administration, the workings of large organizations, accounting, or auditing.

Unlike Dawes, McCarl did not limit his tenure to a single year; he remained in office his full fifteen-year term to the middle of the New Deal. But until the New Deal, he was not a widely known public figure. He was not a great innovator, and the initiation of change was not a distinctive feature of the General Accounting Office under his leadership. Indeed, McCarl brought fewer changes to the workings of the GAO and federal accounting in fifteen years than Dawes did to the budget system in his first month. Among those who knew him or had to deal with him whether they knew him or not, there was a wide disparity of opinion. His admirers described him as righteous and honest, imbued with the belief in economy and legality, independent, unafraid—the ultimate opponent of bureaucratic miscreants, thieves, and later, New Dealers. One journalist called him "the only official in Washington who obeys the law."[19] His critics, of whom he had many, particularly in the executive

18. Harvey C. Mansfield, *The Comptroller General: A Study in the Law and Practice of Financial Administration* (New Haven, 1939), 71.

19. Herbert Corey, "A Conscience in Black," *Collier's*, November 29, 1924, p. 26. In the same article, Corey wrote: "Mandarins jump in the air and snap at their peacock feathers when they speak of him. He compels them—think of the odious inference of this—to obey the law."

branch, would more likely use such words as self-righteous, stubborn, personally ambitious, arbitrary, despotic, humorless, a reactionary ideologue, nitpicker, and manufacturer of red tape and delay.

He inherited a sizable going concern—the offices of the comptroller of the treasury and the auditors in the treasury building plus about twenty other rental offices scattered around Washington, a number of ongoing functions, and a staff consisting of a handful of lawyers and a large number of clerks. The General Accounting Office employed very few if any who had backgrounds in accounting, a profession that was almost unknown in Washington in those days. At the start, the staff totaled about 1,700, but it soon grew to over 2,000 when GAO assumed responsibility for accounting, as well as auditing, for the Post Office. The size of the staff remained virtually stationary until the New Deal, when it grew sharply to more than 5,000. It peaked near the close of World War II at nearly 15,000, largely because of its responsibilities for monitoring and auditing war contracts.

The lion's share of GAO's work was a heritage from the six auditors of the treasury, all of whose positions were abolished. (Most or all of the incumbents were Democrats who were therefore fired.) The best known and least popular of these activities was the review and checking of the accounts of the thousands of federal disbursing officers around the government and of the supporting documents and vouchers that accompanied them. These accounts were shipped in periodically from all over the world, and freight carloads of them were frequently backed up in the yards of Washington's Union Station. The vast majority of them were records of transactions already completed—payments or receipts made. A few were unpaid vouchers to be preaudited prior to payment. GAO's responsibility was to check that each payment was properly authorized, legal, accurate, signed by the right people in the prescribed form, correctly added, and so forth. If any error or irregularity was discovered, GAO would write the appropriate responsible officer for clarification or correction, and a lengthy correspondence might follow. Transactions not cleared up to GAO's satisfaction were "disallowed," and the responsible disbursing officer was held personally responsible for making up the funds to the government, whether or not he was at fault. After all transactions had been checked and cleared, GAO "settled" the account, which then went into its voluminous records. There was usually a large backlog of accounts awaiting review and settlement, and some were held up for years in argument and bickering, resulting in a nearly continuous clamor about bureaucratic delays.

In terms of working time as well as demands for space, the second biggest responsibility of GAO was the maintenance of financial records—going back to the year one. It also:

reviewed and approved or disapproved government contracts and audited the payments made against them

reconciled all canceled checks against the records and depository balances of the responsible fiscal authorities in the agencies

reviewed and decided upon claims for or against the government and
provided a system for collecting payments due the government

directly settled the transportation bills of the agencies and paid the
common carriers

reviewed requisitions from the agencies and their disbursing officers
for advances of appropriated and other funds that, after its approval,
were the basis of warrants constituting legal authorization to expend
(or receive or transfer) funds

countersigned all the warrants themselves, which were drawn in the
Treasury Department and were signed initially by the secretary of the
treasury

The volume of paper involved in these operations was very large even at the
start; it became nearly incredible during the New Deal and totally impossible
in World War II. Even at the outset, disbursing officers' accounts numbered in
the thousands, postal money orders audited in the millions, and checks reconciled in the tens of millions. And one must remember that there were no computers then.

The potentially more discretionary and challenging tasks of the GAO included, first, the rendering of advance decisions requested by departments
and agencies on the legality of proposed financial transactions in terms of
laws, appropriations, court decisions, executive orders, and previous decisions of the comptroller. Such determinations became in effect a vast body of
law, the Bible and verse of all financial officers of the United States government. The impact of some of these rulings went well beyond the strictly legal
and financial. For example, an opinion limiting the use of funds for purposes
of training prevented the development of federal employee training programs
for nearly thirty years, and a McCarl finding in 1924 forbade married women
to use their maiden names on federal payrolls, a decision adhered to for fifty
years that was finally reversed by Comptroller General Staats in 1975, the
International Women's Year.

A second potentially creative function of the GAO derived from the Budget
and Accounting Act of 1921. Its section 309 provides, "The Comptroller
General shall prescribe the forms, systems, and procedure for administrative
appropriation and fund accounting in the several departments and establishments." This provision would soon become, and would long remain, a source

of bitter contention, both in principle (that the function should be in the executive branch) and in practice (the way in which the GAO carried it out). In that first year, General Dawes complained bitterly about the quality of accounting in the government as a whole, which he bluntly characterized a "disgrace." He was hardly less critical of the GAO's work in the accounting field. In his notes for April 30, 1922, he wrote:

> Executive power is here needed, and it exists in the Comptroller-General under the new law. Power is useless, however, without the knowledge of how to use it, and McCarl is therefore devoting himself to thorough study. I am confident that McCarl will master his place and task. He is bright and studious and I believe him to be strong. He is proceeding carefully, surrounded by timid assistants, grounded or rather "stalled" in the old system. He is gradually rising above them. But the delay in the inauguration of correct methods is exasperating. McCarl may finally have to do what in the Budget work I did from the first—club some heads. That would wake some of his people from a deep sleep, and result in a temporary activity on their part which would at least make it possible to pass judgment upon their intelligence.[20]

GAO, with the help of representatives of the Treasury Department and the BoB, did produce in 1922 a standard classification of expenditures by object (personnel, supply, transportation, and so forth). In 1926 it issued a bulletin that included a statement of procedures and a chart of accounts, and this bulletin was succeeded in 1943 by a more general regulation. Neither of these was well received in the agencies or by professional accountants, mainly because they were allegedly directed to meeting GAO's auditing needs, not the managerial needs of the executive branch.

The third responsibility involving potential creative contributions by GAO was one that Congress, in its own deliberations, had heavily emphasized. Section 312 of the Budget and Accounting Act provides, "The Comptroller General shall investigate, at the seat of government or elsewhere, all matters relating to the receipt, disbursement, and application of public funds," and "he shall make recommendations [to Congress] looking to greater economy or efficiency in public expenditures." For this purpose and also to develop general accounting standards, McCarl set up a small investigations office that later grew to become a sizable division with its own battery of field offices. However, it was staffed not with accountants or analysts but primarily with sleuths, including some alumni of the FBI, in search of fraud and overt mismanagement. It later became a source of considerable embarrassment to the GAO and was abolished in the 1950s.

20. Dawes, *The First Year of the Budget*, 213.

The GAO was also required by the Budget and Accounting Act of 1921 to make annual reports to Congress as well as special reports on particular subjects to the president, Congress, and congressional committees at their request or on its own initiative. During his first decade, McCarl submitted few reports other than the mandatory annual ones. His (and his successors') most consistent recommendations were that GAO be provided more adequate office space and that its audit jurisdiction be broadened to include government corporations. In other words, there were relatively few recommendations directed to greater economy and efficiency of governmental operations, and there is little evidence that GAO's reports in fact had much influence on either Congress or the executive agencies.

Being ignored may be one of the costs of being independent. The congressmen who planned the GAO sought, perhaps most of all, that it would be independent of the president and the executive branch generally. There seems to have been some assumption that it would be at least partly accountable to the Congress, but this was not mentioned in the act, and no individuals or bodies within those divided collegial houses were designated as overseers of such accountability. The comptroller general stood pretty much alone out in left field, with broad and not very carefully defined powers, including the authority to organize his operation as he saw fit, to build up or not build up field offices, to name his lieutenants (except for the assistant comptroller general, whom he could use or not use as he wished). He could issue letters and reports as he pleased and sign them on his own authority. And, for practical purposes, he could not be fired. Nonetheless, he was under certain constraints. Like most federal agencies, GAO depended upon the Congress for its annual funding, and this meant a degree of accountability to the appropriations committees of the House and Senate. Furthermore, its responses and reports to committees and subcommittees and individual members of the Congress or its failure to respond to their requests, could be a source of public criticism, embarrassment, and even congressional investigation. Since most comptrollers general, because of their long terms in office, would have to serve during Congresses controlled by both parties, their long-range effectiveness depended upon their demonstration of nonpartisanship and ideological neutrality, a lesson that J. Raymond McCarl may have learned a little too late.

Although independent of the president and the executive branch in most respects, the Budget and Accounting Act provided (in section 306) that "all laws relating generally to the administration of the departments and establishments, shall, so far as applicable, govern the General Accounting Office." This made it subject to the Bureau of the Budget with respect to its own budget, to the Civil Service Commission with respect to its personnel, to the agency superintending federal buildings (now the General Services Administration) with respect to its office quarters, and to others with respect to supplies, printing, and other matters. This provision has been a source of considerable argument almost to the present day. It was not until after Congress, in the Reorganization Act of December 20, 1945, pronounced that the comptroller general and the GAO were "a part of the legislative branch of the government" that the Bureau of the Budget ceased to review its budget estimates. It was not until passage of the General Accounting Office Act of 1974 that the comptroller general obtained control of the GAO building. And on February 15, 1980, the GAO finally escaped the jurisdiction of the Civil Service Commission (which had become the Office of Personnel Management) for most personnel purposes through passage of the General Accounting Office Personnel Act.[21]

The job of the auditor in the best of circumstances is not designed to encourage popularity among those audited—any more than is that of the budget examiner. Its purpose, as narrowly but usually perceived, is to find fault with the work, the decisions, the products, and the ethics of others, and too often an auditor's effectiveness is measured by the number and seriousness of the faults uncovered. The relations between auditors and auditing organizations and those who are audited are therefore likely to be personally distant and formal, suspicious if not hostile, and anxious. The extraordinary powers of the GAO exacerbated these "normal" difficulties of auditing: the powers to give final interpretations of laws and appropriations, to disallow payments and require that errors be repaid to the government by those who made them, to dictate the forms and procedures whereby transactions would be recorded and reported. The early GAO was deliberately distant, impersonal, and disliked. McCarl's posture of righteousness and his frequent challenges to the propriety and thrift of the executive branch did not improve the relationship.

GAO's relations with two departments with generalized jurisdiction, Justice and Treasury, and with government corporations were particularly contentious. Controversy with the Justice Department was virtually inevitable since both had powers to render opinions on matters of law. In the case of GAO, the Budget and Accounting Act made its judgments final upon the executive branch. Habitually, the departments (including the old comptroller of the treasury) had accepted the attorney general's opinions as final unless contested in the courts. The comptroller general, as early as 1923, declared the attorney general's opinions only advisory upon him; indeed, he said the same about the decisions of lower federal courts.[22] The comptroller general and the

---

21. Public Law 93-604, January 2, 1974; Public Law 96-191, February 15, 1980.
22. See his letter to President Harding in 1923, quoted in Albert Langeluttig, *The Department of Justice in the United States* (Baltimore, 1927), 159.

attorney general were at a standoff, a condition alleviated principally by the reluctance of the attorney general to raise an issue on any but major questions. The comptroller general could disallow payments, but at that time, only the attorney general could carry cases in behalf of the government to court. These issues have not been fully resolved to this day.

Until the end of World War II, the GAO and the Treasury Department were frequently at odds over the form and substance of governmental accounts and financial reports. The latter organization complained that GAO's requirements of the departments were useful only for its own auditing purposes and not for Treasury reporting purposes and that it issued directives about accounting classifications and forms without first clearing them with the Treasury Department. The accounts of the two could never be reconciled because they recorded transactions at different stages and times in the financial process.

Almost from GAO's beginning, McCarl (like his successors would be later) was in conflict with some of the federal government corporations, most of which were explicitly or implicitly set up outside of, or in only partial subjection to, the regular audit procedures and powers of the GAO. In 1922, Congress directed GAO to audit the Emergency Fleet Corporation "in accordance with the usual methods of steamship or corporation auditing"; McCarl protested for years that he should have his usual powers to review individual vouchers and to disallow faulty payments. He never won the battle; nor did he win a later one on essentially the same issue when the Reconstruction Finance Corporation was set up in 1932 (with Charles G. Dawes as its first director). The most celebrated of these conflicts, however, came with the establishment of corporations during Roosevelt's New Deal. The most notable of these was the recurring row between the GAO and the Tennessee Valley Authority (TVA), which led to a congressional investigation and was finally resolved by a treaty negotiated by the two agencies in 1940–1941, long after McCarl had left the scene. In retrospect, the conflicts may be seen as having some benign effects because they led to the first step in the first internal revolution of GAO, which began in earnest at the close of World War II (see Chapter 3).

In its first quarter century, GAO initiated remarkably little change in the federal government—despite, or in defiance of—the New Deal and World War II. Until that war it continued to operate very much as its predecessors in the Department of the Treasury had. The war brought new responsibilities to audit war contracts, and this occasioned a multiplication of staffs and establishment of field offices nationwide to perform audits on industrial sites. But the basic objectives and modes of operating did not change. McCarl and perhaps others in GAO's leadership—staunch believers in fiscal conservatism, balanced budgets, and small government—were outraged by the New Deal on ideological grounds, and this probably influenced some of their rulings. After his mandatory retirement on June 30, 1936, McCarl wrote two inflammatory articles entitled "Government-Run Everything." [23] Rumor had it that he had wanted to run for president against Roosevelt in 1936. After McCarl's departure, Roosevelt, who wanted to change the office itself, did not appoint a successor for nearly three years. The post was filled by Assistant Comptroller General Richard N. Elliott until the appointment in 1939 of Fred H. Brown, a former senator from New Hampshire. Brown retired for reasons of health only fourteen months later and he was succeeded by Congressman Lindsay Carter Warren of North Carolina in 1940.

The GAO's continuing skirmishes with the executive branch were from time to time capped by criticisms and confrontations with presidents. Although the presidents rarely had direct contacts with the comptroller general or others in the GAO, they were sometimes moved to criticize it or recommend basic changes in its locus or its powers by subordinate officials in the executive branch or by outside study groups. Wilson, it will be recalled, had vetoed the first budget and accounting bill because it denied him authority to remove the comptroller general—unconstitutionally, he believed. Harding, in 1923, in response to a request of the Joint Committee on the Reorganization of Government Departments, transmitted a draft of reorganization proposals to the Congress, noting in his accompanying letter that "with few exceptions . . . [the changes] have the sanction of the cabinet." [24] Among his proposals was one that the GAO be returned to the Treasury Department and another that the Bureau of the Budget be made an independent agency. These must have been among the "few exceptions"; Secretary of the Treasury Andrew W. Mellon testified vigorously against both proposals. Nothing came of these or any other Harding recommendations on reorganization.

Congress authorized President Hoover, in June, 1932, to prepare executive orders for reorganization to bring about economies in the executive branch, subject to a possible veto by either house of Congress within sixty days. In December of the same year, a month after his defeat by Roosevelt in the 1932 election, Hoover submitted eleven reorganization orders to Congress, the lower house of which was in Democratic control. Although the order perti-

23. See the *Saturday Evening Post*, October 3, 1936, pp. 8–9, 52, and October 17, 1936, pp. 8–9, 70–74.
24. Joint Committee on the Reorganization of the Executive Branch, *Reorganization of the Executive Departments*, 34, 49. This report contains both the committee's final recommendations and those offered the group by President Harding.

nent to this discussion was somewhat vague, it would at least have transferred from the GAO to the Bureau of the Budget the powers to prescribe and superintend accounting forms, procedures, and audits in the departments and agencies.[25] All of these orders were promptly voted down in the House of Representatives. President Hoover would later have another chance to air his views about the GAO when he chaired the Commission on the Organization of the Executive Branch of the Government in 1947-1949. That commission split in four different directions on the GAO organization issue. But Hoover himself, with a bare majority of seven of the twelve members, supported a somewhat more emphatic proposal to transfer all accounting and settling responsibilities from GAO to the Treasury Department. Nothing came of that proposal either.

The most determined presidential assault on the GAO was that undertaken by Franklin D. Roosevelt in the late 1930s and grew out of the recommendations in 1937 of the President's Committee on Administrative Management (also known as the Brownlow Committee). Roosevelt would have substituted an auditor general for the comptroller general, given him responsibility for postaudit, and returned all the other GAO powers to the executive branch. He lost that battle (see Chapter 3), but posthumously, he won the GAO war when Comptroller General Lindsay Warren defanged his critics by quietly, gradually, and almost totally redefining GAO's mission.

In the years between 1920 and 1952, the two presidents who had kind words to say about the GAO were Calvin Coolidge and Harry S. Truman. In his annual message of December 8, 1925, Coolidge must have shocked the leaders of the Bureau of the Budget when he said: "The purpose of maintaining . . . the Comptroller General is to secure economy and efficiency in government expenditure. No better method has been devised for the accomplishment of that end." He followed by urging the Congress to "resist every effort to weaken or break down this most beneficial system of supervising appropriations and expenditures. Without it all the claims of economy would be mere pretense." And in 1951, on the occasion of the dedication of the new GAO Building, Truman asserted that the GAO "has handled the biggest auditing job in the history of mankind and has done it well. It has continuously improved its operations so it could serve the people of this country better and more efficiently." But he was speaking about a much different GAO than was Coolidge. It is interesting and probably significant that no president since Truman has had much if anything to say about the GAO, at least not for public consumption.

25. "Special Message to Congress on Reorganization of the Executive Branch" (December 9, 1932), *Public Papers of the Presidents: Herbert Hoover, 1932–1933*, pp. 882–89.

Control by Detail

As pointed out earlier, the BoB explicitly and repeatedly denied that it had any interest in national policy, that policy was a matter for the Congress, the president, and the heads of the agencies. In one of his more colorful statements to the Business Organization of the Government, Dawes said, "Much as we love the President, if Congress, in its omnipotence over appropriations and in accordance with its authority over policy, passed a law that garbage should be put on the White House steps, it would be our regrettable duty, as a bureau, in an impartial, nonpolitical and nonpartisan way to advise the Executive and Congress as to how the largest amount of garbage could be spread in the most expeditious and economical manner." [26] As noted earlier, there was a certain amount of delusion, or self-delusion, in such statements. Yet, it is true that the federal budget was a mass of details—over a thousand pages of them. It was a line-item budget, organized according to spending agencies and items of expenditure: a position or a railway ticket, a fiber box or a bar of soap, with a numbered quantity of each such item, a unit price, and a total amount. The dollar amounts were usually calculated to the last penny. Thus, among the savings Dawes reported to Congress for fiscal year 1922 were these:

AGENCY	ITEM	SAVING
State Department, Division of Far Eastern Affairs	3 telephones discontinued at $3.00 per month	$ 27.00
Treasury Department, Surveyor General of Real Estate	Housing of two motorcars in army base garage, Boston, November and December	72.00
War Department, Chief of Air Service	Reduction of civilian personnel	23,069.20
Interior Department, General Land Office	Omission of a proposed edition of maps under the Homestead Act	679.00
Interior Department, Rio Grande project	Use of a lower-priced lubricant for gas engines on dragline excavators	7,316.51

26. *Addresses . . . at the Second Seminannual Meeting of the Business Organization of the Government,* 14.

The Bureau of the Budget itself provided the model for detailed statements of its savings. It announced proudly in 1921 that it had saved a large amount (which was, however, not specified) using discarded furnishings discovered in the basement of the Treasury Building. Later, in its annual report for 1924, it reported economies resulting from:

> picking up the printing type from the previous year's budget and using it again ($1,900)
>
> special care in turning off lights
>
> finding and using a bookcase in storage and having the Treasury carpenter make another of plain boards ($90)
>
> requiring that only one pencil be issued at a time and that the unused portion be returned before issue of a new one
>
> using scratch pads made of waste, including obsolete forms, used reference slips, and used envelopes
>
> saving of wrapping paper and twine
>
> saving jackets of inactive files and using them in active files ($18)[27]

Obviously, the bureau practiced what it preached.

The quantity of detail that swamped the budget process was dwarfed by the items on the vouchers, the receipts, the canceled checks, and the postal money orders that were reviewed by the clerks in the GAO. Every aspect of every financial transaction, however small or large, was supposed to be checked and approved or questioned—the accuracy of the price, that the item or service paid for was the cheapest available, that all the steps required for soliciting and examining bids were complied with, that there was authority in law and regulation to buy every item, that funds had been advanced by the appropriate warrant, that each paper was properly authenticated and signed, and so forth. The comptroller general issued rulings on almost every imaginable question arising from the interpretation and application of laws and rules to individual contracts and other transactions—several hundred every year, more in number than all the United States courts combined.

McCarl's strong personal concern with the detail of transaction approvals and audits, coupled with his equally fervent zeal for economy, became virtually legendary during his lifetime. Many examples of his rock-ribbed penny-pinching became well known. On one occasion, when "a special committee appointed by President Coolidge returned from a tour of the national

27. U.S. Bureau of the Budget, *Third Annual Report of the Director of the Bureau of the Budget to the President of the United States* (1924), 217.

parks, a project in which the President was interested deeply, the Controller [*sic*] General refused to put his o.k. on their joint expense account of $3,000. He held there was no statute on the books to substantiate the expenditure. A similar tour planned for the following year was not started." In addition, "seafaring diplomats also felt the sting of his rulings. He decreed cabin and dining-room stewards were entitled to tips not exceeding $5 and refused to sanction expense accounts containing $10 expenditures for these services."

But perhaps most remarkable and most indicative of McCarl's approach to his responsibilities are two other examples of his individual crusade to insure compliance through detailed control. "In one instance he refused to pay a luncheon bill for $1.50 submitted by a government employee who had traveled across the Potomac one afternoon on business." On another occasion he shocked employees of the Bureau of Engraving "when he ruled that the government would not pay for the wooden shoes they must use to protect their feet from acids." [28]

GAO's work only occasionally involved questions of general management, efficiency, or policy. A few times, heads of departments or bureaus might ask its advice on how to carry out a certain law or executive order, such as the drawing of contracts for milk purchases, or alternative methods of managing housing contracts or of reorganizing a specified operation. After the launching of the New Deal, its auditing and settling powers made possible its intervention in policy matters, such as the comptroller general's disallowance of TVA's purchase of a prize mule for its agricultural demonstration program. McCarl particularly aroused the ire of President Roosevelt when, in 1936, he refused to sign a letter authorizing the allocation of some of the funds appropriated to the National Emergency Council for the proposed Committee on Administrative Management, which was to be an adjunct to the council. The letter of authorization had in fact been drafted in McCarl's office. Several months later, the president was granted authority in a deficiency bill to allocate $100,000 to the work of the committee. In Brownlow's own slyly mordacious words, "Finally, however, Mr. McCarl did acknowledge by his signature the validity of an act of Congress passed unanimously by both Houses and signed by the President." [29]

The review and pursuit of details are no guarantee of accuracy and honesty

28. All these examples are from "J. R. McCarl Dead," New York *Times*, August 3, 1940, p. 15.

29. Louis Brownlow, *A Passion for Anonymity*: (Chicago, 1958), 343–55. Vol. II of *The Autobiography of Louis Brownlow*, 2 vols. Actually the committee had the use of only a little more than half of the $100,000, with the rest going to committees of the House and Senate and to the Brookings Institution.

in the large. The leaves can obscure the trees just as the trees can obscure the forest. While the BoB was reviewing and trimming the estimates for individual items and costs and GAO was checking the accuracy of individual vouchers and contracts, the worst financial scandals in the federal government in a century were building almost under the noses of the two agencies—scandals involving bribery, payments for illegal preferences, excessive payments for goods often not delivered, contracts entered into without competition as required by law, income tax violations—crimes that sometimes culminated in suicide or possibly murder. I am not aware that either of the two new agencies, BoB or GAO, knew about or reported on the criminal activities of 1921– 1924 in the Veterans Bureau, the Department of Justice, the Department of the Interior, and possibly the Department of the Navy, which were collectively referred to as Teapot Dome (the name of the navy oil reserves in Wyoming leased to private concerns by the secretary of the interior). Teapot Dome should have warned us of the limits of control by detail, no matter how thorough. But there is little evidence that it did—then or for many years thereafter.

In their first stages, the GAO and the BoB contrasted sharply with each other in many respects. The operations of one were old, its habits, attitudes, and most of its personnel going back many decades. The other was new; its staff were fresh to civil government (the majority being military officers); its routines and memories were built from scratch. One was independent and distant—from the president, from the agencies and people in the executive branch, and even from the Congress. The other was close to, and totally dependent upon, the president and with his support was powerful, respected, and even feared in the executive branch and probably widely disliked in the Congress partly because of its relative independence from the legislature. The work of one was oriented primarily to the past, to deeds already done. The other, while it looked to and relied upon the past for information and guidance, was oriented to problems and decisions for the future. Finally, one had stodgy, distant, authoritarian leadership, while the other, especially at the beginning, was led by enthusiastic, decisive, men who were likewise authoritarian.

The likenesses of the two agencies are as striking as their differences. Both were oriented to matters of finance and particularly the saving of money. Both were devoted to law and rule, and they seemed to share and operate upon the questionable premise that economy and legal compliance were not only compatible but nearly synonymous. Both placed a high value upon centralization and standardization, not only within their own organizations but in the government as a whole. Dawes and his successors repeatedly complained of the decentralization of the federal agencies, each going its own way without common direction and discipline; indeed they viewed the centralization of control under the president high among their missions. Both agencies sought common forms, standards, procedures, classifications, and reports. And both pushed the idea that economy and compliance should share at least equally with substantive goals of the different agencies. Neither did much to carry out its responsibilities in the Budget and Accounting Act with respect to improving management and organization in the executive branch. Both agencies exercised great power, but their influence was essentially negative. BoB conceived its mission in terms of cutting things back or out, not in terms of building, and GAO saw its task as finding fault with the way things were done and paid for. Finally, I would venture the thought, though with little corroborative evidence, that the overwhelming concern with details and with numbers on paper discouraged in both agencies a viewing of the big picture: the directions and problems of society and the things the government could and should—or could not and should not—do in response to them, other than economize.

CHAPTER 3

The Agencies Transformed

The world requires at least ten years
to understand a new idea, however
important or simple it may be.
SIR RONALD ROSS, 1923

By the end of their first decade, the Bureau of the Budget and the General Accounting Office were well established, going institutions. Their basic objectives of economy and legal compliance were clear and accepted; their practices were routinized and well understood; their employees, experienced and mature. Neither of these agencies—any more than the rest of government— was in any sense prepared for the cataclysmic depression in which the nation was already mired and still sinking. Their responses were perhaps predictable—greater economy, stricter compliance. In 1932, President Hoover was given authority by Congress to issue executive orders for federal reorganization in the interest of economy. For the first time he asked the Bureau of the Budget to study and develop such orders, subject to legislative veto. Eleven were prepared and submitted to the Congress after Hoover's defeat in the 1932 election. All were promptly defeated in the House. In the same year, at President Hoover's request, Congress had authorized creation of the Reconstruction Finance Corporation (RFC) with authority to lend up to two billion dollars for purposes of economic recovery. Almost immediately the new corporation and the Department of Agriculture, through which some of its funds were to be loaned to farmers, were at war with the comptroller general because he was not authorized to audit their transactions. Both President Hoover and candidate Roosevelt campaigned on the theme of economy in government. Roosevelt won, and then came the New Deal.

The programs that comprised the New Deal received little from the GAO or the BoB except warnings and opposition. Comptroller General McCarl laid some land mines and shot off some rockets in the media before he retired in mid-1936. After an unsuccessful try to induce a prominent congressional leader, Democrat Lindsay Warren of North Carolina, to accept appointment to that post, Roosevelt, probably in expectation of basic changes in the organization and powers of the GAO, nominated no one for nearly three years. The GAO rocked along basically as before under the acting (previously assistant) comptroller general, Richard N. Elliott, a 1931 Hoover appointee. Then, on

March 30, 1939, the same day that Congress passed the Reorganization Act of 1939 empowering the president to transfer functions and agencies subject to congressional veto, FDR named former senator Fred H. Brown, a New Hampshire Democrat, to the post. The coincidence was probably not an accident. Roosevelt had yielded to congressional pressures to exempt the GAO from the provisions of the Reorganization Act. However, Brown was not there long enough to do much more than learn his job before he was forced to resign due to poor health in mid-1940. A few months later, Roosevelt nominated Lindsay Warren, who accepted only on condition that the president cease trying to change the organization and powers of the GAO. But when Warren was installed on November 1, 1940, Pearl Harbor was only a little more than a year away. Before he could undertake much alteration in the course or the posture of the GAO, the nation was immersed in war.

One might have expected a more active role in the framing and implementation of New Deal measures by the Bureau of the Budget, but it was not to be. Roosevelt ended the military dynasty of bureau leadership when he named Lewis W. Douglas to replace Colonel J. Clawson Roop as director of the budget. Douglas, a businessman, politician, and for six years a Democratic congressman from Arizona, resigned after less than a year and a half because of disagreement with Roosevelt's policies of deficit financing.[1] He was replaced by Daniel W. Bell, a longtime career and later noncareer official in the Treasury Department who refused to serve as director of the budget except in an acting capacity. He served in this role until the revolutionary reorganization of 1939 and in fact began that revolution in 1938. But the contributions of the bureau in those turbulent years from 1933 to 1938 were limited to continuing restraint on the spending programs, which was consistent with its traditions, and its role was virtually nil in the emergency programs.

The New Deal agencies were largely conceived and led by a scattering of trusted Roosevelt appointees around the government, the Brain Trust, and for several years by a more formalized organization known as the National Emergency Council (NEC), which consisted of most of the heads of the major domestic departments and agencies (including the director of the budget) and a few other persons at the president's discretion. Roosevelt set up and utilized the NEC, first, as a forum for discussion of problems and policies; second, as a device to air and resolve interagency disputes; and third, as the apex of a pyramid of counterpart NECs in each of the states. It met, usually with the president, every two weeks in 1934 and 1935. For those two years, the NEC

1. Douglas was the only budget director with congressional experience until President Reagan appointed David Stockman to the job in 1981.

was very nearly the hub of the recovery effort. It was equipped with a staff whose executive director for most of its active life, Frank Walker, was a trusted and close adviser to the president, and to it from time to time were attached a number of other temporary agencies. It was probably not an accident that the NEC gradually ceased to be active during the period when the Brownlow committee was developing its report, which would recommend central staff agencies rather than a collegial body to develop and coordinate presidential programs. The NEC officially went out of existence when the Executive Office of the President was established in 1939.

Among the problems occasionally discussed at NEC meetings were roadblocks to programs set up by the comptroller general, who was a *bête noire* to many NEC members.[2] The director of the budget does not appear to have contributed much to these meetings except on questions of a specifically financial or budgetary nature. But even then, there was confusion as to the role of the BoB on policy questions in connection with its clearance of testimony and legislation in the Congress. In an interchange at one of the later NEC meetings between Secretary of Labor Frances Perkins and President Roosevelt, she asked: "Why should one refer to the Bureau of the Budget a question of policy? It seems a peculiar thing to do." And later: "If it is the NEC staff that is to work out these details, why should the Budget Bureau handle it? It has no relationship to policy, ordinarily, except as to whether the income will stand the outgo." The president replied that a project that involves expenditure of money is cleared through the director of the budget. "He passes it up to me with a memorandum saying, 'On our present budget, we cannot afford it; but if you want to break the budget and approve it, it is up to the President.' He gives me factual information about finances; that is all."[3]

Of course, at that time the BoB was simply too small to be of much help, quite aside from its accustomed practice of economizing. Following the precedent of General Dawes to provide an example of internal parsimony for the rest of the government, its staff still numbered under thirty-five when Roosevelt came in, and it grew to only about forty-five by 1939.

The Brownlow Report and Its Sequels

Studies of the modern development of both the BoB and the GAO often begin with the 1937 report of the President's Committee on Administrative Manage-

2. Most of this information about the NEC is drawn from the minutes of NEC meetings as assembled and edited by Lester G. Seligman and Elmer E. Cornwell, Jr., in *New Deal Mosaic: Roosevelt Confers with His National Emergency Council* (Eugene, 1965).
3. *Ibid.*, 493–94.

ment.[4] The report provided the rationale, though not the specifics, for the existence of the Executive Office of the President (EOP) and the central role therein of the Bureau of the Budget. At the same time, it contained the most thoroughgoing attack on the GAO as it was then constituted yet published and the argument, which still prevails in some quarters, that the comptroller general should become an auditor general, reporting on executive finances and transactions to the Congress.

There is neither space nor need in these pages to summarize the Brownlow report, since it is abundantly described and analyzed in many other books and monographs. But at the risk of brief repetition, certain of its points should be mentioned since they are so fundamental to the study of the two agencies treated in this book, especially the Bureau of the Budget. The central premise of the report was that one of the president's three basic functions is to superintend the management of the government and that this responsibility is encompassed in the constitutional expression "executive power."[5] (The other two presidential functions, according to the report, are his responsibilities as political leader and head of state.) The president, stated the report, was not adequately staffed or equipped to carry out this responsibility of administrative management; he "needs help." For this purpose he should have not more than six immediate aides, and these "should be possessed of high competence, great physical vigor, and a passion for anonymity." Here were planted the seeds of what was to be known as the White House Office. Furthermore, the president should have direct control over the "great managerial functions of the government . . . personnel management, fiscal and organizational management, and planning management"; and for this purpose three managerial institutions should be made part of the executive office: "the Civil Service Administration, the Bureau of the Budget, and the National Resources Board." The only one of these that was subsequently placed in the Executive Office of the President and survived there beyond a few years was the Bureau of the Budget. The report envisaged a much different and greatly enlarged BoB from the one then operating. To the new bureau would be assigned fiscal policy and planning, execution as well as preparation of the budget, administrative research, information services, coordination of field activities, as-

4. U.S. President, President's Committee on Administrative Management, *Report of the Committee with Studies of Administrative Management in the Federal Government* (1937).

5. The Brownlow premise that executive and administrative powers of the president are one and the same or interchangeable was a matter of intense controversy at the time in both academic and political circles. One of the leading opponents of that view then was W. F. Willoughby of the Brookings Institution, who was, as described in Chapter 1 above, a principal author of the Budget and Accounting Act of 1921. The debate continues unresolved to this day. For a recent discussion of it, see James L. Sundquist, *The Decline and Resurgence of Congress* (Washington, D.C., 1981), esp. 47–51.

sistance to the departments and agencies with their internal organization and management, and clearance of proposed legislation, testimony, reports, and presidential directives.

The tenets of the Brownlow report would soon become basic doctrine for students and practitioners of public administration and would so remain for decades to come. They were the beacons for various governmental study groups, beginning with the two Hoover commissions, at the federal, state, and local levels. But at the beginning, the sledding of the Brownlow report was pretty rough. While President Roosevelt endorsed it heartily, select committees in both houses of Congress and then a joint committee of both questioned parts of it, as did the Brookings Institution in a report commissioned by Congress. The basic underlying issue was, as it long has been, the division and sharing of powers between Congress and the president in the management of the executive branch. This issue was reflected in two principal questions. First, should the president be granted power to reorganize by executive order part or all of the executive branch by transferring, consolidating, or abolishing agencies and powers? Second, which branch should have what powers with respect to the administration of finance, once appropriations and taxes had been adopted? More specifically, what should be the powers of the GAO with respect to setting up accounting systems, reviewing and settling accounts, authorizing disbursements, and so forth? The Brownlow committee and the president thought these were properly administrative functions within the executive powers of the president and that the needs of Congress would be satisfied by an independent postaudit. Some Brookings scholars and a good many members of Congress thought that GAO's powers should be retained or even expanded.

President Roosevelt's first reorganization bill, drafted in 1937 by the Brownlow committee itself, authorized the president to bring about reorganizations by executive orders. It narrowly failed of passage. After two years of argument, members of the House of Representatives, with help from the Legislative Reference Service, drafted a compromise bill that provided authority to the president to propose "reorganization plans" that would go into effect unless vetoed by concurrent resolution of both houses of Congress. In the words of Republican Congressman Everett Dirksen of Illinois, this bill had "never been profaned by coming before the eyes of . . . leaders in the executive branch—or members of the Brownlow Committee." The Reorganization Act of 1939, the legislative veto provision, and the psychosemantics of using the term *reorganization plan* instead of *executive order* were thus congressional contributions.[6] Congress, however, protected some of its favorite agencies by

6. Specifically, they were contributions of Missouri Democratic Congressman John J. Cochran and of Lindsay Warren, who would the following year become comptroller general of

exempting them from the law. These included GAO, the Civil Service Commission, and most of the regulatory commissions, thus negating some of the Brownlow committee's key proposals. That first Reorganization Act, like all of its several successors, was temporary, lapsing on January 21, 1941. GAO has been exempted from every reorganization act since.[7]

Once the Reorganization Act was passed, the Roosevelt administration lost no time. In the spring of 1939, it began bringing to Washington consultants in public administration to work on organizational problems in various agencies. On July 1, 1939, the first and second reorganization plans in American history became effective. Part 1 of Plan No. 1 established the Executive Office of the President, consisting of the Bureau of the Budget (transferred from the Treasury and including the Central Statistical Board) and the National Resources Planning Board. And on September 11 of that same year, one of the most famous of all executive orders—No. 8248—was issued. It established the divisions of the EOP and prescribed their duties: the White House Office, including the secretaries to the president, the executive clerk, and the six "anonymous" assistants to the president; the Bureau of the Budget; the National Resources Planning Board; the Liaison Office for Personnel Management, which would be headed by one of the six assistants; and the Office of Government Reports. It also authorized what was later established as the Office of Emergency Management. The duties of the BoB were a somewhat elaborated version of the Brownlow recommendations, plus the improvement and coordination of statistical services.

Executive Order No. 8248, which was drafted in the BoB with the help of Brownlow himself, seemed a fairly accurate expression of the concepts and the words of the report of the Committee on Administrative Management. Actually it went considerably beyond the boundaries of administrative management as the term was enunciated by that committee and as it is usually understood, and it set the stage for even further extension in the future. It provided mechanisms for immediate presidential oversight of political and public relations, policy planning, program development—as well as for the efficient management of going concerns. The precedents for most of the activities of the White House staff and the other units in the Executive Office of the President to this day were set in place by Roosevelt in 1939.[8] So

---

the United States. Louis Brownlow, "Reconversion of the Federal Administrative Machinery from War to Peace," *Public Administration Review*, IV (Autumn, 1944), 309–26.

7. During World War II, the president was granted almost complete authority to reorganize in the First War Powers Act (Public Law 77-354, December 18, 1941), but GAO was exempted from that act, too.

8. The Reorganization Act of 1939 (Public Law 76-19, April 3, 1939) and Executive Order No. 8248 (September 8, 1939) established and defined the functions of the units that would comprise the Executive Office of the President—the presidency's institutional arm. James Sterling

were some of the problems, including those to be discussed below, of the BoB/OMB.

The Born-Again Bureau of the Budget

In retrospect, it seems surprising that President Roosevelt moved as slowly as he did in refashioning the Bureau of the Budget. In 1919, as assistant secretary of the navy, he had vigorously supported a strong, centralized budget system. Beginning in 1929, as governor of New York, he had contributed to the strengthening and broadening of that state's budget division—a part of the governor's executive department—to the point that the budget director became very nearly the administrative manager of the state: a de facto vice-governor.[9] Yet, he was three years into his first term as president before he began to move toward a strong, managerial-staff budget agency and six years—a full decade after he was elected governor of New York—before he forcefully acted on the idea. The Brownlow committee gave him a publicly persuasive rationale, but it seems quite probable that he and the members of that committee were essentially agreed in advance on a budget agency that would act as a general staff for the president. The reincarnation of the Bureau of the Budget in 1939 was surely as much a product of the ideas of Franklin D. Roosevelt as of the Brownlow committee. And over the long pull, the reincarnation of 1939 was very nearly as important as the incarnation of 1921.

Roosevelt began rebuilding the Bureau of the Budget even before his reorganization plan had gone into effect on July 1, 1939. In 1937 and 1938, Acting Director Bell developed an organizational plan for a new bureau and requested and obtained funds for a much larger staff. Effective April 1, 1939, Roosevelt appointed Harold D. Smith director of the budget on the recommendation of Brownlow. Smith, a registered Republican, had for some years been secretary of the Michigan Municipal League and was at that time direc-

---

Young has shown that Roosevelt had effectively institutionalized many of the functions of the EOP as early as 1934–1935. See his *The Puzzle of the Presidency: An Inquiry on Political Leadership in America* (Baton Rouge, forthcoming).

9. The New York state budget system, including the budget division that ran it, was then probably one of the strongest, if not the strongest, in this country. Its origins lay in the state's constitutional convention of 1915, all of whose recommendations were voted down. But most of them, including the executive budget, were picked up and pushed through by Governor Alfred E. Smith during the 1920s, and when Roosevelt succeeded Smith as governor in 1929, he further strengthened them in practice. Frederick C. Mosher, "The Executive Budget, Empire State Style," *Public Administration Review*, XII (Spring, 1952), 73–84.

tor of the budget for the state of Michigan. He would serve Presidents Roosevelt and Truman as budget director until mid-1946, the longest tenure of any director to the time of this writing. He would build its staff rapidly from about forty-five to over six hundred in 1944, which is about as large as it is today. More than that, he almost completely changed the posture and mission of the agency from that of solely an instrument of economy in government toward that of a general-staff agency to the president, an institutional, nonpartisan source of information and advice to presidents, Congresses, and executive agencies, and the central memory of the government's administration. Smith's success in transforming the BoB may be attributed to a number of things: the vacuum of management knowledge and skill that it undertook to fill; the growing demands for such a central staff agency and the challenge to it in the preparation for, and conduct of, the greatest war in history; the confidence and experience of FDR with agencies of that sort; the personal trust of Roosevelt in Smith and later of Truman in Smith's successors, James E. Webb, Frank Pace, and Fred Lawton; and the quality and loyalty of the bureau's staff, characteristically young, enthusiastic, loyal, smart, and, after some experience, perhaps the most knowledgeable people in the government about the government. The relative subordination of economy as the dominating motivator of BoB was no doubt facilitated by the war, for in conditions of all-out war, the key ingredients are not dollars but manpower, critical materials, weaponry, administration, strategy, intelligence, and, perhaps most of all, time.

Under Bell and Smith, the BoB was reorganized into five divisions, each expressive of major functions. Most of what had been the Bureau of the Budget became the Division of Estimates, which handled the supervision, review, consolidation, and execution of the budget. The Division of Administrative Management was Smith's first new one, organized and led by Donald C. Stone, who joined the bureau from the Public Administration Service in Chicago early in 1939. The Division of Statistical Standards handled the coordination of statistics within or required by the government, a function inherited from the defunct Central Statistical Board. The Division of Legislative Reference coordinated and cleared proposed bills, executive orders, proclamations, enrolled bills (prior to their signature or veto by the president), and executive branch communications to Congress on proposed legislation. The Fiscal Division was designed to provide information and advice on the economic implications of budgetary actions and to advise the president on economic policies generally. In addition to these standing divisions there was during the war a War Projects Unit to examine, review, inspect, and consider appropriation requests for construction projects of war agencies.

ADMINISTRATIVE MANAGEMENT

From the standpoint of the reformers who proposed it and the top officials of
the Bureau of the Budget at the time, the most significant development in the
late thirties was the birth and growth of the Division of Administrative Management. Acting Budget Director Daniel Bell began hiring investigators in
the mid-1930s to look into federal management problems, but the real seeds
that were to flower in the Division of Administrative Management were not
planted until early 1939, some months before the transfer of the BoB to the
Executive Office of the President and even before the arrival of Harold Smith
as budget director. It started on problems mostly unrelated to the budget,
problems sometimes referred by the president or others in the White House,
sometimes coming to its attention from other sources: an organizational mess
in the Wages and Hours Division, a jurisdictional problem between the War
Department and the Civil Service Commission, relationships of several different departments on territorial government, and others. Soon it was deeply
involved in planning, organizing, and funding emergency agencies in connection with war mobilization and later most of the nonmilitary war agencies
themselves: the Office for Emergency Management (which was a kind of umbrella for many of the others), the War Production Board, the Office of Price
Administration, the War Manpower Commission, the Office of War Information, the Office of Economic Stabilization, and others. Until 1943, with the
establishment of the competitive Office of War Mobilization (OWM), the
BoB through its arms in administrative management and defense projects provided the principal support for managing the civilian side of the war effort.
The staff of the Division of Administrative Management grew in size from
zero in 1938 to seventy-seven in 1942.[10]

By the close of World War II, administrative management in the BoB was a
sizable (more than one hundred persons), widely respected, going concern.
After a few skirmishes over jurisdiction and power with the Office of War Mobilization and Reconversion (the OWM became the OWMR) and some misun-
derstandings as to its scope and mission among a few near the top, the division
became increasingly involved in presidential problems. When the first Commission on Organization of the Executive Branch of the Government (the first
Hoover commission) was established, a number of its staff were assigned to
help the commission generally and also to help some of its individual members. As general monitor of presidential reorganization plans, it drafted the

10. Larry Berman, *The Office of Management and Budget and the Presidency, 1921–1979*
(Princeton, 1979), esp. 16–30.

plans proposed to implement the commission's recommendations in and after 1949, the majority of which became effective.

ESTIMATES

At the time of the Brownlow committee and indeed from the beginning of the national budget system itself, the principal responsibility of the BoB was to come up with reliable estimates of future expenditures. Most of its staff time was devoted to reviewing, negotiating, and making decisions or recommendations on expenditure estimates submitted by the various federal agencies and to the preparation of the president's budget. The committee proposed no significant changes in the budget process; it would remain the principal engine of the BoB, as indeed it is today. But the words used to describe how the engine should be operated and where its vehicle should be steered were quite different from those utilized by budget directors and presidents theretofore. Only once in the Brownlow report, and then incidentally, does the word *economy* appear. The purposes of the budget system are described as "to provide in financial terms for planning, information, and control." While acknowledging the accomplishments of the bureau, the committee criticized its failure to develop "its important complementary functions," mainly those relating to administrative research, reorganization, and oversight of budget execution. These shortcomings were attributed to the totally inadequate size of the BoB staff, its excessive attention to detail, and by implication, the limited perspectives and qualifications of its professional personnel. The committee urged that BoB have a staff of "unusual competence, breadth of vision, keen insight into governmental problems, and long acquaintance with the work of the Government." [11]

President Roosevelt had already provided the BoB with a significant tool to control budget execution when, by Executive Order No. 6166 in 1933, he authorized its "making, waiving and modifying apportionments of appropriations" to the departments and agencies. Apportionments are in effect allotments of funds that may be spent in each time period, usually months, out of appropriated funds. They had originated in 1905 in the Deficiency Act to require each agency to schedule the obligation of its appropriated funds over the year and thus reduce or eliminate year-end deficiencies. [12]

But the major steps taken to strengthen the budget management activities

11. President's Committee on Administrative Management, *Report*, 16, 18.

12. Public Law 58-217, March 3, 1905, as amended by Public Law 59-28, February 27, 1906.

were in the area of recruiting. Even before 1939, Acting Budget Director Bell received appropriations sanction to double the size of the bureau, and thereafter the staff grew in almost geometric proportions for several years. Some of the new recruits were persons of experience and established reputations in and out of government. More were drawn from the lists of junior management assistants that the Civil Service Commission had developed to attract top-grade college graduates and holders of graduate degrees. They came from many fields—business and public administration, economics, other social sciences, statistics, and the humanities. The majority would become budget examiners.

The BoB maintained the general directions suggested by the Brownlow committee until after the war. But basic changes came as a result of the recommendations of the first Hoover commission, whose reports were published in 1949. One of that commission's most important and most influential recommendations was the adoption throughout the government of what it called a performance budget—a term reputedly coined by President Hoover himself. Such a budget would "analyze the work of government departments and agencies according to their major functions, activities, or projects. It would thus concentrate attention on the work to be done or service to be rendered rather than on things to be acquired such as personal services, contractual services, supplies, materials, and equipment." [13] The commission further argued that this kind of budget would facilitate congressional and executive control by relating the scope and magnitude of work to costs. It also cautioned that it would entail a simplified and rationalized appropriation structure.

The performance budget idea caught on, not only in Washington but all over the country. Even in 1949 it was legally required for the military departments in the National Security Act Amendments, and in 1950 the Budget and Accounting Procedures Act incorporated its major features. [14] At least partly in consequence of the first Hoover commission's recommendations, there occurred in the late 1940s and early 1950s the most comprehensive revisions of the structure and content of federal budgeting in American history to that time. The number of different appropriations was reduced by 70 to 90 percent in some agencies, which meant, among other things, that most of them became lump-sum, related to larger functions and programs, rather than detailed and based on things and services purchased. Attention was directed more to

13. U.S. Congress, Commission on Organization of the Executive Branch of the Government, *Concluding Report* (May, 1949), 15.
14. Public Law 81-216, August 10, 1949, title 4, sec. 403; Public Law 81-874, September 12, 1950.

work done and outputs than to prices paid for inputs. The details were retained in the budget process, as they still are; congressional appropriation committees continued to require the detail (the "green sheets") as in all probability did most of the BoB examiners. During that postwar period, the budget documents themselves were made more meaningful to those not intimately involved in budgeting and assumed formats not very distant from those of the 1980s.[15] From the standpoint of the work of the examiners in OMB, one result was their growing concern in matters like work measurement, accrual and cost accounting, production planning and management, and productivity.

FISCAL ANALYSIS

Apparently from the very beginning, the born-again budgeteers had in mind that the budgeting operation should be supported and influenced by economic considerations. Those were days when Keynesian economics was just beginning to take hold, and the techniques for calculating the gross national product had been developed only a few years earlier. Yet Harold Smith, already convinced of the impact of economic developments upon federal finances and vice versa, sought a stable of qualified economists to assess and anticipate economic conditions and needs and to analyze the impact of alternative federal programs upon the economy on both a macro and a micro basis. In 1939 and 1940, he formed a small Fiscal Division consisting of several economists, many of whom were or soon would become eminent in their field. It was his hope that this division would become the primary source of advice to the president on economic policy. That hope was frustrated, despite his efforts and to his great disappointment, when the Council of Economic Advisers (CEA) was established in 1946. The CEA's initial staff leader, Gerhard Colm, and some others were actually transferred from the BoB, and the relations of the economists in the two agencies remained close and cordial. The Fiscal Division itself continued until 1952, and OMB's fiscal analysis work continues to this day, though under different organizational auspices.

15. The principal U.S. budget documents consist of *The Budget of the United States Government*, which includes the president's budget message and general statements and tables about all aspects of the government's finances; *The Budget in Brief*, a brief summary statement of the major governmental programs, illustrated with charts and diagrams, designed for the general public; *The Budget Appendix*, a detailed and official statement of proposed appropriation language, official duties and statistics of each agency and fund, and other data (this is not for reading but for reference, since it is about the size of the Manhattan telephone directory); and *Special Analyses*, a detailed but still readable account about crosscutting aspects of the budget, the content of which changes somewhat from year to year (recent subjects have included grants-in-aid, loans and loan guarantees, tax expenditures, and research and development).

STATISTICAL STANDARDS

In 1931, President Hoover had established a Federal Statistics Board as part of the Federal Coordinating Service. It consisted of representatives of the principal federal agencies that collected statistics from the private sector. Its mission was to review and coordinate statistical activities, eliminate duplication, and assure maximum utilization of statistical information. That board, along with all the others in the Coordinating Service, was abolished by Roosevelt in June, 1933. However, the following month the president set up a new Central Statistical Board by Executive Order No. 6225, issued July 27, 1933, likewise composed of representatives of federal statistical agencies and with a substantially comparable mission, though with greater emphasis upon the development of standards, schedules, classifications, and so forth. A major difference was that the later board was empowered to hire its own staff. The board was subsequently given statutory status and its powers somewhat enlarged in 1935. When the reborn Bureau of the Budget was established by Reorganization Plan No. 1, the entire board and its staff were moved into it, and its chairman became head of a Division of Statistical Standards, responsible to the director of the budget.

LEGISLATIVE CLEARANCE

The coordination of legislation and other official documents on behalf of the president is one of the oldest and most institutionalized of BoB/OMB's functions, but it has changed fundamentally since the agency began, most profoundly during Roosevelt's second term. The clearance of legislation was not provided in the Budget and Accounting Act, and it was undertaken on the suggestion of the House Appropriations Committee, not the Bureau of the Budget. In 1921, the chairman of that committee wrote the budget director a letter about the diversion of funds requested by a federal agency from the purposes for which they had been appropriated, and he suggested that such requests should be reviewed and controlled by the bureau. Accordingly, the bureau issued a circular in December, 1921, directing agency proposals for, or comments on, legislation that would create obligations on the Treasury to be submitted to BoB to ascertain whether they had the president's approval; if this was not done, new proposals could not be submitted; in addition, comments on legislative proposals were to state whether they had presidential approval.[16] Hard pressed by objections from the agencies, Dawes and President

16. Budget Circular No. 49, December 19, 1921.

Harding did not push for enforcement of this procedure. But under Presidents Coolidge and Hoover, it was exercised vigorously—and negatively. It became a major device for turning down or disapproving legislation that would cost money. After the inauguration of President Roosevelt in 1933, the clearance procedure was largely ignored until the Budget Bureau itself reestablished it more or less along the old lines in early 1934. But Roosevelt had different ideas about legislative clearance. He was concerned about statements and opinions emanating from different agencies that expressed views differing from his own or from each other on substantive policy matters. At his personal direction, a new procedure was instituted providing that all proposed legislation or reports on legislation from the agencies go to BoB.[17] Matters of policy would be referred to the staff of the National Emergency Council; matters of fiscal importance BoB would handle itself—in both cases after consultation with the president.[18] But since the National Emergency Council ceased to be active in 1936, the entire function fell to the BoB. Acting Director of the Budget Daniel W. Bell began in 1937 to build up the bureau staff in response to the recommendations of the Brownlow committee, and permanent staff were assigned to legislative clearance. The following year, he organized them as the Division of Coordination, which later became the Office (now the Division) of Legislative Reference.

An important step in the progression of BoB's role in this area was its assumption of responsibility (made official in early 1939) for coordinating agency views and recommending presidential signature or veto of enrolled bills—that is, bills passed by the Congress that would become law if signed by the president.[19] The jurisdiction over enrolled bills capped the BoB's influence in the three-step process of legislative clearance. First, it was to coordinate legislation initiated by federal agencies throughout the executive branch and advise, with the concurrence of the president, whether or not they were in accord with his program or of no concern to it. Second, when committees of Congress solicited views of federal agencies on legislation under consideration, agency replies and testimony normally had to undergo much the same process. Finally, when bills were passed, the most crucial review occurred on the question of whether the president should sign or veto them. Through this process, the BoB built up an administrative history of each piece of legisla-

17. FDR made this decision at a meeting of the National Emergency Council, on January 22, 1935. Seligman and Cornwell (eds.), *New Deal Mosaic*, 415ff.

18. This procedure was prescribed in Budget Circular No. 336, issued December 21, 1935.

19. This section relies heavily on Richard Neustadt's authoritative article "The Presidency and Legislation: The Growth of Central Clearance," *American Political Science Review*, XLVIII (September, 1954), 641–71. Official recognition of BoB's responsibility as presidential agent in the handling of enrolled bills came in Budget Circular No. 346, issued January 19, 1939.

tion unmatched elsewhere in the government. The bureau over the years acquired a comparable role with respect to executive orders, proclamations, and other formal presidential announcements, formalized in Executive Order No. 10006, issued October 9, 1948.

The effectiveness of the BoB role in legislative reference and its impact upon public policy varied a great deal over the six decades after it was begun without official congressional sanction. At first, it was purely a negative fiscal restraint, used to prevent administrative agencies from seeking or endorsing legislation that would cost future dollars. Under Roosevelt it was first used, also negatively, to assure that the administration spoke with one voice—or at least without too many discordant voices. Its influence during World War II was reduced partly because legislation during wartime became less important than administrative action, partly because of influential figures in the White House and agencies (notably the Office of War Mobilization) with better access to the president and greater clout than the BoB. But subsequently, as President Truman's confidence in Budget Director James E. Webb and his staff became clear, BoB's legislative clearance function grew increasingly influential and positive. Bureau professionals worked closely with White House staff, and some of them were even transferred to the White House. Both worked together and sometimes teamed in working groups with representatives of the agencies in coordinating and modifying legislative proposals and in shaping the president's legislative program (see Chapter 4). Truman was apparently the first and only president who spelled out his legislative program in the annual budget message and posted it for all to see. This close association with the president greatly enhanced the image and prestige not alone of legislative reference but of the Bureau of the Budget itself during Truman's years.

The influence of the function carried over into the Eisenhower administration. In fact, Ike relied perhaps even more heavily on the director and career staff of the bureau to participate in informal sessions with congressional committees and staffs and to testify on proposed bills in which the president was interested.

Such activities in connnection with legislation have continued to the present time, though some believe that BoB's influence on the substance of legislation has declined. Work in legislative reference occasioned contacts with presidents, congressional leaders, presidential staff, and leaders in the departments and agencies. It is therefore hardly a coincidence that the position of deputy director of the budget, normally the highest post to which a career officer in BoB/OMB can realistically aspire, was filled by three graduates of the

Legislative Reference Division (or Office) in the years from 1950 to 1953 and then from 1958 to 1969.[20] Since 1969, only one career person has been appointed to that post.

The Born-Again General Accounting Office

The first transformation of the GAO was, if anything, more comprehensive than that of the Bureau of the Budget, but it came nearly a decade later—after rather than before World War II. But some of the groundwork for the change to come was laid before and during the war. The Brownlow committee's recommendations on auditing were effectively neutralized by the GAO and its supporters in Congress, who included the new comptroller general, former congressional leader Lindsay Warren. But they probably alerted some of them that all was not well and that the organization's operations were vulnerable to criticism not only by spokesmen for the administration. In the midst of the war (1943), a committee on government accounting of the American Institute of Certified Public Accountants (AICPA) convened a conference on federal accounting in which the GAO, the BoB, and the Treasury Department participated. Its proceedings, which were widely circulated, included a damning statement about the GAO. An observer summarized what occurred.

> Following the formal papers there was extended general discussion, in which the General Accounting Office representatives found themselves frequently on the defensive. Objections were voiced to the GAO's legalistic pre-audit procedure, involving the shipping of vouchers and supporting documents to Washington, and the open-ended liabilities imposed on certifying and disbursing officers until payments had been approved; to the general absence of accrual accounting; to the lack of financial audits, of the kind common in industry, even of business-type operations of the government; to the absence of coordination and consistency in the requirements of the General Accounting Office, the Treasury Department and the Bureau of the Budget; and to the fact that the GAO made administrative determinations and then audited payments which it had already determined could properly be made.[21]

But even before the war, Warren demonstrated a greater willingness than had his predecessors to work cooperatively with the executive branch. As in-

---

20. The three were Elmer B. Staats, who served during 1950–1953 and 1959–1966; Roger W. Jones, 1958–1959; and Phillip S. Hughes, 1966–1969.

21. John L. Carey, *The Rise of the Accounting Profession: From Technician to Professional* (2 vols.; Washington, D.C., 1969), II, 421.

dicated earlier, he participated in negotiations with the TVA that led to full agreement about commercial-type audits of that government corporation. A similar agreement was worked out a little later with the Commodity Credit Corporation. By force of necessity, Warren broke McCarl's rule of centralization of everything in Washington. Because of shortages of office space, he moved the entire accounting and auditing operation for the Post Office Department to Asheville, North Carolina, where he had once gone to school. After the Congress passed legislation requiring GAO to audit military expenditures on war contracts, GAO established a number of zones across the country and as many as 276 on-site locations for contract audits.[22] After the war, these would become the nucleus for GAO's field operations and regional offices. However, unlike the practice of the comptroller of the treasury in World War I, no central auditing organizations were established overseas.

Much of GAO's work during World War II was more of the same as before—much more. Although the staff trebled to nearly fifteen thousand, the backlog of accounts, vouchers, contracts, and money orders to be audited reached unbelievable proportions. Most of this work was still carried out in Washington, and aside from a handful of lawyers, the staff continued to be even less professional than before, if that was possible.

The first break in the dam of custom, tradition, and attitude occurred just before the end of World War II with the passage of the George Act of 1945, an amendment to which provided for commercial-type audits of all government corporations by the GAO. It was soon followed by the Government Corporation Control Act of 1945, which tightened government controls over corporation budgeting and financial management as well as auditing.[23] Both were products of collaborative work by staff of the GAO and the BoB under the aegis of Senator Byrd's Joint Committee on Non-Essential Federal Expenditures. Those acts began the professionalization of GAO in the field of accounting. Starting with the establishment in July, 1945, of a Corporation Audits Division, it hired dozens of experienced commercial accountants, many of them CPAs who were at the time being discharged from the military services. The conspicuous success of the new division in its extensive early investigations of the Reconstruction Finance Corporation and the Maritime Commission (not itself a corporation) encouraged Comptroller General Warren to extend a similar kind of auditing later to noncommercial activities of federal agencies.

A second and probably more important source of GAO's transformation

22. Public Law 77-703, July 12, 1940.
23. Public Law 79-4, February 24, 1945; Public Law 79-248, December 6, 1945.

arose from the many efforts to improve and integrate accounting systems in the government. These began before World War II, largely on the initiative of the Treasury Department, which sought to develop a system that would better serve the needs of agency management, government-wide financial reporting, and budgeting. In 1939 and 1940, certain officials of the Treasury, the re-vamped BoB, and GAO agreed to work together to plan such a system, and in 1940 the president issued an executive order directing its development.[24] One purpose was to encourage the GAO to adapt its requirements to the needs of the executive branch, and there were apparently some joint efforts in that direction. But preparation for, and then conduct of, the war prevented further progress at that time. Evidently, Warren became increasingly aware of the problems of accounting and auditing during the war. In 1950 he recalled, "On the day after the surrender of Japan, I called a meeting of my staff and told them the No. 1 problem in the General Accounting Office from that date was improvement of accounting in the government." [25] It should be borne in mind that at the end of the war, GAO had about a four-year backlog of unaudited papers with which to contend. Two years later, with the encouragement of the heads of both the Treasury Department and the BoB, Warren established an Accounting Systems Division and appointed as its director an academic leader in accountancy who had worked in both the Treasury Department and BoB, but not previously in GAO. The new division, with a freshly appointed pro-fessional staff that grew to about seventy accountants, proceeded to develop proposals that would revolutionize the GAO and stimulate roughly comple-mentary changes in accounting practices in the various agencies of the execu-tive branch. The philosophy underlying the proposed changes was the con-verse of that of J. Raymond McCarl, which had prevailed within GAO since 1921. Its major features were these:

The GAO should prescribe principles and standards to govern all fed-eral accounting and auditing.

But the initiative in developing and maintaining accounting systems should rest on the operating agencies of the government.

Basic responsibility for control and for internal auditing of financial operations would lie in the operating agencies.

The warrant system could be abandoned or foregone whenever the

---

24. Executive Order No. 8512, August 13, 1940.
25. U.S. Congress, Senate, Committee on Expenditures in the Executive Departments, *Hearings on S. 2054 to Improve Budgeting, Accounting, and Auditing Methods of the Federal Government* (1950), 81st Cong., 2nd Sess.

comptroller general and the secretary of the treasury agreed it was not necessary.

Audit procedures of the GAO should be directed to the effectiveness of internal accounting in the agencies and the Treasury.

GAO should provide for audits, primarily audits of methods, through sampling augmented by voucher audits where needed, at the site of agency operations, not centrally.

GAO should dispense with most of its central records, accounts, and ledgers.

All GAO operations not essential to its general audit responsibilities should be eliminated.

These recommendations, when circulated among GAO's division chiefs, elicited predictable responses. They were favored by the head of the Corporation Audits Division and, with qualifications, by the head of the Audit Division; they were vigorously opposed by the chiefs of the Accounting and Bookkeeping, Investigations, Reconciliation and Clearance, and Postal Accounts divisions. Thus, almost all of the old-time leaders within the GAO opposed the proposals. They thought them in violation of law, of congressional intent and powers, and of governmental principles. Nonetheless, in October, 1949, the comptroller general issued an administrative order directing that the changes be implemented substantially as originally contemplated, and the following month he appointed a team to plan the reorganization of the GAO and designated another group to draft necessary changes in legislation. The first transformation of the GAO was thus enunciated almost exactly a decade after that of BoB.

The first Hoover commission (Commission on Organization of the Executive Branch of the Government), with its task force on fiscal, budgeting, and accounting activities, was considering the GAO and related agencies at about the same time that these developments were occurring in 1947–1949. By a slim majority of seven to five, the commission voted to recommend a professional accounting service under an accountant general in the Treasury Department and to change the title of comptroller general to auditor general. President Truman did not endorse the proposal, and it was voted down unanimously by the oversight committees of both houses of Congress. In 1949, Congress enacted the Federal Property and Administrative Services Act, which set up the General Services Administration (GSA). The section of the act dealing with property accounting was virtually a repeat of the GAO's concepts as they had been set forth the previous year. In 1950 the Post Office

Department Financial Control Act returned postal accounting from the GAO to the Post Office and likewise repeated the newly framed concepts on accounting and auditing. And later that year, Congress passed the Budget and Accounting Procedures Act, which President Truman, at the time of signing it, pronounced "the most important legislation enacted by Congress in the budget and accounting field since the Budget and Accounting Act, 1921, was passed almost thirty years ago." [26] As noted earlier, probably its most important financial feature was the requirement of a performance budget (based on functions and activities of the government), the central recommendation of the Hoover commission. But for GAO's purposes, more important was the approval and go-ahead it gave to the changes already under way in that agency, including particularly the thrusting on the agencies of responsibilities for development of their own accounting systems and for internal auditing, to be carried out according to GAO standards, with its guidance, and subject to its review.

GAO's transformation between 1945 and 1954, when Lindsay Warren resigned for reasons of health, was astonishing in its scope:

> It changed its primary focus from checking the accuracy and legal compliance of individual transactions to propounding principles and reviewing auditing systems and management effectiveness.

> It changed from an almost completely centralized operation to one in which the central headquarters did very little operative work; most of its effort was removed to offices "on site" in the various departments and agencies, to regional offices across the United States, and to overseas offices in Europe and later the Far East and Latin America.

> It reduced its total personnel strength from nearly 15,000 to just under 6,000; but at the same time, it increased its professional accounting personnel from a handful to almost 1,500.

> It eliminated enormous stocks of financial records, whole buildings full.

When GAO's ponderous new headquarters building was completed in 1951 after thirty years of pleading, it was too big. Most of the people who were to have occupied it were elsewhere, and almost all the records it was to have stored had either been destroyed or removed. It was a new organization with a long tradition and the same old name.

26. Public Law 81-151, June 30, 1949; Public Law 81-712, August 17, 1950; Public Law 81-784, September 12, 1950.

82 A TALE OF TWO AGENCIESA TALE OF TWO AGENCIES

The Effort at Collaboration

Until the late 1930s—that is, until the appointments of Harold Smith and Lindsay Warren—the relationships between the GAO and the executive branch, particularly the Bureau of the Budget, had been characterized by almost constant annoyance and occasional confrontation. The beginnings of more collaborative relations between BoB and GAO have already been described. Before the war, these agencies had attempted abortively to work together on a program to improve federal accounting systems. Soon after the war, officials of both institutions, joined by some from the Treasury Department and the Senate Committee on Executive Expenditures, held a series of informal conversations on how they might best coordinate their efforts to improve and integrate accounting methods in the agencies.

The major breakthrough occurred as a product of the congenial relationships of the heads of the three principal financial agencies, Treasury, BoB, and GAO. James E. Webb, appointed by President Truman to succeed Smith as director of the budget in 1946, had been executive assistant to Secretary of the Treasury John W. Snyder and was a long-standing friend of fellow North Carolinian and Comptroller General Lindsay Warren. Webb later recalled his effort to persuade Warren, during a walk at a dinner party, that GAO should collaborate with Treasury and BoB on a program to improve accounting throughout the government. According to Webb, Warren immediately responded, "What you are asking me to do is to reorganize the General Accounting Office and nobody ought to be asked to do that." [27] But do it he did—with the encouragement and support of BoB and Treasury. The three top officials agreed in late 1947 to collaborate in the development and leadership of a Joint Accounting Improvement Program (JAIP). In October, 1948, Warren wrote a letter to the heads of all departments and agencies announcing the JAIP and urging their participation in the development of an accounting system suitable to the needs of each and tied within a government-wide framework. The principal leader and spokesman for JAIP thenceforth was the comptroller general, and it was provided intermittent staff by GAO, augmented from time to time by staff detailed from Treasury, BoB, and other agencies. Many of the changes initiated by GAO's new Accounting Systems Division were made and announced under the umbrella of the JAIP. The Budget and Accounting Procedures Act of 1950 provided the program with the official recognition and blessing of Congress.

27. The story is told in Webb's speech "Leadership Evaluation in Large-Scale Efforts," in U.S. General Accounting Office, *Improving Management for More Effective Government* (1971), 26.

For a period of about ten years following its inception, the JAIP served as a major stimulant and lubricant for the improvement of accounting and auditing practices in the government, including the development of an accounting staff in the Bureau of the Budget, the promulgation of standards, the growth of internal auditing within the departments and agencies, and the encouragement—though with only scattered success—of accrual accounting. It became moribund in the late 1950s and early 1960s. But following the appointment of Comptroller General Elmer B. Staats in 1966, it was revived under a broader name, Joint Financial Management Improvement Program (JFMIP), and added a new member, the chairman of the Civil Service Commission, to help to improve the caliber of accounting personnel throughout the government. Later, it set up a permanent office of executive director with a small continuing staff (supported by GAO) and undertook a variety of projects, some within individual agencies, many government-wide. The latter have included training programs in financial management, productivity measurement, electronic fund transfers, sampling procedures for audit purposes, cash management in federal agencies, and the improvement of auditing practices in state and local governments. The JFMIP continues today as one of the most conspicuous organizational expressions of collaborative efforts of a congressional agency, the GAO, with the BoB/OMB and other agencies in the executive branch.

One may note, in reviewing this chapter, that it devotes about twice as much space to the changes in BoB as to those in GAO, even though the latter agency was many times the former in size. This is because the variety of activities that the bureau came to undertake was greater—and also more interesting—than was that of the GAO. It does not mean that the transformation of BoB was any more fundamental or complete than was that of GAO. If anything, the reverse was true. The bureau had (and retained) the drive shaft of the budget process to which it could attach new wheels and a new frame. It was moving into a vacuum in which it had no competition. It had the endorsement and guidance of a distinguished committee and the enthusiastic support of a president who had successful earlier executive experience with a central budget agency. It was a time of crisis and a time for building. The winds outside were strong and favorable.

For GAO, few of these advantages pertained. The war was over, and the agency was in a period of rapid contraction. It had to virtually abandon a financial system more than a century and a half old, to change the jobs of most of those who stayed in the organization, to disgorge mountains of records and carloads of paperwork. It had to do this both in Washington and in offices all across the country. It had no popular president to support it, only the nudges of two friendly lesser officials—the director of the budget and the secretary of the treasury. Mostly it was an inside job, led by a comptroller general who was highly regarded in the Congress, and engineered by a small minority of rebels at the second and third levels of its organization. GAO's transformation was a remarkable achievement.

Perhaps the most significant aspect of both transformations was the changes in attitudes and images—of what the agencies were, what they did, for whom, and for what purposes. The BoB approached the posture of a general-staff agency for the president, one not restricted to a single process like the budget. Furthermore, it became one of the first institutional (as distinguished from personal or political) agencies—and the most lasting one—immediately attached to the chief executive and operating through a director highly re-spected by and accessible to the president—a Smith, a Webb, or a Pace. It could issue directives on all sorts of topics "by order of the president," and its staff (not all of whom were bathed in humility, and in this they were like some on the White House staff in later years) could often speak with the authority of the president. The BoB became the principal fount of knowledge and, it hoped, wisdom about the United States government.

Changes in attitudes in and about GAO were equally as thoroughgoing al-though they came more slowly. First, the comptroller general from the begin-ning took the position that he and his organization were completely indepen-dent, not simply from the president and the executive branch but also from the Congress and everyone else. His annual reports to the Congress consisted in part of reports of his activities, in part of specific complaints against execu-tive agencies, and mainly of requests for accretions to his power, his jurisdic-tion, and his building space. There was not, in the original act, any outright statement that the GAO was responsible to Congress, and it was not until the end of World War II that the Congress, in exempting the comptroller general and the GAO from the reorganization plans of the president, declared that they were "a part of the legislative branch of the government." [28] Thereafter, though the great bulk of GAO reports were self-initiated, there was increasing attention to Congress and response to its requests. There was no such sense of dependence of the GAO upon Congress, as there was of BoB upon the presi-dent, but it was beginning and it would grow.

A second and perhaps more important change was the increasing pride and professional spirit of GAO's personnel. Most of them were no longer clerks but accountants, indeed the ranking accountants in the federal government.

28. Public Law 79-263, December 20, 1945.

Finally, the geographic and physical decentralization of the GAO personnel, both in Washington and in the field, meant increasing contact and probably better communication and understanding between GAO personnel and the staffs of the agencies whose operations they were reviewing.

The Treasury Building, where they both began. *Courtesy U.S. Department of the Treasury*

Where They Have Been

I've always felt that architecture was
most important. You can tell a lot
about a country by the kind of building it has.

PRESIDENT HARRY S. TRUMAN

A great deal has been written about the interrelatedness of geography and
politics on the grand scale: on geopolitics among nations, political boundaries
within and between nations, regionalism, national and state and local relations, and many other facets of the subject.[1] There has been rather less attention to what might be labeled microgeography—the impact of an agency's
scattered or consolidated offices within the same city or within the same building, of space allocation in relation to function, status, communications, interpersonal relations, and prestige. Nor has there been much concern about the
effect of organizations and people upon their physical settings and surround-
ings.[2] The architectural past as well as the present physical situations of the
Bureau of the Budget–Office of Management and Budget and the General
Accounting Office are not only fascinating stories in themselves but also tell
us something about them as organizations. Both started their lives on the same
floor of the same building. Although that edifice, the Treasury Building, was
one of the most distinguished in Washington and occupied some of the city's
most prestigious grounds, located only a few hundred feet east of the White
House, it does not appear that either agency was very happy about its situs.
Both moved to ancient, ornate pieces of American public architecture during
the following two decades, and after World War II both found new, more modern quarters for all or part of their headquarters personnel.

The original Treasury Building, which was on about the same site as the
Treasury Building of today, was the first federal office building constructed in

1. Most of the historical and architectural information and quotations in this section are drawn
from two works prepared by the General Services Administration: *Pension Building*, Historical
Studies Series No. 1 (January, 1964), and *Executive Office Building*, Historical Studies Series
No. 3 (Rev. ed.; September, 1970). I have also used some unpublished miscellaneous notes on
the Executive Office Building compiled and revised by H. A. Daugherty and dated September
25, 1959.

2. A distinguished exception in political science literature is James Sterling Young, *The
Washington Community, 1800–1828* (New York, 1966).

Washington. Its location near the President's House (which was close to the site of today's White House) rather than near the Capitol was decided at the insistence of George Washington for very pragmatic administrative reasons. On March 25, 1798, he wrote, "The daily intercourse which the Secretaries of the Departments *must* have, with the President, would render a distant situation extremely inconvenient to them; and not much less so would one be close to the Capitol." [3] Washington's view prevailed over that of John Adams, who at the time was president and would have located the departments on Capitol Hill. In those days and for a good many years thereafter, the Capitol and the White House were separated by about two and a half miles of muddy road, Pennsylvania Avenue, which crossed a stream, known as the Tiber, that sometimes overflowed and became impassable.

The first Treasury Building was begun in November, 1798, and completed in 1800. It was matched by a twin building for the War Department to the west of the President's House on part of the site of the present Executive Office Building. Within a year, both buildings were severely damaged by fire. They were succeeded by a series of different buildings, repeatedly destroyed by fire or demolished for replacements, variously housing the War and Navy departments (always on the west side of the White House), Treasury (always on the east side), State, the Patent Office, and others, some of which at one or another time were on both sides. The present Treasury Department building was begun, and a substantial part of it finished, before the Civil War. It was completed in stages during and immediately following that war. In fact, the inaugural ball for President Grant was held in the Treasury Cash Room in 1869. [4]

The accounting officers of the Treasury, as the comptroller(s), auditor(s), and register were commonly called, presumably occupied offices in the Treasury Department east of the White House. As their staffs and their financial records grew in size, they were forced to scatter among various rental quarters around Washington. Thus, when the GAO was established in 1921, the new comptroller general and his deputy, together with a few of his top staff, occupied the former offices of the comptroller of the treasury and the several Treasury auditors in the main building. But much of the work was performed, and the records stored, in about twenty other buildings in Washington for GAO's first thirty years.

These physical arrangements were a source of repeated complaints by the first comptroller general, J. Raymond McCarl, and his successors, partly because of the awkwardness of managing operations so scattered and partly

3. Quoted in General Services Administration, *Executive Office Building*, 5. He wrote this sentence in a letter to Alexander White, one of the District of Columbia's commissioners.
4. *Ibid.*, 23.

Interior of the Pension Building, home of GAO, 1926–1951. *Courtesy National Building Museum, Washington, D.C.*

because of the symbolic connection with the Treasury Department and the propinquity to the president. The GAO, for obvious reasons, sought to emphasize its independence in every way. McCarl's objections were partly assuaged when in 1926 GAO's headquarters and the larger part of its staff were moved to the Pension Building on Judiciary Square at Fifth and F streets. That building, which became GAO's home for the following quarter century, is located about equidistant from the White House and Capitol, at the angle of two roughly equal sides of an isosceles triangle, the base of which is Pennsylvania Avenue. The building was, and is, an extraordinary and unique structure, originally built a century ago (1882–1885) to house the bureau that dispensed pensions to veterans or their widows. The service of some of these veterans dated all the way back to the American Revolution. Constructed of some fifteen million bricks and designed by General Montgomery C. Meigs, retired quartermaster general of the Union army, who also contributed to the design of the Capitol dome, it is one of the largest brick office buildings in the world. It probably contains more wasted space than any other office building, since its interior is in the shape of a huge box (most of which is hollow), rising the equivalent of a dozen stories, with the roof supported by eight 75-foot columns also made of brick. In terms of floor space usable for offices, it is at the same time one of the most efficient; its central cavity is surrounded on each of its four floors by a ring of offices connected by galleries overlooking the main floor. Fully 80 percent of the floor space is usable. Built partly as a memorial to the warriors of the Civil War, the basic design motif is expressed in a three-foot bank of sculptured relief between the first and second floors on the exterior—a 1,200-foot strip of infantrymen, cavalry, artillery, sailors, and others. The bulk of GAO's green-visored clerks and typists worked on the 80,000-square-foot base floor while the officers worked in the galleries up above. "Meigs's old brick barn," as it was dubbed, is probably most famous as a site of inaugural balls for Presidents Cleveland, Harrison, McKinley, Theodore Roosevelt, and Taft, and more recently Nixon, Carter, and Reagan.[5] Inside, it is a magnificent, awe-inspiring sight.

But Comptroller General McCarl and his successors remained unhappy about GAO's quarters. They wanted a single building large enough to house all their employees and the ballooning financial records, which were still scattered in various structures around Washington. Finally, a few months before Pearl Harbor, Congress authorized construction of a large new GAO Building that would cover most of the block just across G Street from the Pension Building. Plans were drawn, the site was cleared, and a hole was dug. Then

5. After the GAO departed in 1951, the building was used by the Civil Service Commission and assorted other federal and District of Columbia agencies until 1981.

came World War II, and construction was abandoned for the duration. The excavation remained as a reminder. Construction was resumed after the war according to the original plans, and the building was completed and occupied in 1951. The "new" building, which is now thirty years old, is a ponderous, concrete mass, unrelieved and undistinguished by inner courts or decorations, standing seven floors above ground and two below. But GAO's mission and mode of operating and organization radically changed in the years immediately after the war (see Chapter 3). It lost its responsibility for both accounting and auditing for the Post Office; it set up regional offices across the United States; in Washington, a large part of its work was conducted "on site" in offices allotted to it by the departments and agencies; most important of all, it dispensed with the bulk of its once treasured financial records—to permanent federal storage, to the National Archives, or through destruction. As a consequence, a building designed to house thousands of feet of file space and thousands of people turned out to be far larger than necessary. This must have been one of the few times in American history when a permanent federal building turned out bigger than needed rather than smaller. In fact, GAO has never fully occupied its own building. In the late 1970s, about two-fifths of its space was used by agencies in the executive branch. And however psychologically desirable its distance from the executive buildings and the Congress may be, its site in a decaying area of Washington has not simplified its relationships, its administration, and its recruitment. On the other hand, there may be a certain appropriateness in its location one block north of Judiciary Square, a Washington park, surrounded largely by buildings housing federal and district courts.

The Bureau of the Budget with its minuscule staff remained in the Treasury Building for its first eighteen years—until 1939. Its location on the third floor, one floor above the secretary of the treasury, occasioned a famous statement by General Dawes concerning the position of the budget director relative to the treasury secretary: "I am glad to say that the Secretary of the Treasury walked upstairs to my office . . . because he regarded it as necessary in connection with a call from me for information needed by the President of the United States. That will be an historic walk in the annals of the Budget Bureau." [6] Obviously Dawes, like his successors, did not want to be considered to be *under* the secretary of the treasury.

President Franklin D. Roosevelt's first reorganization plan and the executive order following it made the Bureau of the Budget the central unit of the Executive Office of the President. In the same year (1939), the bureau was

6. Charles G. Dawes, *The First Year of the Budget of the United States* (New York, 1923) 9–10.

The GAO Building, headquarters of GAO since 1951. *Courtesy U.S. General Accounting Office*

moved from the Treasury Building on the east side of the White House to the enormous structure on the west side, originally known as the State, War, and Navy Building and since known as the Executive Office Building (EOB). Through much of the nineteenth century, the property to the west and southwest of the White House had been a repeated source of contention and the site of a variety of public buildings, fires, demolitions, and architectural competitions. The War Department had been there in one form or another almost from the beginning; Navy came along a bit later, and at times State and some other agencies occupied structures in that area. The idea of joining War, Navy, and State in a single, connected building was apparently hatched during Andrew Jackson's administration, but it did not materialize until after the Civil War. Congress passed the initial authorizing legislation for the building in 1871. But the design and redesign by a succession of architects and the actual construction took many years. Different wings for the three departments were completed and occupied at different times, and there were long delays between periods of construction. The building was not completed until 1888.

The Executive Office Building is very probably the most elaborate, ornamental, and intricate of all the larger office buildings in Washington today, both on the exterior and the interior. Originally, many of its structural and border designs, mansards, doors, windows, and stairways were different from one another and almost unbelievably ornate. So were its chandeliers, lamps, fireplaces, mantels, doorknobs, sculpture, ironwork, and other decorations. (Many of these have been removed or covered by more modern and utilitarian substitutes.) Its style is described as French Renaissance, and the Pension Building's is described as Italian Renaissance. The two buildings are unlike each other, but both are even more strikingly unlike the neoclassic Greek and Roman styles of many of Washington's other public buildings. To an extent greater than the Pension Building, the Executive Office Building has been the object of effusive praise, ridicule, and abuse, beginning from the time of its original design and carrying on to the present day. It has been variously described as "second in architectural importance and beauty to no building in the United States," "magnificent," the "finest office building in Washington" and "one of the finest . . . if not the finest in the world," and "the grandest among many other grand monuments of the artistic taste and skill of its official designer." A less extravagant but also favorable appraisal in 1930 held that "she's plump and she's square and, boys, she's purty."

On the other hand, it has been attacked as "a reproach to our architects"; an "architectural infant asylum" (according to Henry Adams); "a monument of incompetency" in which "simplicity, proportion, dignity and beauty, those fundamental principles . . . went by the board"; and "Washington's worst eyesore—the ugliest heritage of the nineteenth century in America." President Harding described the building as "the worst I ever saw." President Truman was quoted in 1958 as saying, "They've been trying to tear this down for twenty years, but I don't want it torn down [he chuckles]. I think it's the greatest monstrosity in America." Perhaps the most amusing derogation of the building is that attributed to William Tecumseh Sherman, who, as commanding general of the army, had approved the original architectural plans. On being told the building was fireproof he is said to have remarked, "What a pity." The same reaction has also been attributed to President Coolidge. A similar statement ("It's too bad the damn thing is fireproof") is credited to either Sherman or General Philip Sheridan about the Pension Building. Both remarks are apocryphal. The EOB survived a number of attempts to demolish it or remodel it along either modern or classical lines, and it retains today much of its ornate splendor (or ugliness, if you prefer).

It has provided office space for some of the most important leaders in American government for nearly a century—several presidents or presidents-to-be (including both Roosevelts), vice-presidents, the top officials of its three original departments, and officials of the agencies that make up the Executive Office of the President. In 1918, Navy moved out, and it became the State and War Building. Then, in 1938, most of its War Department occupants moved to the "temporary" Munitions Building up Constitution Avenue (on their circuitous route to the Pentagon), and shortly thereafter the State Department moved to its new quarters one-half mile to the west in Foggy Bottom. In 1939, the Bureau of the Budget and other units of the newly created Executive Office of the President moved in, and it became the Executive Office Building.

The evacuation of the State Department was not made without resistance. The State people argued that there was not enough space in their new quarters, apparently making particular reference to their extensive active files. President Roosevelt wanted to see for himself. He was wheeled into the old building under the escort of Budget Director Harold D. Smith and Undersecretary of State Sumner Welles. He began pulling out file drawers, and the first file he looked at was labeled "Wild Horses in China." Thereafter, he advised Welles that a good many of the files could safely be removed to the archives and directed that the move to Foggy Bottom be made as planned.[7]

With the enormous growth of the Executive Office of the President during and after World War II, it became apparent that more office space was required to house staff of the BoB/OMB and other units; indeed some offices

7. This story was related by Harold Smith to Herbert Emmerich, who recounted it in his *Federal Organization and Administrative Management* (University, Ala., 1971), 77.

The Executive Office Building, headquarters of BoB/OMB since 1939. *Courtesy U.S. General Services Administration*

had already been forced out. So a New Executive Office Building (like the Pension Building, made of red brick, but in no other respect distinguished), located across Pennsylvania Avenue and a half block up Seventeenth Street from the old one, was completed in 1965. The joke is told in Washington that Bureau of the Budget leaders planned the new building to replace the old one so the latter could be demolished but that, once the new one was approved, they forgot to demolish the old one. Actually, the leaders of the Kennedy administration Budget Bureau sought to have the old EOB rejuvenated at about the same time as the new one was being built up the street. They sought to have the exterior of the old EOB cleaned by sandblasting. In this they succeeded. But their other efforts—to have the interior restored to its original character, and to provide an underground parking area, a tunnel between the old and new buildings, a fountain, and some other things—failed because President Johnson suddenly changed his mind and because the architect of the proposal died. At any rate, the division between the old and new executive office buildings has had the unfortunate effect of accentuating the cleavage between the political and professional career staffs of BoB/OMB. Virtually all of the former continue in their offices in the elite old building, and virtually all the career personnel work up the street in the new building. The separation is awkward because movement from one to the other requires crossing Pennsylvania Avenue at one of its busiest intersections. More recent proposals for a tunnel have been stymied, I was told, because a tunnel might undermine one or both of two of Washington's historic landmarks—the original Corcoran Museum (now the Renwick Gallery) and the Blair House.[8] Thus does the OMB stand, a house divided. The older, more permanent staff are in the newer building; the newer, more transient people are in the older building. But the latter are closer to the White House, physically as well as politically.

The two old buildings, the GAO's Pension Building and the BoB/OMB's Executive Office Building, are monuments associated with many great events in our nation's history. The Congress in 1980 recognized this in the case of the Pension Building by creating in it a National Museum of the Building Arts to be operated by a nonprofit corporation with matching grant-in-aid funds.[9] The Executive Office Building is unfortunately too heavily used by the vice-president, the top layers of the OMB, some members of the White House staff and other units of the Executive Office of the President, and sometimes the president himself to permit setting it aside as a museum (even though some in

8. This, too, is probably a myth. The early plans for a tunnel, which might yet be funded, provide that it go down Jackson Place and cross Pennsylvania Avenue, well removed from either the Renwick Gallery or the Blair House.
9. Public Law 96-515, sec. 306.

The New Executive Office Building, since 1967 the home of most of the career staff of
BoB/OMB. *Courtesy U.S. General Services Administration*

the opposition party might from time to time so describe it). It seems unfortunate that, as things now stand, the average citizen not on official business finds it virtually impossible—without a special act of Congress—to get by the guards at the building's entrances to see its interior.

One of the many laws penned and enacted single-handedly by C. Northcote Parkinson provides that "a perfection of planned layout is achieved only by institutions on the point of collapse. . . . Perfection [in planned headquarters], we know, is finality; and finality is death." [10] It does not appear that either of the agencies that are the principal characters of this tale is now or has ever been on the point of collapse. Yet, in some ways Parkinson's observation is apt. When GAO's headquarters were moved to its new building in 1951, the organization was in the midst of its first transformation. Most of the first GAO was in fact dying and being replaced by a quite different agency—different people, different objectives, different activities, different methods but under the same name. It was a time of "death and transfiguration." And the move of the career professionals of BoB into the New Executive Office Building in 1967 presaged and probably contributed to a decline in the influence of its civil service staff, a decline that may yet prove a slow death, which may also be accompanied or followed by a transfiguration.

10. C. Northcote Parkinson, *Parkinson's Law and Other Studies in Administration* (Boston, 1957), 60–61.

The BoB/OMB Since 1950

Management, Policy, Politics, and the Budget

The Budget, strange fish and monster vast
To which from all sides the hook is cast.

VICTOR HUGO

If there ever was a group of tight-fisted public officials who would squeeze the last little drop of compassion and charity out of anything, they are the group in the Office of Management and Budget.

HUBERT H. HUMPHREY, 1977

In contrast to much of its earlier history, the development of the Bureau of the Budget (or the Office of Management and Budget, as it has been labeled since 1970) has demonstrated no consistent philosophy in the last three decades. To be sure, the agency has had certain continuing responsibilities, notably the budget and the budget process themselves. But even the budget has changed greatly in scope, nature, and size and in form and detail of presentation. It has gone through a succession of phases, each representing a somewhat different perspective, procedure, and emphasis: the performance budget in the early fifties; the cost and accounting emphasis in the late fifties; planning-programming-budgeting systems (PPBS) in the sixties; management by objectives (MBO) in the early seventies; and zero-based budgeting (ZBB) in the late seventies. Federal budgeting has adapted to these to varying degrees and· borrowed some pieces from each of them.

In addition, there have been three developments immediately affecting the budget process that have had major impact upon BoB/OMB. First was the enormously expanded role and staffing of the Office of the Secretary of Defense (OSD) with respect to the military budget, which began about 1950 and has continued to this day, and the accommodation of the BoB/OMB and its procedure to that role. During the Korean War, when the defense budget was half or more of total federal outlays, the review and major hearings of the components of the Defense Department were conducted within that department. BoB examiners attended those hearings and could raise questions, as could those of OSD.[1] Then the defense budget was submitted to BoB/OMB, as were those of other agencies. It could be, and was, reexamined by the central budget group, and hearings and discussions might be held on particular questions. But the basic and comprehensive review and hearing of the defense budget was conducted in the Pentagon, not the Executive Office Building, and under chairmanship of top officials of Defense, not BoB. Thirty years ago, this writer was told that this modification in BoB procedure, which normally forbade participation by its own examiners in agency budget-making lest they prejudge and precommit their agency, weakened its ultimate influence on the defense budget. More recently, I have been advised that OMB examiners have in fact been more effective because they were informed and involved earlier— well before the OSD review—in substantive questions that would significantly affect the defense budget. It is likely that, in times of war or alarm, BoB/OMB has had little influence on military budgets. In peacetime, its influence has probably been less than upon civil programs. Its concerns have, perhaps very properly, been matters like bases and stations, logistics in the United States, the inflation rates of military versus civilian goods, the pay of military personnel, and the economic impact of defense programs, not the number and deployment of divisions, ships, aircraft, and nuclear weapons. It is interesting that the GAO has for many years been less reluctant to investigate and evaluate merits and demerits on purely military subjects such as weapons systems, deployments, states of readiness, and strategies than has BoB/OMB.

The second development of major concern to the budget process was the report of the President's Commission on Budget Concepts, which was appointed by President Johnson in 1966 and in which both GAO and BoB played prominent roles. The recommendations of that commission, most of which were promptly carried out, comprehended some of the most far-reaching changes in the content, format, and process of the federal budget since 1921. They included putting into effect a comprehensive and unified budget that would encompass almost all federal transactions, including trust funds,

1. This practice was begun following passage of the National Security Act Amendments of 1949, which gave the secretary of defense full authority over defense budgets. While he was building his own budgetary staff, he asked BoB to provide him staff help.

lending operations, and other categories, whether or not requiring annual appropriations.[2]

During the dozen years following the installation of the new budgetary concepts, many of them were weakened or dissipated by actions of the president and Congress. A number of public and quasi-public enterprises were established outside the budget process, and an increasing number of federal objectives were sought through regulations, tax expenditures, and loan guarantees. These and other developments have led to recent proposals for the establishment of a commission to develop new and more inclusive budgetary principles for the future.

The third development with major impact on the budget process, and on both OMB and GAO during this period, was the passage of the Congressional Budget and Impoundment Control Act of 1974 (Public Law 93-344). That act, among many other things, provided a new budget calendar and procedure, and new committees and staff, with the intent of creating a more orderly, rational, and influential role for the Congress in the budget process and of reducing what Congress considered excesses in the execution of the budget. It added new responsibilities for both OMB and GAO—but at the same time set up a new congressional unit, the Congressional Budget Office, which would coexist and in some ways compete with both of them. It also provided a mechanism for reconciling federal outlay targets with substantive authorizing legislation, thus potentially enlarging the area of congressional controllability of budget items.[3] The act established procedures whereby presidential impoundments of appropriated funds could be regulated and negated by the Congress, working through the GAO. Since impoundments are normally handled through OMB, this provision also had considerable impact upon its work.

The main focus of this chapter is not the budget process itself, important as that subject is, but the organization that superintends that process and its related—or unrelated—responsibilities: the BoB/OMB in its potentially broader role as a general-staff agency to the president. This subject will be treated under three headings: its role in the general management of the executive branch; its responsibilities in the development, review, implementation, and evaluation of federal policies and programs; and its part in presidential politics.

2. U.S. President, President's Commission on Budget Concepts, *Report* (October, 1967). The unified budget replaced the three different budgets previously used—the so-called administrative budget, the consolidated cash budget, and the national income accounts budget.

3. Paradoxically, the act, which was basically intended to enhance congressional influence vis-à-vis the president and the executive branch, provided through its reconciliation machinery the means whereby the president could effectively shape congressional action on the budget in 1981. See Epilogue I.

Administrative Management and the Budget

The relationship of management with finance and of the powers and responsibilities with respect to each has been a source of controversy from the beginning of the Republic. The issues attendant upon the relationship were largely
ignored in the Constitution and were to a considerable extent fudged in the
legislation enacted by the First Congress. Subsequently, with the exception of
a few strong executive leaders (such as Hamilton, Jackson, Lincoln, and Theodore Roosevelt), it seems to have been accepted that finance and management are closely related and that the seat of authority and supervision over
both rests in the Congress, especially its committees. The Budget and Accounting Act of 1921 recognized a relationship between the two activities and
gave both branches some jurisdiction with respect to each, though many,
probably including most of the principal authors and sponsors of the act, regarded the powers as basically congressional, while acknowledging that for
practical reasons some of them should be delegated to the executive. Both the
GAO and the president's agency, the BoB, were authorized, in addition to
their financial functions, to make studies and reports on organization and
management, with the goal of encouraging greater economy and efficiency.[4]

Neither BoB nor GAO picked up their potential managerial responsibilities
until their great transformations in the late 1930s and 1940s. But then and
thereafter, the issues associated with the relationship of management and finance assumed center stage, and they remain there today. Most of them are
generic problems, common to the governments of most nations and in no
sense unique to the two institutions treated in this study. Among the germane
ones applicable to the presidency are these:

> Is the president the general manager of the executive branch? Beyond
> the specific constitutional authorities (such as the appointing power
> and his status as commander-in-chief of the military), is his man-
> agerial responsibility derived from the Constitution (implicit in the
> "executive power" or in taking "care that the laws be faithfully ex-
> ecuted") or from delegation by the Congress?
>
> Assuming that the answers to the first question above are affirmative
> either by Constitution or delegation or both, of what does his manage-
> ment responsibility properly consist?
>   Organizing and reorganizing?
>   Developing or reviewing and approving programs, including design
>   of implementation?

4. The relevant sections of the act are quoted in Chapter 2.

Coordinating program operations?
Evaluating program effectiveness?
Directing agency heads?
Advising and assisting agency managers in the performance of these
duties?

To the extent that any or all of these activities are proper responsibilities of the president, to what degree should they be delegated to
staff? And should such staff be

continuing, institutional, and professional?
transitory, personal, and political?
authoritative or advisory in relation to the operating agencies?

If there are to be staff assistants to the president for purposes both of
general and financial management, how should they be related organi-
zationally?

In two or more separate agencies?
In different units of the same agency?
Or merged within the same units and even perhaps in the same peo-
ple of the same agency?

The same kinds of questions, slightly reworded, apply to the Congress vis-
à-vis its role in overseeing the administration of finances, for which it passes
the laws and the appropriations, and the management of the agencies, most of
which it establishes and empowers by law and for many of which it prescribes, in varying degrees of detail, internal organization structure and procedures. The powers, nature, and limits of congressional oversight are not
prescribed in the Constitution any more than are those of presidential management. These questions as they pertain to Congress will be discussed in Chapter 5.

The prevailing answer to the first question above, whether the president has
a role and responsibilities in the management of the executive branch, has
been yes for more than sixty years. It was implicit and in some ways explicit
in the debates that led to the Budget and Accounting Act and in the act itself.
It was the central theme of the Brownlow report and of many studies dealing
with the presidency since. Most recently, it was the basic assumption of the
report developed by a distinguished panel of the National Academy of Public
Administration for the winning candidate of the 1980 presidential election.
But that report, like virtually all of its predecessors, was somewhat am-
bivalent as to how far "presidential management" should go: "Controversy
over the nature and extent of executive authority is frequent, and opinion
differs widely regarding the degree to which the President should function as

a 'general manager' in directly supervising and being responsible for the government."[5]

In fact, the arrangements within the BoB/OMB and between it and other agencies have been repeatedly changed over the last three decades. The initial phase, which was briefly summarized in Chapter 3, was the period 1939–1952, roughly the decade of the 1940s, when the Division of Administrative Management was a separate, self-contained unit reporting to the director of the budget. During its early years, that division handled the budget estimates of some of the newer, nonmilitary war agencies, and from 1945 to 1950 it reviewed the estimates of the Department of State and other international agencies. Otherwise, it was completely divorced from the Division of Estimates, which handled the rest of the budget.

Aside from its international work, the responsibilities of the Division of Administrative Management were divided between two branches. One concerned government-wide organizational and procedural matters, including the preparation and processing of presidential reorganization plans; the other and larger one concerned setting up and improving management systems within individual agencies. It handled *ad hoc* managerial problems, many coming from the president himself (Roosevelt or Truman), and was a fruitful source of information and intelligence about incipient problems, many of which were relayed through the division's head and the budget director to the White House, some to the president personally. Through its reputation and prestige, it was able to recruit top-grade personnel. Furthermore, it became a major source of managerial know-how and information as well as a bastion of qualified personnel available for detail or transfer to other parts of the bureau and to other federal agencies, not excluding the White House itself. Through the personal and frequent contacts of the director of the budget and the president—often accompanied by the division head and staff responsible for the problems under consideration—it had direct communication and liaison with the very top of the executive branch of the government. The division had certain other advantages, most of which would not be replicated in subsequent decades. During the war, when it essentially won its spurs and developed its modes of operating, it had little competition in the Executive Office of the President, then quite small. The gospel of winning the war was virtually universal, and until the postwar period, partisan politics were not of great importance. Budgeted dollars were more an implement than a limitation. It is little wonder that alumni of the Administrative Management Division still look back on the forties as the acme of the BoB.

5. National Academy of Public Administration, *A Presidency for the 1980s: A Report by a Panel of the National Academy of Public Administration* (Washington, D.C., 1980), 8.

But from the perspective of some outside the division and even a few within it, the view was not quite so roseate, and it became less so after the problems of war were succeeded by those of demobilization. In the years 1944 to 1946, the Office of War Mobilization and Reconversion (OWMR) became increasingly influential with respect to administrative matters, and for a brief period, it seemed that the BoB might be reduced to a mere budget-processing agent. But in 1946, at about the same time that the ailing Harold Smith resigned as budget director, the OWMR went out of existence. BoB's Division of Administrative Management had already begun to decline, quantitatively if not qualitatively. When the first Hoover commission came along in 1947–1949, it was staffed at significant points by members or graduates of that division. Furthermore, as noted above, its major recommendations were translated into legislative action or reorganization proposals by the same staff. But neither the commission nor its task force on budgeting and accounting was enthusiastic about the performance of the bureau's Administrative Management Division. The task force attack was acidulous. It criticized the division's absence of relationships with the Estimates Division and its lack of authority to enforce its recommendations and affirmed the need for an overall program of management improvement. Acknowledging that the division "has done some good work," it nonetheless complained that the work "has been done on a casual basis" without any "comprehensive approach looking toward organizational and management improvement." The task force then proposed that the Estimates, Fiscal, and Administrative Management divisions be merged, reorganized on a program basis, and focused on the budget.[6] The Hoover commission itself did not go nearly so far, but it did propose that budget reviews be done "from first to the final stages in conjunction with representatives of the Administrative Management and Fiscal Divisions."[7]

As BoB had grown in size, the functional scheme of organization had become more and more cumbersome. Representatives of up to five different divisions might be concerned with the same problem in the same agency. Each would bring to it his own predisposition, loyalty, and hierarchical responsibility. Officials of the federal agency concerned would have to deal with several different representatives in BoB. Differences between the divisions that could

6. U.S. Congress, Commission on Organization of the Executive Branch of the Government, *Task Force Report on Fiscal, Budget, and Accounting Activities* (January, 1949), 52, 40. The task force report had actually been prepared by A. E. Buck of the Institute of Public Administration, who had long believed that the budget was essentially a financial process and should be run by the Treasury Department. On this matter, he was totally out of step with the commission itself, which strongly endorsed the role of the bureau as a general management tool of the president.

7. U.S. Congress, Commission on Organization of the Executive Branch of the Government, *Report on Budgeting and Accounting* (February, 1949), 81st Cong., 1st Sess., 23.

not be settled between them had to go to the office of the budget director for resolution. Such differences were most frequent between the Estimates and the Administrative Management divisions.

This problem—common in all sizable, functionally structured organizations that deal with problems crossing functional lines—had been noted as early as 1942, and its essence was reiterated in several later internal studies and reports on BoB organization.[8] Finally, on March 14, 1952, Budget Director Frederick J. Lawton ordered a reorganization that set up five operating divisions, each covering a broad spectrum of federal programs, and four staff offices on the old functional basis, each to handle government-wide problems and to coordinate, guide, and assist the operating divisions in its sphere.[9] The new operating divisions would consist predominantly of personnel from the old Estimates Division, each augmented by a few analysts from the Division of Administrative Management and a smattering of economists from the Fiscal Division. This would leave a much smaller staff in central management work, thenceforth known as the Office of Management and Organization (OMO), while the remaining economists in the old Fiscal Division became part of a new Office of Budget Review (OBR).

The reorganization was planned by Charles Stauffacher, then the executive assistant director, the third-highest ranking post in the bureau; he had previously been director of the Division of Administrative Management. The reorganization's purposes were several. First, the branches of the old Estimates Division, which had been organized on the basis of federal departments and agencies, would now be structured on the basis of broad programs so that activities crossing organizational lines or otherwise related might be treated together. Second, the intimate knowledge of budget examiners concerning agency developments and problems could be utilized on managerial and other projects. In addition, their budgetary workload was to a considerable degree seasonal; their services might now be drawn upon for other work during off-seasons. Conversely, the knowledge and talents of the management and fiscal analysts could be applied to reviewing budgets during the appropriate seasons. Finally, the new and far smaller Office of Management and Organization would be encouraged to provide leadership on the larger managerial questions

8. See the 1942 memorandum of V.O. Key, who had just joined the bureau's staff. It is particularly interesting that one of these analyses was undertaken by Elmer Staats, who as comptroller general twenty years later would direct a reorganization of GAO comparable to that of BoB in 1952. (See Chapter 5.)

9. The five operating divisions set up in 1952 were Commerce and Finance, the International Division, Labor and Welfare, the Military Division, and Resources and Civil Works. The four staff offices were Budget Review, Management and Organization, Legislative Reference, and Statistical Standards. The latter two were not significantly affected by the reorganization.

of government-wide organization, interagency relationships, and common administrative processes such as procurement, work measurement, transportation and travel, and others. This would encourage and even entail the development of managerial talent within the departments and other agencies to handle their own internal problems.

However effective the 1952 shift was in meeting many of these goals, some of those then involved in management work look back on it as a disaster. The few management-oriented staff that remained in the central organization (OMO) —about 10 percent of the BoB staff—rocked along with government reorganization plans, servicing outside agencies from time to time, backing up the financial improvement program described in Chapter 3, and developing special studies. The majority were transferred to the operating divisions, where some were separately organized in management analysis units. Even these proved temporary. Soon all of them were sucked into the budget cycle, the work of the budget examiners. Here was a classic illustration of what has been termed the Gresham's Law of Administration: the routine, deadlined, required work drives out the nonroutine, unscheduled work; the short-range, normal work drives out the long-range, unusual work. There is no doubt that the driving engine of the operating divisions was the budget process, and for about fifteen years after 1952, it became again the motive force of most of the Bureau of the Budget.

Thus, the organization and management activities, which had probably been the major source of BoB's fame during the 1940s, assumed less importance during the Eisenhower, Kennedy, and Johnson administrations of the 1950s and 1960s. This decline was probably due as much to the changing nature and interests of BoB's top leadership as to its internal organization. Eisenhower's budget directors—bankers and accountants—were certainly more concerned with dollars than they were with the sticky problems of general administration. And in a much different way, the same was true of the economists appointed by Kennedy and Johnson.

Soon after his election, President Eisenhower set up a three-man President's Advisory Committee on Government Organization (PACGO).[10] At about the same time, the second Hoover commission was established. The Budget Bureau's OMO provided both groups with information, analytic help, and other services. The second Hoover commission and its task force on budgeting and accounting recommended that BoB's management staff and responsibilities be substantially enlarged; indeed, the task force (not the com-

10. The members were Nelson Rockefeller (chairman), Arthur Flemming, and Milton Eisenhower.

mission) recommended that the title of the bureau be changed to the Office of Budget and Executive Management. Both the commission and its task force laid great stress on the improvement of accounting in the federal establishment and proposed that central responsibility for this activity be lodged in a new office of accounting under an assistant director of the budget. Only this last recommendation was carried out. The proposal gave rise to an Office of Financial Management, and it resulted in further weakening of the OMO by transferring from it the small group of accountants (about eight) that it already had.

Between 1957 and 1961, the PACGO group made a series of proposals, all designed to strengthen the president in his managerial role. It first recommended a director and an office of administration whose jurisdiction would comprehend all managerial responsibilities of the EOP, including those of BoB. This was resisted by the director of the budget because it would have interposed a layer between him and the president. A substitute idea, an assistant to the president for management, was opposed for the same reason. A later proposed office of executive management—though actually recommended by Director of the Budget Maurice Stans—was vigorously resisted by the head of the OMO. So no change came to pass.[11] The impression prevailed on PACGO's staff that the bureau's staff was negative, obstructive, and anxious to preserve its status. It is no secret that PACGO's chairman, Nelson Rockefeller, then undersecretary of health, education and welfare, was very critical of the bureau's management work.

Meanwhile, in 1959 Budget Director Stans ordered a self-study by staff of the bureau, perhaps partly as a defense against PACGO proposals and criticisms. The study was conducted by a number of old-timers, veterans from the 1940s. It urged nothing very specific but a return to the creativity, flexibility, positiveness, anticipation, and preparedness its authors associated with that earlier period. The group recommended that the bureau serve as a strong institutional staff arm to the president and that the management work of the operating divisions be increased—with, however, no significant change in the OMO.

Neither Presidents Kennedy nor Johnson was much interested in organization and management. Their dominant concern as presidents was new ideas, new policies, new programs, and politics, not implementation and mechanics. Nonetheless, during their two terms in the 1960s, there were established two new departments and a large number of new agencies, to many of which

11. Much of this information is drawn from Larry Berman, *The Office of Management and Budget and the Presidency, 1921–1979* (Princeton, 1979), 58–66.

the Bureau of the Budget made significant contributions. But during most of the hyperactivity of the Great Society period, BoB's management arm was bypassed, and management considerations were widely and unfortunately neglected. President Johnson, under criticism for alleged inefficiency and extravagance in the implementation of an avalanche of new programs, launched in the mid-1960s several undertakings to encourage order and economy in the administration. One was a cost-reduction program; a second was the development and use of the so-called planning-programming-budgeting system (PPBS) in most of the domestic agencies of the government.

He also designated two successive task forces or committees to study the organization and management of the Great Society programs and make recommendations thereon. Each was composed of high government officials as well as knowledgeable people from outside. Like the multitude of other Johnson task forces, both operated in secret; their reports were filed away without any action and have not been published to this day. The first of these, chaired by Dean Don K. Price of the Kennedy School of Government at Harvard, in its report of 1964 did not address its recommendations directly to the problems of administrative management in BoB. The second, which was known (by a few people) as the President's Task Force on Government Organization, was chaired by Ben W. Heineman, prominent Chicago lawyer and business executive, and directed its first report in June, 1967, to the management of domestic social programs.[12] It was vigorously critical on a number of grounds: fragmentation and lack of coordination among agencies in Washington and in the field; lack of institutional staff to evaluate existing programs and to anticipate, study, and plan ahead; lack of channels of communication between the White House, governors, and mayors; overcentralization of decision-making power in Washington; and lack of common centers and boundaries of field organizations in the various departments and agencies concerned with related domestic programs.

The task force recommended changes both in the operating departments and in the Executive Office of the President, but for present purposes the latter are more important. First, it proposed a new office of program coordination in EOP but *outside* the Bureau of the Budget.[13] This office was to have a permanent regional organization with power to mediate interagency disputes in the

12. The committee's report is duplicated from typescript. Its staff included, among many others, Charles L. Schultze, then the director of the budget; Kermit Gordon, the last previous director; and William M. Capron, then an assistant director.

13. The expressed need for such an office was unanimously endorsed, but three members, including Chairman Heineman and Budget Director Schultze, thought it should be inside the BoB.

field, to provide the president intelligence, and to facilitate liaison with state and local political executives. A second proposal was an office for program development in a reorganized BoB. It would stimulate, design, and coordinate new or changed programs. Another recommendation was that the central offices and the boundaries of the various departmental regional structures be harmonized.

The president filed the Heineman report in his drawer, from whence it eventually found its way to the Johnson Library in Austin. Indeed, rumor has it that President-elect Nixon and his transition team were denied a peek at it following the 1968 election. Yet, it has been the basis for a great deal of discussion in Washington up to the time of this writing, and its recommendations about regional organization were partly, but not completely, carried out.

Before the report was completed, Deputy Director Philip S. Hughes and senior members of the BoB staff initiated another self-study of the bureau, which apparently bore no relation to the Heineman task force. That study was begun early in 1967, and its summary report was issued in July, a month after the first Heineman report was submitted.[14] Basing its findings partly on responses to internal questionnaires filled out by a substantial number of bureau staff, the study was highly self-critical on grounds not far different from those offered by the Heineman group. It found the management work of the bureau deficient, routine, negative, and not very creative. In the first place, it recommended eliminating or transferring elsewhere "functions and activities which do not *directly* support the bureau's responsibility as a permanent staff to the Director and the President," including some of the work of the Office of Management and Organization. And to replace the OMO it proposed a new Office of Executive Management (OEM), which would have five major responsibilities: improvement of government organization structure; systems design with emphasis upon interagency and intergovernmental programs like grant simplification and consolidation, and realignment of field organization; operational coordination, particularly the handling of immediate and short-range problems; financial management and accounting; and special government-wide projects. Later on, it was hoped, the new office would undertake the analysis of general personnel problems and provide advice and assistance to the top management of departments and agencies.

The Heineman task force and the BoB self-study group thus roughly agreed on a more ambitious program of operational coordination of domestic pro-

14. U.S. Bureau of the Budget, "The Work of the Steering Group on Evaluation of the Bureau of the Budget: A Staff Summary" (July, 1967).

grams, particularly those involving grants-in-aid. The former group would have created a new agency for the purpose outside the Bureau of the Budget. The two groups did not agree on the program development organization within the bureau as proposed by the Heineman group. The self-study group insisted that responsibility for program development should remain in the White House staff and that BoB should provide only support services.

Budget Director Charles L. Schultze chose the alternative proposed by the self-study group and in August, 1967, established an Office of Executive Management under a noncareer assistant director of the budget. The position, however, was not filled until 1969, when Dwight Ink, then assistant secretary of the Department of Housing and Urban Development, agreed to assume it. Work was already well under way under the leadership of Philip S. Hughes when Ink arrived and with a rejuvenated staff developed an ambitious program known as Federal Assistance Review (FAR) involving common centers and boundaries of departmental regions, grant simplification, decentralization, federal regional councils, and related changes. Over the next few years, this proved to be the most energetic and effective program of innovation in the field of management that the BoB/OMB had undertaken since the 1940s. It may be noted that, like the earlier wartime and postwar programs, it was initiated and largely carried out by management people quite independent of the estimates (later known as the program) divisions of the organization. Unlike the earlier efforts, however, that of the Office of Executive Management was directed primarily to the federal field establishments and their relationships to state and local governments. This was an appropriate change of focus since most of the new federal domestic programs after World War II, including practically all of those encompassed in President Johnson's Great Society, were and are carried on by state and local agencies.

Yet, the Office of Executive Management fell some distance short of the Heineman proposal for an office of program coordination. It provided no continuing presidential presence in the field, though representatives of the BoB/OMB were assigned to the regions on travel status and attended the meetings of the regional councils. The delegations of decision-making authority to regional representatives were uneven among the different agencies and departments. But significant progress on problems of enormous complexity was begun under the aegis of the office, and some of this work continued, though with less central impetus and drive, in subsequent years.

But the 1970s would bring a succession of differing objectives, new directors, new positions, reorganizations, and even a new name to the staid (and some said tired) old Bureau of the Budget. Soon after the first inauguration of

President Nixon in 1969, he appointed an Advisory Council on Executive Organization, better known for its chairman, Roy Ash, as the Ash council.[15] That council's first recommendation was the establishment of a domestic policy council immediately responsive to the president, acting as a liaison between him and the agencies on policy matters. It also called for the creation of an office of executive management to encompass the Bureau of the Budget and serve in a variety of ways as the president's chief management arm. The council envisioned a new organization with a charter encompassing but going well beyond the bureau's emphasis on the budget to include organization and management improvement, program coordination, program evaluation, executive personnel development, and other responsibilities.

Following consideration and approval by the president, the council's recommendations, substantially unchanged except in the names of the two organizations, were submitted to the Congress for consideration in Reorganization Plan No. 2 in March, 1970. The name domestic policy council was changed to Domestic Council (out of deference to John Ehrlichman, who would be its director and who thought the word *policy* was too restrictive); the office of executive management became the Office of Management and Budget (out of deference to certain congressmen who wanted the word *budget* in the title). The president's message accompanying the plan stated that the council "will be primarily concerned with what we do; the Office of Management and Budget will be primarily concerned with how we do it and how well we do it"— an interesting reversion to the familiar dichotomy between policy and administration. The plan was vigorously opposed by some leading career officials of the Bureau of the Budget who viewed it as a mistaken effort to separate budget formulation from budget execution and as an attack on the old bureau's effectiveness and power. It was also resisted in the Congress, though for different reasons. Some legislators, for example, fought it because the director of the council would not have to testify before Congress or because all the powers of BoB would be transferred to the president, who could delegate them as he pleased. It was supported with equal vigor by the White House, the Ash council members and staff, many members of the Congress, and some current and former high officials in the executive branch, mainly, it appears, because of dislike of the BoB and its alleged "entrenched powers" and "negativism." A leading proponent of the reorganization plan was in fact Democratic Senator Abraham Ribicoff of Connecticut, then chairman of the Senate

15. Unlike most of the study groups before it, the Ash council was composed almost exclusively of men whose primary experience was in private business, though one of its six members, John Connally, had held a number of government posts.

Subcommittee on Executive Reorganization, who had been secretary of HEW a few years before. He declared in the subcommittee hearings: "The most frustrating agency in the government is the Bureau of the Budget. . . . I think that the most backward bureaucracy in the Federal Government is the Bureau of the Budget. Nothing moves when it gets there. They stalemate. They are people without imagination." [16]

The House subcommittee on Executive and Legislative Reorganization voted to disapprove the proposed reorganization, but in a most unusual reversal for reorganization plans, the whole House overruled its subcommittee; it approved the plan, as had the Senate. [17] So on July 1, 1970, the Domestic Council was formally established under the leadership of John Ehrlichman, and the Bureau of the Budget was renamed the Office of Management and Budget. At the same time, the president appointed a new director of OMB, George P. Shultz, and a new deputy director, Caspar W. Weinberger. The operating parts of the organization were bifurcated, with Weinberger heading up all of the budget activities and an associate director all the rest under the general heading of management. [18]

It is ironic that the effects of all these changes in 1970 were perversely opposite to the professed intent of their initiators. Shultz, first director of OMB, took an office in the White House and became a principal adviser to the president on policy matters, leaving him little uninterrupted time for leadership of OMB. Ehrlichman, first director of the Domestic Council, was soon immersed in operating problems and calling on individual members of the OMB staff for assistance. Furthermore, while "management" was given a place, indeed first place, in the title of what had been the Bureau of the Budget and was separated from, and given status nearly equal to, the budget on the organization chart, its importance in OMB's work declined, though with some interruptions, for at least the following seven years.

In 1973, a new director and deputy director, Roy L. Ash and Frederic V. Malek, reorganized OMB again but in the opposite direction. Unaware of the unhappy consequences of the reorganization of 1952, they in effect did it all over again—integrating management personnel into management divisions, one for each of the four major program areas, alongside the examiners. For

16. U.S. Congress, Senate, Subcommittee on Executive Reorganization, *Hearings on Reorganization Plan No. 2 of 1970*, 91st Cong., 2nd Sess., 31.

17. The votes were actually to disapprove resolutions to reject the plan.

18. These changes brought several new or newly named divisions: Organization and Management, Program Coordination, Executive Development and Labor Relations, Statistical Policy and Management of Information Systems, and Legislative Reference.

this purpose a number of new personnel were hired and given the title of management associate. They were typically young (about thirty), with graduate education (about half in business administration) and some government experience. The names of these units were subsequently changed to special studies divisions, and they were assigned to miscellaneous tasks, usually associated with the budget. Their management functions gradually evaporated. At about the same time a number of those functions regarded as administrative details were transferred to the General Services Administration (GSA), along with the personnel who had performed them in OMB. These included activities related to procurement policy, travel regulations, and property management, and some in automatic data processing, financial management, grant simplification, and management systems. Dwight Ink, theretofore assistant director of OMB on the management side, was transferred to GSA as its deputy director. These responsibilities were never fully assimilated within GSA, and their transfer aroused vehement protests among some members of Congress. By early 1976, most of these functions and the personnel assigned to them were returned to OMB, where they did not receive a very warm welcome. Some observers believed that the purpose behind both these actions—the setting up of management divisions and the transfer of personnel to GSA—was to provide vacant positions in OMB that could be filled by persons responsive to the new OMB leadership.

Following the election of President Jimmy Carter, OMB was again reorganized in 1977, apparently to reinvigorate and redefine the management functions. Budget and management were each once again given a "side" of the organization, this time under executive associate directors, one for budget, one for reorganization and management. Partly this seems to have been to lend emphasis to Carter's vigorous campaign rhetoric on the need for reorganization and to his promise to streamline the entire federal government. For a period at least, the word *management* was nearly equated with reorganization by those within OMB and indeed in the government as a whole. The administration's original ambitious reorganization goals were later abandoned because of political roadblocks, and the ultimate results were mixed. A few boxes were shifted in and out of the Executive Office of the President itself; the new Departments of Energy and Education were established, but both would later be marked for extinction by President Carter's successor; and massive changes were made in the organization and basic elements of civil service administration, based on the reports of a series of task forces. OMB shared leadership in this latter undertaking with the chairman and others of the Civil Service Commission. During the Carter administration, there was also some expansion of activities and staff for many of the familiar and older functions of the OMB.[19] It should be added that Congress in 1974 directed OMB to establish an Office of Federal Procurement Policy, which was intended to operate practically independently of the rest of the organization.[20]

Yet, in 1980 it still appeared to many observers that management was a very unequal partner to the budget within OMB, however they might appear on an organization chart. In the 1980 study on the presidency by the National Academy of Public Administration, one entire chapter was devoted to the strengthening of OMB.[21] Four of the five recommendations listed there were directed to activities other than the budget itself—organization and management studies, program evaluation, intergovernmental assistance, and regulatory decision-making. The panel complained that after the reorganization of 1970, "both its budget and management sides were being weakened" and that "the agency's normal preoccupation with the budget became ever more dominating." A later study by another panel of the academy in 1981 emphasized nine areas of management requiring high priority in OMB.[22]

1. intergovernmental management and relationships
2. organization policy and planning, particularly intergovernmental and interagency
3. administrative planning to assure that managerial considerations are factored into program changes
4. management assistance to agencies

19. These included, for example, improvement of government-wide management systems; providing support when called upon in the budget process; providing a limited amount of consulting service to agency heads; encouraging interagency coordination on both policy and operational matters; program monitoring in intergovernmental relations; and review and clearance of reorganization plans and major intradepartmental reorganizations, executive orders, legislative proposals from other departments and agencies, proposed new regulations, and federal forms.

20. Public Law 93-400, August 30, 1974. Establishment of this office was the first of 149 recommendations of the Commission on Government Procurement of 1969–1972, a blue-ribbon body of which the comptroller general was the only statutory member. So dissatisfied was the commission with the way OMB had handled, or neglected, procurement policy that it sought to make the new office virtually autonomous within OMB and required that its head be appointed by the president with the advice and consent of the Senate.

21. National Academy of Public Administration, *A Presidency for the 1980s*, ch. 4.

22. National Academy of Public Administration, *Strengthening OMB's Role in Improving the Management of the Federal Government* (Washington, D.C., 1981). With only one exception, every member of the seventeen-person panel had worked for BoB, OMB, or both. Most had been at the level of director, deputy director, assistant director, or division chief. The majority were old-timers who had served during the Eisenhower period or earlier. About half had served under Roosevelt, and at least four went back to the very beginning of the revitalized BoB of 1939. The only one who was then on the OMB staff headed the Division of Management Improvement and Evaluation under the associate director for management.

    5. more effective standards of procurement
    6. strengthened coordination of statistics policy, paperwork manage-
       ment, automatic data processing, and governmental communica-
       tions
    7. improvement in financial management
    8. more emphasis and help to agencies in program evaluation
    9. leadership in interagency relations

It is evident from this capsule sketch that no enduring answer has been provided to the questions raised at the outset about the president's role in management, the proper part of BoB/OMB in that role, and the appropriate
relationship of managerial and budget activities within BoB/OMB. A number
of different arrangements have been tried, none with great success. Much of
what has been written and said about the agency's management work since the
1940s both by outsiders and by some insiders has been rather critical. Some
proposals, like those of the Heineman task force, were never tried, and the
Reagan administration is now providing a different twist and emphasis (see
Epilogue I). Some observers have recommended that management work be
completely divorced from budget work in a separate unit of the Executive Office of the President. There is some precedent for this in the old Bureau of
Efficiency of 1916–1934, but its experience was not very encouraging.

Policies, Programs, and the Budget

In 1921 General Dawes indicated that major reductions could be made in the
budget without significant changes in public policies and programs, and many
political leaders down to the present have confidently pronounced that if only
"fraud, waste, and abuse" could be eliminated, the budget could be sharply
reduced. Economy has long been a convenient shield for those who would
cut programs and change policies, including officials of supposedly policy-
neutral budget agencies. Yet, it has been quite clear for a long time that significant changes in public expenditures usually entail significant changes in
public policies or in conditions and workloads, whether or not they are under
the control of government officials. Therefore, those who make budgets and
those in central offices who review and modify them are to some extent necessarily involved in policy and programs, of which the budget itself is an expression and instrument. But as Aaron Wildavsky suggested many years ago,
most public programs are ongoing, and most changes in them in the normal

course of the budget process are incremental.[23] In fact, developments since World War II have further reduced the proportion of items that can be significantly changed in the budget-appropriations cycle: the growth of entitlement programs, long lead-time commitments on contracts and procurement, and formula grants-in-aid to state and local government (subsidies). That is, at least until 1981, the scope of budgetary discretion available to the president, the agency heads, the OMB, and indeed the Congress was declining.[24]

If the BoB/OMB were to satisfy the objectives of the Brownlow committee and the many groups since, it would be a general-staff agency of the president, advising and assisting him on the development and carrying out of programs in most areas of government (not of politics). Important but not exclusive among its tools would be the budget, and an implicit aspiration was that the budget itself, its process, its content, and its format would be relevant to and expressive of the president's program. This philosophy contributed to most of the variously labeled reforms mentioned earlier—performance budget, MBO, ZBB, and others. All of those expressions had to do with associating programs with dollars, though in procedurally and, to a limited extent, in conceptually different ways.[25] It is of some interest that none of these efforts—or gadgets—originated in BoB/OMB.

In addition to the normal budgetary routine, other related channels and tools have been used by BoB/OMB to influence the course of federal policies and programs. These have included the direct contacts of budget directors and their top staffs with presidents and their key advisers; the development and coordination of legislation and the president's legislative program; the development of fiscal policy; program analysis and evaluation; and the review and coordination of proposed federal regulations. Each of these five will be explored briefly.

23. Aaron Wildavsky, *The Politics of the Budgetary Process* (3rd ed.; Boston, 1979). The first edition of this book was published in 1964.

24. The reconciliation process (described in Epilogue I) has at least temporarily halted this trend.

25. The origins of these various labels and movements are interesting. The performance budget came from the naval and air force arms of the defense establishment, though the name itself is attributed to former President Hoover. The accounting emphasis in cost-of-performance budgeting came from the accounting fraternity and, within the government, from the GAO. PPBS was a product of microeconomists, particularly those in RAND, which reached the civil government by way of the Department of Defense. MBO was a product of mixed ingredients—certain savants in the business fraternity, notably Peter Drucker, and some from cultural anthropology, however indigestible the mixture might seem. Finally, ZBB was an experiment originating in a private research and development firm transferred to the federal government by way of Georgia.

PRESIDENTS, BUDGET DIRECTORS, AND STAFFS

Until President Carter's appointments of Bert Lance and James McIntyre as directors of OMB, not one of the directors of BoB/OMB had been a personal intimate of the president who appointed him. A number of them had been selected on the recommendation of others and had had little or no prior acquaintance with the appointing president. Yet, a very substantial number of them became frequent—some almost daily—and trusted if not intimate advisers of the presidents whom they served, not only on budgetary and financial matters but also on questions of basic governmental policy.[26] Obviously, there was a wide variance among presidents and among budget directors in the frequency, depth, nature, and influence of their advice. Presidents who were wise would talk with them and listen to them, for they had certain advantages that no one else in the chief executive's entourage could claim. They were loyal to the president, for their institution's standing and their own appointments and retention depended solely upon him; they were objective because they represented no constituency; they were broad-gauged because their purview extended to the whole of government; they could be widely informed because of the information networks beneath them; and they had recourse to the depth, knowledge, and institutional memory of one of government's most experienced organizations. Until quite recently—since roughly the late 1960s—the budget directors also had the advantage of relative anonymity, since their identities were usually unknown to the great mass of the American public. Their information and advice was seldom divulged or leaked to the media. Since 1932 they have issued no annual reports and produced few documents for public distribution other than the budget itself and materials immediately related to it, and these were of course the president's, not OMB's. Frequently presidents also had the benefit of drawing directly on the expertise of the budget directors' subordinates, for many of the budget directors brought with them to meetings with the president their deputies and/or other officers, and a few (notably James Webb, Frank Pace, and Frederick Lawton) made it a practice to invite staff members, career and noncareer, who had worked on problems on the immediate agenda.

But some obstacles worked against the influence of the budget directors. Some were effectively blocked by White House factotums and seldom saw their presidents. Some were not in office long enough to realize their advan-

26. Among the budget directors who fit this category must certainly be included Dawes, Smith, Webb, Pace, Lawton, Dodge, Stans, David Bell, Gordon, Schultze, Shultz, Ash, Lance, McIntyre, and Stockman. I may have missed some who should be included in this list for want of adequate information.

tages or even to get adequately acquainted with their staffs and the resources of their organization. Few, in fact, almost none, of the budget directors have been part of the inner advisory "kitchen cabinet." This has meant that their access to the president has depended upon his desire to see them or, in a few cases, on the willingness of his gatekeepers to admit them. The degree of influence of budget directors upon presidential policies and programs appears to have depended upon the esteem and confidence in which they were held by the presidents they served, even when not grounded in prior personal friendship and association. It also depended inversely on the relative influence on the president of his other advisers in the White House office who were usually closer in proximity and political dependence than were the directors of the budget.

Although the role of BoB/OMB was officially one of advice and not authority, it did, from the very beginning, make decisions on budgetary and program matters, most of which were in effect final. In theory, unhappy agency heads could appeal to the president, but in practice such appeals were usually limited to the most basic disagreements on matters that could be properly regarded as presidential. During some periods, even these were effectively blocked by the White House "guards." This meant, among other things, that a great many decisions on lesser matters were in effect delegated down the line within BoB/OMB because they were not of enough import to be appealed to higher echelons within that organization or within the aggrieved departments. In some areas and at certain times, presidents specifically or implicitly delegated their decision-making powers to BoB/OMB. Thus, during World War II, President Roosevelt relied heavily on Budget Director Smith to "run" the nonmilitary parts of the government. During the Watergate period, after the departure of Ehrlichman and Haldeman, Budget Director Ash and his staff essentially filled the vacuum of presidential leadership in the domestic aspects of the administration.

THE LEGISLATIVE PROGRAM

Another important entrée of BoB/OMB into substantive matters, second only to the budget itself, is its responsibility for the development and coordination of the president's legislative program. This responsibility grew out of its power to clear legislative proposals and agency comments on legislation under consideration in the Congress. The growth of BoB influence in this area has already been recounted—how staff members were increasingly relied upon to steer, coordinate, modify, and compromise with various agencies in the government, in the White House, and indeed in the bureau itself. In the later Truman years, a procedure was developed and institutionalized whereby the president's annual legislative program might be produced on a systematic basis. Like the budget, the legislative agenda is disciplined by the calendar. During the first weeks of every calendar year the president must transmit to the Congress at least three basic messages: the report on the state of the union, the budget message, and the annual economic report. The first of these is normally prepared by a high official in the White House (the special counsel or equivalent) assisted by staff; the second, by BoB/OMB—since 1952 its Office of Budget Review; and the third, since 1947, by the Council of Economic Advisers. It is obviously imperative that these documents be consistent with one another. It is important, too, that they reflect statements and pledges made by the president, especially if they follow a presidential election campaign; that they anticipate important legislation and budget changes that may follow; that they be based at least in part upon consideration of proposals from the departments and agencies; and that they reflect a consciously designed legislative strategy.

It is not too surprising that until the end of World War II, the drafting of presidential messages was a rather hit-or-miss affair. The budget message was heavily financial and lifeless, and the state of the union report was drafted by one close to the president on the basis of the latter's interests augmented by selected suggestions from the departments and agencies. Beginning about 1947, through a process of occasional initiatives and gradual routinization, a procedure was built, principally by BoB career staff in the Legislative Reference Division but under the leadership of the special counsel to the president. The annual call for budget estimates, which the bureau sent to the various departments and agencies in the late spring or early summer every year, included a section requesting a listing of legislation expected to be sought the following year. Later, in the fall, the president signed a letter to every agency head asking for his proposals for legislation. All these documents were reviewed, sifted, and coordinated by bureau staff, mainly the Legislative Reference people, further studied where necessary by teams guided or monitored by BoB personnel, and finally made the common basis for all three messages. In this work, the Legislative Reference personnel were working more directly for the White House than for the bureau itself.

The first test of the procedure, which was not spelled out in any law, was the transition to President Eisenhower in 1953. He and his staff adopted it *in toto* and continued to rely heavily upon BoB's Legislative Reference staff, not only in the preparation of the president's legislative programs but also in connection with the coordination, review, and content of individual items of legislation. To a lesser extent, the same process continued during the Kennedy and Johnson administrations. There was more leadership and involvement from the White House and more input from outside groups in the multitude of task forces that both Presidents Kennedy and Johnson employed. But much of the staffing of the task forces and the implementing of their reports came from the Bureau of the Budget, specifically from its career Division of Legislative Reference, working with the appropriate budget examiners. The relatively small staff (eight to twelve professionals) in that unit worked on both the procedural and substantive aspects of proposed legislation and testimony and enrolled bills. Most of the time, their superintendents were not the budget directors but the policy advisers in the White House—such as Sorensen for Kennedy and Califano for Johnson.

This procedure and this relationship effectively ended during the Nixon administration for two essentially political reasons. First was the establishment and the staffing in and after 1970 of the Domestic Council (later the Domestic Policy Staff), which in effect took charge of significant domestic policy development. Second was the naming of noncareer associate directors above the career divisions in OMB in the early 1970s. Thenceforward, the staff of the legislative reference group in OMB, still entirely career personnel, would receive, refer, handle, and coordinate all legislative materials, as before. But significant or controversial matters of policy and politics would be referred to the politically appointed officers in OMB or in the White House or both. The volume and the complexity of materials still processed by the legislative reference group is enormous. But for better or worse, the group's influence on significant substantive matters is less than it once was.

FISCAL POLICY

The first responsibility imposed upon the Bureau of the Budget by President Roosevelt's Executive Order No. 8248 in 1939 was "to assist the President in the preparation of the Budget and *the formulation of the fiscal program of the Government*" (emphasis added). Accordingly, Acting Director of the Budget Bell and after him Budget Director Smith in 1938 and 1939 began employing a small number of top-grade economists to analyze, and give advice on, the economic aspects of the budget. They constituted the Fiscal Division of the bureau. As noted earlier, in 1952, when the BoB was reorganized, the Fiscal Division was abolished, and the macroeconomists of its economic policy staff became a branch of the Office of Budget Review. The program analysts (microeconomists) were transferred to the various program divisions. There remains today a substantial fiscal analysis branch in the Division of Budget Review as well as a small Office of Economic Policy under the director.

Those Budget Bureau economists during the war and early postwar years were apparently the first policy and program analysts in the BoB in the modern sense of the term. After creation of the Council of Economic Advisers, they began informally meeting with staff of that council and of the Treasury Department. Such meetings were later regularized to discuss and then prepare periodic reports on the state of the economy. These meetings witnessed the birth of what later—during the Eisenhower administration—became known as the Troika. Customarily, the career staff officials of the three agencies met first. Their findings, conclusions, and policy options were then sent forward and considered in meetings of the appropriate assistant heads of the same agencies. After that, the secretary of the treasury, chairman of the CEA, and director of the budget would meet to discuss and finalize decisions and, in case of disagreement, forward the unresolved problems to the president. Normally, the final report of the Troika was drafted by representatives of the BoB/OMB, though the chairman and spokesman of the top group was the secretary of the treasury, the ranking official of the three and the ranking economic official in the government. The late Arthur Okun, former chairman of the CEA, is said to have described the rationale for the Troika in these words: "Treasury had the revenue, Budget had the expenditures, and CEA had the deficit." [27] A less cryptic explanation might be that Treasury had the overall financial picture, private and public, as well as the public revenues and debt; BoB/OMB had the information and analysis on public programs, including their costs and benefits; and CEA had the professional economists' information and analysis of the general economic situation.

The Troika was subsequently enlarged on occasion to include the chairman of the Federal Reserve Board in view of the concern with monetary policy, and this larger group was labeled the Quadriad. Additional agencies were also included in the 1970s in a succession of formal and informal groupings—Agriculture, Commerce, Labor, State, and others. But the core group, the most intimate and the one least influenced by parochial interests, remained the Troika, augmented sometimes by the vice-president, the president's policy director, and others. Through it the BoB/OMB has had a channel of communication to the president, the Congress, and the people. But one cannot generalize about BoB/OMB's influence on governmental economic policy, which fluctuates greatly with changing budget directors, leaders of the sister agencies, presidents and presidential staffs, and other factors. It is likewise guesswork to try to calculate how much influence economic considerations have

27. See Herbert Stein (later a chairman of CEA himself), "The Chief Executive as Chief Economist," in American Enterprise Institute, *Essays in Contemporary Economic Problems: Demand, Productivity, and Population* (Washington, D.C., 1981), 53–78.

had on the other divisions of BoB/OMB and on the budget itself. Some have declared that the real intent of hiring economists at the start was to counteract the negative and conservative tendencies of the budget examiners. Many of the first arrivals were Keynesians, and in all probability many of the later arrivals were, too.

There can be no area of more potential political contention than economic policy, and it is interesting that to this day there has not been a single non-career, political officer on the fiscal analysis staff—or in the whole Office of Budget Review. But in the early 1970s there was established a new noncareer office of assistant director for economic policy, who came to be the top OMB representative, under the director, in the Troika structure. This office has a very small staff and works with the economists in the Office of Budget Review. Incumbents in the economic policy post typically change with administrations. Interestingly, the first one was Arthur G. Laffer, who was brought in as a special assistant by Budget Director George Shultz, and who, more recently, became famous as a leading proponent of supply-side economics and the architect of the Laffer curve.

PROGRAM ANALYSIS AND EVALUATION

In 1961, the new secretary of defense brought in a group of microeconomists, largely from the RAND Corporation, to revamp the financial management systems of his department. They had long prior experience with budgeting and finance in the defense area and were ready with a new system that they styled a planning-programming-budgeting system (PPBS). It was initiated basically as a device to relate the military plans to the budget through program structures. The design was nearly the ultimate in microeconomic rationality as applied to the going problems of organizational decision, and its elements are much easier to define than to perform. As applied to civilian problems, PPBS involves the following steps:

the determination of governmental objectives in a given area in terms as precise as possible

the conception of alternative means of attaining those objectives—that is, alternative programs

the analysis and comparison of each alternative program against others in terms of their effectiveness in attaining the objectives (or benefits) against their costs

the choice of the best program

the translation of that program into a budget

the implementation of the program and budget in operation

the evaluation of results in terms of their effectiveness (or benefits) against their costs

on the basis of such evaluation, the beginning of the process again

Since few programs (let alone their effects) are completed within a year, PPBS required projections for several years in advance. It also required that programs with related or interdependent purposes and effects be grouped and considered against one another, which led to the need for a program structure consisting of program packages with ready crosswalks to the budgets that would provide the resources for the programs.

PPBS in the mid-sixties was widely heralded as a highly successful innovation in the Department of Defense. In 1965, President Johnson, under considerable criticism for alleged inefficiencies in his Great Society programs, ordered that it be installed and used in almost all federal agencies, excepting principally the regulatory commissions. He instructed Director of the Budget Charles L. Schultze to supervise the undertaking. PPBS probably caused as noisy a disturbance in Washington, its field offices, and ultimately in state and local jurisdictions and foreign governments as any administrative idea since performance budgeting twenty years earlier. There were training courses galore to convert budgeteers (and many others) into PPBSers, a plethora of new monographs, case studies, and texts, and many new university courses and programs in pursuit of the new light. There were also reams of paper endeavoring to analyze programs, replete with charts and graphs, preferably obscure and exotic. These analyses climbed up hierarchies in which they were reviewed and consolidated or augmented and then were propelled to the appropriate examiners in BoB, few of whom had time to examine them even if they wanted to (which many of them did not). For the most part, they did not go on to the appropriations subcommittees in Congress, which preferred to review executive budget requests in their time-honored ways.

The BoB set up a special unit to sponsor and monitor the PPB system and borrowed or hired a few top officers from Defense and elsewhere to provide leadership. But there appears to have been quiet resistance to it as a new method of budgeting in BoB and in other agencies of the government. One heard few laments among the regular budgetary personnel when it was quietly dropped from the budget instructions in Nixon's second year. Although the name of the system and some of its elements survived in a few federal agencies, including parts of the Defense Department, and among some state and local jurisdictions, for most intents and purposes it died in the early 1970s. But PPBS left legacies to both the executive and legislative sides of the government and specifically to the BoB/OMB and the GAO.

It added a significant new dimension to public budgeting. The original and traditional formula for a public budget looked something like this: appropriations to provide *money* to *organizations* to buy *services* of people (salaries for positions) and *things* (supplies, equipment, utilities, and so forth).

The performance budget had moved a long step beyond this formula by focusing on the *activities* and the effective use of the services and things bought. It gave impetus to such matters as work measurement, cost accounting and unit costs, and productivity measurement. Many today may not remember it, but the first flare of interest in productivity in the government occurred in BoB and a few other agencies in the early 1950s. PPBS, too, was concerned with outputs, but it went a step beyond to *outcomes* and effects and their relationship to costs. An oversimplified example might be the appropriation of funds to a police department.

> Under traditional budget: appropriations for numbers, grades, salaries of police; for purchase and operation of police cars, uniforms, and supplies; for rents or depreciation; for electricity.
>
> Under performance budget: appropriations for miles driven by police cars, services rendered to people in trouble, disturbances resolved, arrests made.
>
> Under PPBS: appropriations for maintaining order and reducing crime.

It may be noted that with each successive step, the difficulty of budgeting is increased, the precision of data is diminished. Furthermore, the amounts of effort and research and thought are magnified, because one cannot reach the second stage without the first, or the third without the first and second. Yet, that third stage is undeniably the reason for almost all governmental policy and programs.

PPBS as a system failed for a variety of reasons, both practical and conceptual.

> It was vastly oversold by its early sponsors, who claimed for it many things it could not then (or probably even now) do.
>
> It did not, in either theoretical or operational terms, genuinely link programs and budgets with the activities that were expected to flow from them.
>
> Its intended linkage of plans and programs with budgets on an annual basis was simply impracticable; there was not enough time.
>
> The tools for measuring results and outcomes, particularly in social fields, were largely undeveloped.

There was insufficient recognition of the past and its impact on the present and future; there seemed to be an assumption that every program began with the first round of PPBS.

It was too comprehensive, insufficiently selective of the critical problems, which resulted in mountains of paperwork.

There was insufficient consideration and tolerance of factors beyond the realm of economic rationality—political, social, bureaucratic, human.[28]

The basic element of PPBS that did not die was its focus on results and outcomes (rather than, or in addition to, resources and means), on the analysis of policies and programs to attain such results, and on the evaluation of the effectiveness of ongoing programs. Such evaluation and analysis became basic nutrients in the consideration of new or changed policies and of the establishment or continuation of programs. With this explosion of concern came others: multiyear planning of projects and their costs, utilization of increasingly sophisticated tools of analysis, an upsurge in the use of microeconomics and of its practitioners in managerial advice and decisions, temporary rather than continuing authorizations of programs, consideration of sunset laws, and others.

When President Johnson proclaimed PPBS for the civil government, he simultaneously directed the agencies to set up offices to superintend or at least provide analysis for it. After that time, many of these grew in both size and sophistication, though they seem to have declined recently. Almost every major study dealing with BoB/OMB or the Executive Office of the President generally has urged greater effort to provide leadership and coordination of policy and program evaluation, and many have deplored what they judged to be inadequate attention to this activity.[29] It is curious that BoB/OMB, the agency that had much to do with launching program evaluation fifteen years ago, now seems to be lagging behind in both its use and its development.

28. The most virulent critic of PPBS, Aaron Wildavsky, would probably not agree with this list and would no doubt add some other items. See his *The Politics of the Budgetary Process*, 186–202. But it is interesting that Wildavsky changed the name of a new graduate school at the University of California at Berkeley from a school of "public affairs" to one of "public policy." (He was the new school's first dean.) Later he wrote a book entitled *Speaking Truth to Power: The Art and Craft of Policy Analysis* (Boston, 1979). He did not like the system, but he was apparently much enamored of its central-element, analysis.

29. For example, among the studies cited earlier, see the Heineman report and BoB's own self-survey of 1967, the Ash council's report of 1970, and the reports of the National Academy of Public Administration in 1980 and 1981. See also an unpublished OMB internal self-study, "Report of the Task Force on Analysis of Program Divisions Work Load" (March, 1973) and the following unpublished National Academy of Public Administration documents: "The President and Executive Management: Summary of a Symposium" (January, 1976) and "Conference on the Institutional Presidency: Preliminary Papers" (March, 1974).

THE MANAGEMENT OF REGULATIONS

Although there had been federal regulation for a long time, particularly of economic activities of a presumably monopolistic and interstate character and of recipients of federal grants and contracts, it was not until the 1960s and 1970s that generalized regulation became prevalent.[30] It arose from growing popular and political concern about such matters as discrimination against minorities, women, and the aging; threats to the environment; conservation of energy; health and safety of residents, consumers, and workers; and endangered species. Regulations in such areas were applied to industries and businesses in the private sector, nonprofit institutions (including schools, universities, and hospitals), state and local governments, and even individuals. During the 1970s, regulation grew to become a major instrument of federal intervention in both the public and private sectors of the economy.

The direct cost of regulation to the federal government is not large, probably not much more than 1 percent of the budget. Its costs to the economy and to various kinds of enterprises however, may be enormous, and of course, so may be its benefits. But the point is that the federal budget is not very useful in directing the course and extent of regulation except in a negative way. We have known for many decades that the intent of the Clayton Antitrust Act could be effectively negated by the simple budgetary recourse of denying adequate funds to the agency intended to enforce it. Such recourse is not unknown today. But the quasi legislative-judicial-administrative processes of regulation remain largely an area of unresolved argument, as do the degree and nature of presidential control over regulatory agencies, both those that operate as independent commissions and those within the executive branch.

Presidential involvement in regulatory matters has a long history, but until recently it was not a responsibility very demanding of staff time and research in the executive office. This situation changed radically during the 1960s and 1970s as the scope of regulatory legislation exploded and the concern of interest groups grew. Congress increasingly insisted on legislative review and veto of agency regulations; the courts likewise became more interested in matters of policy substance as well as procedure; and the president himself came under growing pressure from businesses and others adversely or favorably affected by federal regulation. BoB/OMB has long been interested in the costs

---

30. Much of this information on the management of regulations is drawn from a report by Charles E. Ludlam, "The Reagan Regulatory Program in Context," issued by the Alliance for Justice in October, 1981; and from Lester M. Salamon, "Federal Regulation: A New Arena for Presidential Power?" in Hugh Heclo and Lester M. Salamon (eds.), *The Illusion of Presidential Government* (Boulder, 1981), 147–73. I am also indebted for the advice and counsel of Peter Petkas.

and budgets of regulatory agencies, and some individual examiners have from time to time been concerned with substantive regulatory questions. In addition, the organization and procedures involved in regulation have been a bone of contention and discussion among management analysts for at least forty years.

But the first major institutional involvement of the budget agency in the substance of regulation dates only from 1971, when President Nixon's OMB director George Shultz initiated the quality-of-life review program in a letter to executive departments and agencies. Shultz originally proposed that regulations in the fields of safety and health, particularly those of the Environmental Protection Agency (EPA), be submitted in draft to OMB for review and clearance. But the White House, apparently nervous about congressional and media reaction to such potential presidential interference in environmental regulation, required that the procedure be severely limited. As finally promulgated, the directive provided that EPA submit its proposed rules to other federal agencies affected and report to OMB on their comments and its own reactions to them. OMB would then examine the comments and reactions and decide whether they required further meetings for resolution. In some cases, where differences could not be resolved, the problems were referred to the OMB director and to John Ehrlichman, then head of the Domestic Council, for *review*, not for decision, which remained with EPA. The evidence on the degree to which this procedure blocked or changed the ultimate content of the regulations is mixed. There is no doubt that it sometimes caused long delays but equally that it did not constitute an OMB veto.

In the decade after inauguration of the quality-of-life review, which itself survived until the last week of the Ford administration, the course of OMB involvement in regulatory activities has been one of unsteady increase. President Ford in November, 1974, issued an executive order (No. 11821) requiring that agencies consider costs of *major* proposed regulations and their potential impact upon inflation and that they submit cost-benefit analyses of their proposals to OMB and the Council on Wage and Price Stability (COWPS). OMB was called upon to develop guidelines for determining what was *major* and what factors should be considered in the evaluation of recommended regulations. But final decision on what was major remained with the proposing agencies. Both OMB and COWPS played some part in monitoring the program and seeing that its requirements were carried out, but neither was empowered to change or overrule an agency's decision.

President Carter built upon and considerably extended the Ford program. His executive order (No. 12044) in March, 1978, established internal review procedures for regulatory agencies, requiring, among other things, involvement of the agency head. It also broadened the analysis required of proposed regulations and required consideration of alternatives, and it provided that a Regulatory Analysis Review Group (RARG) headed by the chairman of CEA must review a small number of regulatory analyses as a kind of quality control. Later, he established a Regulatory Council, consisting of representatives of all the departments and agencies with regulatory responsibilities, to develop better methods, innovative techniques, and interagency programs in the regulatory field.

OMB was increasingly involved in monitoring and policing the program— reviewing, questioning, and debating proposed regulations with the appropriate agencies. Section 3503 of the Paperwork Reducton Act of 1980 established a new and separate unit, the Office of Information and Regulatory Affairs, within OMB for this work and other responsibilities with respect to reports, questionnaires, other paperwork, and data processing. Almost all of the personnel of this group were career OMB employees, and most of them continued in this work after the Reagan transition. Partly to enhance OMB's clout in regulatory matters, a regulatory reform bill that would give legal sanction to Carter's order and add other features was introduced in Congress in 1980. The bill passed the Senate but did not reach the floor of the House; a somewhat revised version was under consideration during the Reagan term.

Political Responsiveness Versus Neutral Competence

The very first principle enunciated by the first budget director, General Dawes, at the first meeting of agency heads on June 29, 1921—two days before the Budget and Accounting Act took effect—was that "the Budget Bureau must be impartial, impersonal, and nonpolitical." The statement was subsequently issued verbatim in BoB Circular No. 1. Insofar as personnel rotation and patronage are an indicator, the Dawes prescription was followed faithfully for nearly half a century. The BoB was one of the safest agencies in the government for professionals and administrators almost to its very top, and to this writing it cannot be said that more than a handful of appointments, if that, have reflected typical patronage considerations, though party alignment and loyalty have frequently been considered. With changes of administration to the other party, directors have always changed and most assistant (since 1953, deputy) directors have also changed.[31] Only one of the directors

31. Assistant or deputy directors who were exceptions to this generalization were Elmer B. Staats, who survived the transitions from Eisenhower to Kennedy and from Kennedy to Johnson, and Philip S. Hughes, who survived that from Johnson to Nixon.

(Frederick J. Lawton) was drawn from the career ranks of BoB/OMB, but almost all (until the Carter administration) had had prior administrative experience in the federal government, and a few were promoted from the assistant or deputy job to the directorship.[32]

Until the Eisenhower administration, virtually all the other personnel of BoB were regular civil servants. Under Eisenhower and his successors to 1968, a few noncareer assistant directorships were established (up to four), but none of these was placed in a line position. Thus, the heads of the offices and the divisions were all career personnel, and all worked immediately under the office of the director. A major break in this situation occurred during the second Nixon term. It was the appointment of four individuals to an equal number of new noncareer positions as program associate directors (PADs), each to head up a cluster of the program divisions. The OMB management and certain other nonbudget activities were already under a noncareer assistant director. Appointments to these posts were not then and have not since been patronage in its traditional sense. Most appointees have had backgrounds of education and experience relevant to their OMB responsibilities. They were to superintend the budget work of the career personnel, provide a channel between them and the political leadership of OMB and the White House, and also provide a filter between them and the federal agencies with which they dealt. The titles of the career division chiefs were changed to deputy associate directors (DADs). Later OMB director Thomas B. ("Bert") Lance added a new wrinkle when he created two executive associate directors (EADs) between the director's office and the operating units—one for budget and the other for reorganization and management. Thus, the top career personnel were separated by two levels of political appointments from the director and his deputy, with whom they had formerly enjoyed direct and frequent contact. Furthermore, after 1967 virtually all the OMB political appointees were housed in the old Executive Office Building, the career personnel in the New Executive Office Building, thus accentuating the cleavage between the two.

There are now about a dozen noncareer officers in the top echelons of the office. They are typically short-termers: virtually all vacate their jobs when the party of the government changes, and most move along to other work within a year or two or sometimes three of their appointment—regardless of party politics. The contrast between them and their career subordinates in respect to years of OMB experience and therefore of knowledge, memory, ex-

32. Examples of such promotions include Roop (after several years in private business), Lawton, Rowland R. Hughes, Brundage, Charles L. Schultze (after a two-year lapse), Zwick, Weinberger, and McIntyre.

pectations, and ambitions could hardly be more vivid. The median BoB/OMB experience of the career division chiefs in 1980 was more than ten years.

A second break against the nonpolitical position of OMB occurred in 1973 and 1974. Watergate temperatures were rising and Congress was becoming increasingly irate about the Nixon administration's impoundments of appropriated funds and its allegedly arbitrary decisions in the execution of legislation. Much of the congressional animus focused upon OMB Director Ash and his deputy Malek, through or by whom presidential impoundments and many other unpopular actions were ordered. Congressional feelings against OMB were accentuated that year as the White House staff became increasingly preoccupied by Watergate and thereby enfeebled in managing the government. Following vituperative hearings, Congress passed a bill requiring senatorial confirmation of both the director and deputy director of OMB and making the requirement retroactive upon the two incumbents, Ash and Malek. President Nixon vetoed it on the grounds that its retroactive feature was an unconstitutional attempt to circumvent the president's power of removal. The Congress was unable to override the veto, but it then passed, and the president signed, an act providing that all future appointments to the posts require the advice and consent of the Senate.[33]

That law carried a greater significance than may superficially appear. From the very beginning of the argument about the Budget and Accounting Act, its principal supporters insisted that the budget agency staff and its two top officers should be uniquely the president's people. They should not be like regular officers of the government with responsibilities both to the president and Congress, and they should not be like members of the White House staff because they headed a career institution. The act in 1974 obfuscated that special status. Henceforth, the nominees have had to undergo the same kind of congressional and political scrutiny, the same kind of pressure, as presidential appointees in line positions. They may now be held directly accountable by Congress as well as by the president. Relieved of the constraints and protections of the Hatch Act, there emerged the possibility, which now seems to have been realized, that they would become political and partisan spokesmen for their administrations. Under such circumstances, whether they or the agency over which they preside could maintain the reality or even the illusion of Dawes's prescription of 1921 was at least questionable. The symbolism of the 1974 act was probably as important as the reality—to those both within and outside the agency. It is interesting that all of the academic witnesses who testified on the bill opposed it, even though it is doubtful that any held any

33. Public Law 93-250, March 2, 1974.

brief for those who were at the time the incumbents of the positions in question. And a few years later, many of the congressmen who had endorsed it suffered some embarrassment because of the allegations about OMB Director Bert Lance's banking experiences. They had approved his nomination without much inquiry.

Another dimension and qualification of the job of OMB director was added in the 1970s. In contrast to the low public profile of prior years, budget directors began to be selected with a view to their being spokesmen for the president's program, particularly to business groups. They give speeches, even campaign speeches, on behalf of the president. OMB directors including George Shultz, Caspar Weinberger, Roy Ash, and Bert Lance all became identified with the political and partisan posture of the president in some degree. It is said that President Carter's hesitation in appointing James McIntyre as director, after keeping him for many months in an acting capacity, reflected his concern that McIntyre would not meet the expectations of the business world. It should be added, however, that none of these appointees of the 1970s was himself a political leader and none became a *major* spokesman for the president before the Congress, the media, and the public. David Stockman, who followed them, was thus sui generis, the first of his kind (see Epilogue I).

The problem of neutrality versus political responsiveness goes well beyond personnel appointments and patronage to questions of personal and political loyalty and social ideology. On the whole, until the 1970s, the problem was effectively handled—or camouflaged. The unflagging dedication of the three Republican presidents from 1921 to 1933 to the cause of economy was thoroughly attuned to that of the military officers assigned to the budget agency. Roosevelt largely let the BoB alone for his most active New Deal years; then, when he was ready to modify it in the late thirties, he completely changed the scenario and the cast of characters. The prevailing BoB doctrine for about three decades after 1939 was that its staff should be concerned with, and involved in, the politics of program and policy as analyzers of options but not as partisan political advocates. Yet, it would have been surprising if the bulk of BoB's professionals were not sympathetic with the objectives of the New Deal and Fair Deal programs when Eisenhower took office in 1953. The transition in BoB was, according to all accounts, remarkably smooth. This may be attributed to a variety of factors: changes in the White House staff; the sensitivity and acumen of Eisenhower's first budget director, Joseph M. Dodge; and the knowledge, cooperativeness, and skill of the top career staff of BoB, who did all in their power to educate the leaders of the new administration to the pros and cons and the backgrounds of all the major issues. The ease of the transition of the Bureau—in sharp contrast with the friction and paralysis in many other places in the government—may also have derived from the traditionally passive or negative posture of many of the budget examiners toward expanded governmental activity and from the fact that Eisenhower's procedures were generally more orderly and the options clearer.

There do not appear to have been serious problems of transition in the bureau between Eisenhower and Kennedy in 1961 or between Johnson and Nixon in 1969. Indeed some found the transition between the two Democratic presidents, Kennedy and Johnson, more difficult than the transitions that preceded and followed it. But the political problems for OMB in the 1970s and 1980s probably began in the decade of the 1960s. Kennedy and Johnson both encouraged their personal staffs in the White House to assume the initiative in the development of public policies. JFK and LBJ both relied heavily on task forces composed largely of outsiders but including some officials of BoB and other agencies, and both used representatives of the bureau to organize, provide services, and write reports for the task forces. The initiative for the new approaches to problems during that period flowed away from the operating agencies toward the White House, its task forces, and the BoB. As far as the programs of the Great Society were, or would become, politically controversial and vulnerable—as most of them did—BoB/OMB could hardly escape some share of responsibility for them. Yet, at the same time, it was criticized for not taking a more aggressive role in planning and developing programs and in supervising and coordinating their implementation. It was damned if it did, and damned if it didn't.

If the 1969 transition caused little trouble, later developments in the Nixon presidency surely did. After formation of OMB and the Domestic Policy Council in 1970, the line between what was institutional and neutral (and thus belonged to OMB) and what was personally presidential, partisan, and political—which had been fuzzy since 1921—became simply a blur. Individual members of OMB's staff were called upon to work for the Ehrlichman group, sometimes with instructions not to tell their supervisors. The situation for OMB was exacerbated during the later months of the Nixon administration when, with the departure of Haldeman, Ehrlichman, and other key presidential assistants, OMB director Ash undertook to use his agency to run the government. According to Ash, after the departure of Ehrlichman in the spring of 1974, "OMB clearly and indisputably became a presidential right hand. It was absolutely a myth to say that the government was not managed in the last few months of the Nixon administration. It was probably better managed in terms of government function than it has been in any other time in American history, except not by the President. We had that place humming." [34]

The humming of which Ash spoke was not very musical to the ears of the executive agencies or to those of Congress. It has already been noted that Congress tried to remove Ash and Malek in 1973. As one of his last presidential acts, Nixon signed the Congressional Budget and Impoundment Control Act, which severely restrained the president's power to impound funds. It also set up a competitive process in Congress for consideration of the president's budget. Some observers felt, and still feel, that the close political ties between the presidential staff and the noncareer staff of OMB during the Watergate period seriously damaged the reputation and effectiveness of that agency. It is good to be close to a president, but not too close, especially to one as controversial as Richard Nixon.

The transition to the Ford administration following the resignation of President Nixon was gradual and not traumatic, though many of the principal noncareer leaders changed during the months following Ford's inauguration. The transition to the Carter administration in 1977 seems to have been well planned and coordinated on both sides, even though there was a sudden change in the incumbents of almost all the top positions on or immediately after January 21. President Carter's first OMB director, Bert Lance, was from the very beginning a principal adviser and confidant of the president—more so than he was the managing head of an organization. In this regard, his role somewhat resembled those of Smith with Roosevelt, Dodge with Eisenhower, and Shultz with Nixon. His difficulties and resignation eight months after his appointment probably caused more trauma (paralysis, some called it) in the White House than they did in OMB or than had the transition in January of the same year.

The posture, the stature, and the "politicalness" of the BoB/OMB have depended on a great many relationships and perceptions. Perhaps most important has been the relationship with, and the view of, the president himself, particularly with respect to the director of the agency. A second has been the nature, strength, and attitudes of the personal staff of the president in the White House—the degree to which they compete or cooperate with BoB/OMB, the ways in which they use or ignore it, the degree to which they direct it or co-opt its resources and individual staff members, and the degree to which they obstruct or facilitate its communications with the president, the departments and agencies, the Congress, and outsiders. The relationships

34. Berman, *The Office of Management and Budget and the Presidency*, 122. The quotation is from his personal interview with Roy Ash on November 6, 1975.

with other units of the EOP and, outside it, of the executive branch have been of the greatest significance—the extent to which it has behaved as, and is regarded as, facilitator, giver of orders, coordinator, standardizer, adviser, critic, obstructor, and "eyes, ears, mouth, and arms" of the president. Finally, OMB relations with Congress and its various elements and committees have become increasingly important, particularly since passage of the Congressional Budget and Impoundment Control Act.

A recent and rather striking example of the use of OMB and the budget itself for political purposes was the inclusion in the 1981 budget document of a 180-page eulogy of the Carter administration's "major accomplishments." Issued in the crucial early stages of the 1980 presidential campaign, this was, according to Allen Schick, "the first time that the president's budget office incorporated a campaign tract into its budget documents." [35]

That there has been substantial politicization of BoB/OMB in the last fifteen years seems to be generally recognized and widely deplored. Yet, there has probably always been a certain amount of mythology about its political neutrality, and the myth has been increasingly stretched as the federal government—and therefore the president—has become increasingly involved in controversial matters touching almost every facet of American society. The BoB's self-study group in 1967 criticized the long-standing distinction between loyalty to the *president* and to the *presidency* as unrealistic. And a later internal study group in 1979 urged that the OMB take more aggressive stands in advocacy of the president's programs. [36] But the institutional posture of OMB is of great, perhaps indispensable, significance. OMB is the only place in the executive branch of the government with a record and memory of issues and their pros and cons, usually above the parochial views of bureaus and divisions, congressional committees, and private interests. Transition from party to party, from president to president, could be total chaos without the institutional continuity of OMB. But OMB's effectiveness in these matters depends heavily upon trust and credibility, and these depend upon the posture of the noncareer leadership and the caliber and integrity of the career staff. The maintenance of these in a viable mix is and will continue to be a delicate but essential requirement.

---

35. Allen Schick, "The Problem of Presidential Budgeting," in Heclo and Salamon (eds.), *The Illusion of Presidential Government*, 105. Schick may have been stretching it a bit. Earlier budgets have glorified accomplishments, though not at such length.
36. Neither of these studies has been published.

CHAPTER 5

The GAO Since 1950

Program Evaluation for a Resurgent Congress

It is the proper duty of a representative body to look diligently into
every affair of government and to
talk much about what it sees. It is
meant to be the eyes and the voice,
and to embody the wisdom and will
of its constituents. Unless Congress
have and use every means of ac-
quainting itself with the acts and the
disposition of the administrative
agents of the government, the country must be helpless to learn how it
is being served. . . . The informing
function of Congress should be preferred even to its legislative
function.

WOODROW WILSON, 1885

All goddamn auditors ought to be in
the bottom of hell!

Attributed to
GENERAL GEORGE S. PATTON

When in the late 1940s GAO launched itself on a program of comprehensive
audits, the meaning and significance of the term was not altogether clear except in the negative sense. It meant an end to the detailed checking of individual vouchers and transactions, accounts, checks, and like matters. At the beginning, the term was apparently equated with *financial*. An audit of this kind
was essentially like those undertaken by public accounting firms in the private
sector; the immediate models were the audits of government corporations that
had begun just a few years before. The models for the corporation audits were
audits of private business. Comprehensive audits were variously and loosely
defined within GAO, but the definition contained in the Budget and Accounting Procedures Act of 1950 was probably as definitive as any.

> The financial transactions . . . including but not limited to the accounts of accountable officers, shall be audited by the General Accounting Office in accordance with such principles and procedures and under such rules and regulations as may be prescribed by the Comptroller General of the United States. In the determination of auditing procedures to be followed and the extent of examination of vouchers and other documents, the Comptroller General shall give due regard to *generally accepted principles of auditing*, including consideration of the effectiveness of accounting organizations and systems, internal audit and control, and *related administrative practices of the respective agencies*. (Emphasis added.)[1]

GAO would soon be issuing manuals of auditing principles for the guidance of its own staff, of internal auditors in the federal agencies, and later of auditors, private and public, of state and local governments.

During the two decades from 1946 to 1966, the two comptrollers general, Lindsay Warren and Joseph Campbell, professionalized the GAO in the field of accounting. There remained a substantial group of about one hundred lawyers, but the number of persons educated in accounting and auditing grew from near zero to about 2,200 during that period. This was the more remarkable since those were years of rapid and painful postwar retrenchment in the total GAO staff, which declined from almost 15,000 to just over 4,000. During the term of Campbell, who succeeded Warren as comptroller general in 1955, GAO established an ambitious professional development program involving aggressive recruiting of college graduates in accounting on the campuses and of experienced accountants in the private sector; a variety of training courses; a rotation program, particularly for junior professional personnel so that they might learn to ply their trade in all sorts of settings; and encouragement of the professional staff to study for and earn CPA licenses.

But even from 1950, the meaning of the word *comprehensive* as applied to GAO audits went well beyond "generally accepted principles of auditing," at least as these were understood in the private sector. The basic principles of commercial auditing are based upon attesting to the accuracy, validity, and legality of the representations of management. GAO's comprehensive audits were not attestations; they concerned the economy and efficiency with which functions were carried out, that is, the wisdom and effectiveness of management. Thus, during the same period when emphasis upon federal management was declining in the Bureau of the Budget, it was beginning and growing in GAO. GAO audits and reports continued to emphasize financial matters

1. Public Law 81-784, September 12, 1950, sec. 117.

but increasingly concerned themselves with more general management issues, reaching conclusions and recommendations in both areas.

Comprehensive was in at least one respect (and in its usual meaning) a
complete misnomer. For by *comprehensive*, GAO really meant *selective*. The
rationale was (and largely remains) that the office could look over an entire
program or agency in a brief, superficial *review* (GAO's term) to determine
where the soft, vulnerable spots were. On these spots, which were usually
aspects where GAO auditors thought fault could be found, they conducted
thorough audits, financial and managerial. To a literalist the comprehensive
audits of the postwar GAO were in fact less comprehensive than the item review of transactions and accounts typical of the earlier GAO. Most of the
studies were—and many of them remain—very restricted in scope and overall significance; they fell far short of being comprehensive.

Insofar as the idea of comprehensiveness went beyond strictly financial reviews of books and accounts, GAO's ambitions in this direction brought on
new problems for itself and new challenges for its future personnel policies.
Education in accounting schools and departments was not particularly good
preparation for general management any more than was experience in public
accounting firms. GAO personnel were vulnerable in two ways. The first is
common to all staff officers who delve into problems of general management,
especially when it applies to the management of particular professional fields
other than their own: the military, economics, education, engineering, and virtually all the others. Their expertise and credibility are doubted, because they
are not trained and experienced in the specialty. The second, applicable particularly to the auditors of GAO, is that most of them have been trained in a
field that, it is charged, overemphasized finite numbers, dollars, and specifics
and is weak on or ignores nonquantifiable and particularly human values and
costs. During the past thirty years, their work must have been a broadening
and, in financial terms, a softening experience. Not very many in the top
echelons, however and wherever educated, regard themselves as accountants
or auditors in the traditional sense. But few have had administrative experience outside the GAO. My guess is that a majority of professionals in GAO
twenty years ago and probably also today would subscribe to the quip "If you
can't count it, it doesn't count," though few would admit it. The reputation
dies hard, but so does the culture that spawns it.

Viewed in retrospect, the two decades between the mid-1940s and the
mid-1960s, with their increasing applications of "comprehensive auditing,"
were probably useful not alone for whatever values their work may have contributed at the time but also as a period of testing, learning, and preparation
for the future. Paul H. Appleby, in an article about the first Hoover commis-

sion, no doubt reflected the view of many public managers and students of public administration when he wrote in 1949, "The pretensions of the General Accounting Office . . . to deal with public management broadly on a basis of accounting expertness are readily subject to question."[2] GAO's outreach in its audits into areas with which it had little familiarity was often very tentative, unsophisticated, platitudinous ("The management of ———— should be improved"), frequently challenged, sometimes refuted, and occasionally disastrous. The ground was much firmer when their reports stuck to numbers. But their potential scope was tremendous. They could get into most of the subjects the government could get into, and this was not too far short of everything. The Civil Service Commission was restricted to civil service personnel. The General Services Administration to civil (as distinguished from military) matters. The Bureau of the Budget and indeed the rest of the Executive Office of the President—like the congressional staff agencies—had only indirect access to what went on in the field, that is, outside of Washington, and this is where about nine-tenths of the government was and is. GAO was unique in that it had most of these matters within its purview and substantial staff resources around the nation and around the world with which to examine them.

The GAO in Washington and the Field: Defense Contracts

For GAO, one of the most significant effects of World War II and the transformation that followed it was the development of continuing staff resources and installations in the field. The development of GAO's resources outside of Washington in the regional offices and overseas was a great advantage in many ways. It provided the central headquarters with information, judgments, and ideas that were not filtered through the hierarchies of other agencies. It provided local know-how and perceptions not readily available to staff in Washington. But it also greatly complicated the problems of cohesive management. Most field personnel are locally recruited in or near their hometowns and spend most of their working lives there. There has been little interregional or regional-headquarters mobility except for the directors and some deputy directors of the regions. Changes in direction, in policy, and in technique were slow to "take" in the field, as is usually the case in scattered organizations, and the postwar transformation (described in Chapter 3) was not really absorbed in the field until many years later.

2. Paul H. Appleby, "The Significance of the Hoover Commission Report," *Yale Review*, XXXIX (September, 1949), 18.

The approaches and skills involved in "comprehensive" auditing were relatively undeveloped among field personnel. But the field personnel had abundant experience and unique advantages in the auditing of contracts with private industries, particularly defense contracts. In this activity, the Washington elements of GAO were at a considerable disadvantage. They lacked experience, and the materials to examine and report on were distant—from Miami and Boston to Seattle and Honolulu. In 1951, Congress granted GAO continuing authority to examine the records of private companies incident to negotiated contracts (Public Law 82-245)—a type of contract that became prevalent during the 1950s. During that period, it should be recalled, about half of the federal budget was allocated to national defense, and a substantial share of that amount was paid to business contractors for research, development, and production. Stimulated by directions and signals from Washington, the regional auditors aggressively audited defense contractors, producing data on the failures of individual firms: excessive profits, cost overruns, delays, and technical inadequacies. Reports on these matters were released with considerable fanfare to the media. By virtue largely of its contract auditors in the field, GAO acquired considerable notoriety or fame as a defender of the public purse against the predators of the military-industrial complex.

GAO's aggressiveness in pursuit of alleged waste or fraud in contract auditing led to passage of the Truth-in-Negotiations Act of 1962 (Public Law 87-653) and to the establishment of the various audit agencies in the Department of Defense. But it also led to criticisms, increasingly virulent, from defense contracting officials and from representatives of industry. These charges climaxed in the hearings held in the summer of 1965 by the Military Operations Subcommittee of the House Committee on Government Operations. The subcommittee was then chaired by Democratic Representative Chet Holifield of California, who would later chair its parent committee for many years, and those hearings became known as the Holifield hearings, one of the most traumatic experiences in GAO's history. From the outset, GAO was on the defensive against a great array of criticisms from both private contractors and top officials of the Defense Department and other federal agencies.[3] It was charged with many misdeeds: being unfair and inaccurate, seeking publicity for itself, finding and disclosing business information that should have been kept confidential, publicizing alleged but unproven deficiencies in the performance of government contracts, naming "culprits" before they had a fair chance of defending themselves in the courts, and many others.

3. One of the few non-GAO witnesses who supported the agency's performance was Elmer B. Staats, deputy director of the Bureau of the Budget. He was not then aware that he would, within a few months, become comptroller general of the United States.

Future historians may view the Holifield hearings of 1965 as the product of one of the noblest and bravest efforts of any federal agency in recent history. GAO there confronted a concerted and probably orchestrated attack by top leaders of both the government and private industry, especially defense industries. In the short run, at least, it lost the battle. Holifield made it clear that GAO was the defendant, and the majority of the subcommittee was inclined to support the prosecution.[4] Comptroller General Campbell, whose health had not been strong for several years, resigned in the midst of the hearings, and subsequent leadership for GAO was assumed by Assistant Comptroller General Frank H. Weitzel, who had barely been on speaking terms with Campbell for some years. In an effort to placate the subcommittee, he wrote a letter that was appended to the subcommittee's official report, making several promises.

GAO's future reports would focus on general causes and deficiencies in contracting, not on individual cases.

These future reports would emphasize corrective changes for the future rather than errors in the past.

They would not reveal confidential business information.

They would not mention names and titles of offenders; nor would they mention specific individuals referred to the Department of Justice for prosecution.

They would be phrased in constructive and not controversial terms.

The report that emerged from the hearings was critical of GAO's contract auditing but welcomed the changes being made under Weitzel's direction. But it was by no means unanimous. One of the most vigorous dissenters was Democratic Congressman Jack Brooks of Texas, who would later succeed Holifield as chairman of the House Government Operations Committee. Brooks contended that the report would inhibit GAO's aggressive and fearless inquiries into defense contracts. There is no doubt that emphasis upon contract auditing declined sharply after 1965 and that the nature of GAO reports on defense became more general. As one outspoken critic later wrote, "The hearings had whacked the GAO in the head, and in some ways it has still not recovered."[5] But others held that the shift in stance of the GAO was due primarily to factors other than the hearings. The new comptroller general,

---

4. Holifield was over the long run one of GAO's best congressional friends. At the time of the hearings, his California district contained no defense plants. On the other hand, he was dean of the Democratic delegation in California, the situs of more defense-supported industries than any other state in the union.

5. Richard F. Kaufman, *The War Profiteers* (New York, 1970), 149.

Elmer B. Staats, who took office a few days after the Holifield report was released in 1966, made no commitment with respect to Weitzel's letter. Later, he told this writer that he did not consider the hearings as important as some others did because the establishment of the Defense Contract Audit Agency in 1965 relieved the GAO of the need for so many contract audits and because of the growing effectiveness of the Truth-in-Negotiations Act. Subsequently, GAO's efforts in tthe defense area, in response to congressional and popular pressures, shifted to broader studies of cost overruns, defense-industry profits, procurement policies in general, and weapons systems, both in terms of costs and substantive merits. These were not usually focused on individual companies. A somewhat later by-product of the Holifield hearings (and other developments) was concern in GAO and in Congress, most notably by Democratic Senator William Proxmire of Wisconsin, about cost-accounting standards of defense contractors and subcontractors. Proxmire's interest led to a GAO study, ordered by Congress in 1968 (in Public Law 90-320), of the feasibility of standardizing cost-accounting procedures for defense contracts. The study in turn led to the establishment in 1970 of a Cost Accounting Standards Board (CASB) to develop and establish standards that might be applied to the development and accounting for such contracts. The board was a unique organization; it consisted of the comptroller general as chairman and four other members appointed by him. Despite hostility and criticism from defense firms from its beginning, the board promulgated some nineteen standards during the 1970s before Congress permitted it to die in 1980.

Viewed in a broader context, the Holifield hearings presaged changes in GAO's priorities and practices that went well beyond the field of defense. They encouraged GAO to broaden its perspectives from review of individual contractors or agencies to projects whose dimensions had government-wide significance. This meant greater care in the choice of projects, in the way in which they were conducted, and in the writing and review of reports. The hearings thus contributed to some of the significant administrative changes that occurred within GAO in subsequent years: a major reorganization that, among many other things, split up the old Defense Auditing Division; the development of an elaborate planning and programming system; the creation of a system, even more elaborate, for documenting and reviewing reports; and the establishment of a system of internal accountability for its own work. Paradoxically, the hearings may actually have assisted Comptroller General Staats in moving the organization in the new directions that he sought.

One knowledgeable GAO official has maintained that the Holifield hearings led to major changes in the relationships and relative strengths of the regional offices and the Washington headquarters.[6] The auditing of contracts was almost entirely a field operation. Few could be audited in or near Washington. Most were done in the regions where the defense plants were located. Furthermore, contract audits that uncovered fraud or abuse were then the principal source of publicity and fame for GAO. The experience and expertise for this work were in the regions, not Washington. On the other hand, the regional auditors were not well trained in the broader activities that were developing in Washington under the umbrella of "comprehensive" audits. As contract audits declined, the stature of the regional organizations and their personnel within GAO also declined. They became fact-finders for, and subordinates to, professionals in Washington, who produced the reports, had contacts with Congress, and for the most part had higher grades and better opportunities for advancement. These problems of field-headquarters relationships are fairly typical of federal organizations. But for GAO, the sharp decline of contract audits, occasioned at least in part by the Holifield hearings, was a major contributor to problems of this type.

The Second GAO Transformation

Unlike in the BoB/OMB, in the GAO change has come gradually and slowly. But it has certainly been no less profound. The first great change in GAO, as we have seen, was delayed by World War II, but even after it was decided upon, its accomplishment took up to ten years. The second transformation can be traced to the appointment of Elmer B. Staats as comptroller general in early 1966, and in some ways it was not yet complete at the end of his term fifteen years later. Staats's credentials for the job were unique. He was neither accountant nor lawyer, and his party affiliation, if any, was not generally known.[7] Unlike any of his predecessors, he had devoted most of his working life to administrative posts in the executive branch of the federal government, beginning before World War II. He had started at the Bureau of the Budget at the time of its great metamorphosis in 1939. Later, he served as its deputy director under four presidents of both parties—Truman, Eisenhower, Ken-

6. Much of this paragraph is based upon an article by Dave Sorando, then director of the Washington Regional Office of GAO, "The Significance of the Holifield Hearings for GAO," in the house organ, *WRO Ledger* (December, 1979–November, 1980), 1–7.

7. In recognition of his bipartisanship, his colleagues at the Bureau of the Budget, in memorializing his departure, presented him with a seat cushion for his desk chair with an elephant on one side and a donkey on the other.

nedy, and then Johnson, who appointed him comptroller general. He subsequently served in the latter capacity during five presidencies, also of both parties—those of Johnson, Nixon, Ford, Carter, and, for about six weeks,
Reagan. Even before he became deputy director of the budget, he had been
the chief of its Legislative Reference Office and was widely known and highly
respected in the Congress on both sides of the aisle. His confirmation hearings
were largely a series of encomiums, just as, fifteen years later, leaders of Congress and other groups held parties in his honor that likewise consisted principally of tributes.

Transitions of leadership in the GAO are not the mad, chaotic affairs one
expects in the executive branch. Few if any people are changed, and there are
no immediate changes in policies, no new announcements in the state of the
union address, and no revised budgets. Staats brought no one with him and
shifted no personnel immediately, though over the five succeeding years he
hired a handful of top personnel from outside, most of whom had worked in
the Bureau of the Budget. The only other noncareer position in the agency, the
post of assistant comptroller general, became vacant in early 1969, when
Frank Weitzel's term expired. President Nixon replaced him at Staats's urging
with Robert F. Keller, who had been GAO's general counsel. During the first
months and even years under Staats, GAO's work went on very much as
usual. Staats himself sought to learn his organization. He met with his subordinates, visited all the regional offices, talked with a great many congressmen, including most of the majority and minority leaders of the committees
and subcommittees. Gradually during Staats's term, there emerged consistent
and compatible but incremental changes in GAO in two major directions. One
was the broadening and deepening of GAO studies from the financial and
strictly managerial toward the evaluation of results in terms of program objectives. The other was GAO's increasing responsiveness and service to the Congress. These two overall directions of change, and some of the particular elements of each of them, will be examined in succeeding sections.

PROGRAM EVALUATION

During the summer of Staats's last full year at the Bureau of the Budget, President Johnson directed the bureau to oversee the installation of PPBS throughout the executive branch. PPBS relied heavily on the review and analysis of
benefits, or effectiveness of programs against their costs. This meant the development and application of techniques to evaluate program results. As
noted earlier, the label of PPBS did not last very long in the Washington
scene, but program evaluation certainly did. GAO had already made a hand-

ful of studies of the effectiveness of individual programs, but after Staats's arrival they became increasingly prevalent until they accounted for about one-half of GAO's reports. One of the first reports done after he came on the scene was a survey of federal discounting techniques in evaluating programs, published in 1968. The following year GAO published a general survey on PPBS in the executive agencies.[8]

A major stimulus in this direction was provided by Congress. In the amendments to the Economic Opportunity Act in 1967, it added a provision, known for its author, Republican Senator Winston L. Prouty of Vermont, requiring the GAO to assess and report on the effectiveness of the principal poverty programs, a task for which at that time GAO was quite unprepared. With the help of consultants and contracts to private firms, it produced about fifty reports on the poverty programs in 1969. This was the painful introduction to program evaluation for many of GAO's auditors. The following year, the Congress in its Legislative Reorganization Act of 1970 made it clear that such work would in the future be a major dish in GAO's diet. The act provided that "the Comptroller General shall review and analyze the results of Government programs and activities carried out under existing law" when ordered by either house or any committee of Congress or on its own initiative. That act, together with the Congressional Budget and Impoundment Control Act that followed four years later, also gave the comptroller general extensive responsibilities to develop methods for evaluation, set up standardized budgetary and fiscal information systems, and create standard terminology, classifications, and definitions of program and budget data, as well as carry out related duties.[9] GAO soon thereafter set up a special staff to focus on program matters and their evaluation; in 1976 that staff became the Program Analysis Division. Then, in 1980, an Institute for Program Evaluation was established to develop methods and techniques for program evaluation, provide technical assistance to other divisions in this field, and conduct demonstration projects of new methodologies.

Thus, there was during the Staats term a transformation in the nature and content of GAO's work almost as profound as the one that occurred during the Warren and Campbell era. Financial auditing, which with legal work had been the bread and butter of its first quarter century, comprised only 7 percent of its total workload in 1980. Management studies in the interest of economy and efficiency narrowly defined, as developed after World War II, dropped

8. U.S. General Accounting Office, *Survey of Progress in Implementing the Planning-Programming-Budgeting Systems in Executive Agencies* (Report No. B-115398), July 29, 1969.

9. Public Law 91-510, October 26, 1970, sec. 204; Public Law 93-344, July 12, 1974.

to about 29 percent. Evaluations of ongoing programs, together with cost-benefit analyses of alternative approaches to problems for the future, comprised just about one-half, and the balance, about 14 percent, was made up of special studies of one kind or another—of methodology, techniques, surveys of needs for internal planning, and so forth.[10]

As careful readers of some metropolitan newspapers know, today GAO's studies cover almost the entire spectrum of government work and many problems that are only partially governmental: the effectiveness of the food stamp program, problems of nursing homes, productivity in shoe manufacture, the war against organized crime, the Clinch River breeder reactor, the fiscal future of New York City, the usefulness of rural post offices, the sale of airplanes to Saudi Arabia, the cost-effectiveness of the B-1 bomber, methods of introducing metric systems, handgun control. It produces an average of about four reports each working day. Its reports and other memoranda go to the Congress—as a whole or to committees or individual members—to the executive agencies concerned, to OMB, and to the media. Most of them contain not only statements of findings of its investigations but also recommendations for action. Their orientation is both to the past and to the future.

It was evident from the outset that, if GAO was going to produce credible studies in the many specialized fields relating to the federal government, it must have professionals and specialists in fields other than accounting and financial auditing. It was further evident that the professionals already there would have to expand their horizons beyond finance and internal management. Yet, almost the entire organization was under the civil service career system—other than the attorneys, who had their own personnel system. Staats did not opt for a wholesale turnover in personnel as, to some extent, some of his predecessors had done; nor did he choose to designate a strong intermediate layer of political or noncareer personnel, as was done in the OMB during the 1970s. But he initiated, soon after his arrival, a program of modest change in recruiting whereby professionals from fields other than accounting would be hired, at both entering and midcareer levels. The recruitment of nonaccountants, which began in 1968, increased almost every year thereafter. In the following decade, while the number of persons originally educated in accounting did not change very much, their proportion among all GAO professionals declined to about 60 percent. The new personnel included, in addition to lawyers, persons in both business and public admin-

10. These statistics are drawn from Roger L. Sperry *et al.*, *GAO 1966–1981: An Administrative History* (Washington, D.C., 1981), and they are based upon records of man-years. I have adjusted his figures to eliminate administrative and support data.

istration, economists, other social scientists, mathematicians and actuaries, computer specialists, engineers, and others. Some came to GAO with long experience in other agencies, such as civilian and officer personnel from the military, personnel specialists, and budgeteers. A rotation program, particularly for junior professionals, permitted broader experience in a variety of functions, but at middle and higher levels, individuals became increasingly specialized in areas such as military ordnance, social security, health services, or land management. The problem of specialism and generalism remains a major one in GAO, as it does in OMB. But there can be no doubt that the agency as a whole became far more cosmopolitan than it had been. Furthermore, it increasingly relied upon private consultants to help and advise in specialized fields in which it had little experience.

In 1971 Staats induced the Congress to change the title of his immediate assistant to deputy comptroller general (Public Law 92-51) and to set up four new positions with the title assistant comptroller general. These moves were exactly comparable to similar ones taken many years earlier in the Bureau of the Budget, but none of the appointments was in the usual sense political. Staats filled some of the new positions with outsiders, mainly alumni from the Bureau of the Budget, and the remainder by promotion of career GAO personnel.

Unlike the BoB/OMB, the GAO has not frequently been studied by outside groups like the Rockefeller, Price, and Heineman committees; nor has it relied upon extensive self-studies by internal task forces. True, the major changes of direction in the late forties were implemented through an organizational study by an internal task force appointed by the comptroller general. Later, in 1955, a study by a special subcommittee of the House Government Operations Committee was conducted under the direction of Republican Congressman Glenard P. Lipscomb of California, himself an accountant and probably a friend of Comptroller General Campbell. At any rate, the bulk of its recommendations, published in a report of November, 1956, had already been implemented earlier that year.[11] The Campbell organization survived with little change until well after the arrival of Staats, so it is of some significance. Campbell sought first of all to make a clean division between line and staff or support roles. He consolidated standards and policy in accounting and auditing in a single staff office. He divided the old Auditing Division into two divisions, one civil, the other defense, in order to give more emphasis to the latter

11. U.S. Congress, House, Committee on Government Operations, *The General Accounting Office—A Study of Its Organization and Administration with Recommendations for Increasing Its Effectiveness*, House Report 2264, 84th Cong. 2nd Sess., (November, 1956).

(including contract auditing). He abolished the Accounting Systems Division and merged its work in the development and review of agency accounting systems with the two new auditing divisions. He did the same with the Office of Investigations and merged all of its scattered field units with the regional offices. To provide general administrative supervision of the field apparatus in the United States, he set up a Division of Field Operations, which with the two audit divisions plus the old Claims and Transportation divisions comprised the line organization of the GAO. To them was added, in 1963, an International Division, which among other duties supervised the overseas offices.

Soon after his arrival in GAO, Staats made a few changes, principally in the staff offices, but in general the organization he inherited remained intact for his first five years. When he was ready to move, however, he was thoroughly prepared and the change was comprehensive. In 1970, he employed Thomas D. Morris to study and make recommendations concerning GAO's organization and management. Morris had many years before directed the management work of the Bureau of the Budget and was a seasoned executive and management consultant in both government and the private sector. After a six-month exploration, Morris recommended a broad management improvement program, which he was subsequently named to head, and the outlines of a reorganization plan to be developed by an internal study group of GAO leaders chaired by the deputy comptroller general. During 1971, this group made a series of proposals, most of which were adopted with some modifications and put into effect by Staats in that year and early 1972. The general plan was similar in concept to the reorganization of the Bureau of the Budget twenty years earlier. The civil and defense auditing divisions were transformed into eight operating divisions, each dealing with different clusters of federal programs and each responsible for the bulk of GAO activities and studies in its designated cluster, whether civil or military, whether in Washington or the field or overseas. The clusters were deliberately designed so that they would cross organizational lines within the government; many were in fact government-wide. For example, three of the new divisions were Manpower and Welfare, Logistics and Communications, and Resources and Economic Development. The building of divisions around broad program categories was intended to encourage broader studies and evaluations of program effectiveness across organizational lines. It was also hoped that there might result a greater degree of expertise and specialization in individual program areas.

Complementing the programmatic line divisions was a series of staff offices established or augmented to handle government-wide problems and internal management: the Offices of Policy, Internal Review, Program Planning, Information, Congressional Relations, Personnel Management, General Counsel, and others. It should be noted that the new type of structure did not directly affect the organization of the regional and overseas offices, for which there is no standard pattern. There have been shifts and additions in the decade following 1972, but the basic organizational design remains substantially as it was then, and it is still comparable to that of OMB (see Appendix).

The introduction of program evaluation more than ever raised questions about the needs of specialization and adaptation. No longer could one rely on the precept that a good auditor could audit anything, already made questionable by the extension of auditing beyond finances to management generally. Clearly, one needs substantive knowledge to evaluate a weapons system, a health maintenance organization, a bilingual educational program, or a mass transportation system. GAO sought to address this problem partly through modifications in its personnel recruitment, training, and placement programs, and partly through the organizational changes summarized above.

But there was another problem—the choice of subjects to audit, the marshaling of organizational resources and people to handle them, and the assignment of responsibility to the appropriate individuals in headquarters and in the field. This problem became more crucial as GAO sought increasingly to respond to, and to anticipate, the needs of Congress. It was further complicated by the scattered nature of GAO's resources. Headquarters divisions, for example, were increasingly specialized according to government program. Auditors at agency sites were obviously organized by federal agency organization. Field offices were relatively unspecialized by program or agency, and overseas offices were often called upon to work on the foreign ramifications of domestic problems.[12] But the ideas and the initiatives on a great many GAO projects, probably most, came not from the Congress or the comptroller general or the top headquarters personnel. Instead, they came from the individual auditors on the sites in Washington and in the regional offices who, in the course of other projects, saw problems in which there might be "pay dirt" in terms of waste or inefficiency. Under the previous system (as again today under the current one), power over selection of major projects and assignments of personnel gravitated to the division and branch chiefs, their deputies and associates, and the heads of the regional offices. Most of these officers in GAO were old-timers, auditors from the "ancien régime." Many of the most important changes introduced and developed in GAO since the mid-1960s

12. There were a few field offices where specialization was encouraged, such as the Houston office, which concentrated on energy problems. But most of the regional and overseas offices were called upon for work in any substantive field.

were in fact efforts to centralize control over planning, assignments, review, standards, and reports at the level of the comptroller general and his immediate staffs. These actions, which inevitably infringed upon accustomed prerogatives and authorities, were not universally acclaimed within GAO, and they have not been uniformly successful.

A year after his appointment, Staats appointed a Program Planning Committee to review short and long-range plans of the divisions. In general, the refinement and extension of that process, so begun, has continued ever since. In 1972, an Office of Program Planning was established. In the same year, the idea of national issue areas was implemented as a device to structure planning and relate it to national problems on the one hand and to GAO operations on the other. By 1980, there were nearly forty approved issue areas, ranging from food, consumer and worker protection, and national productivity to tax administration, military readiness, and international affairs. Each of the issue areas is assigned to one of the divisions as a lead division, though other divisions may be called upon to contribute to it. For each, there is a long-range plan of evaluations. The divisions are later called upon to develop and defend before the Program Planning Committee, chaired by the comptroller general, their specific plans for each issue area and to report upon their progress—a system that GAO labels its own accountability system.

A later step—one hesitates to consider it final—was the adoption in 1977 of team (as distinguished from hierarchical) management of GAO studies. Team management, very simply, is the development of teams for each project requiring the services of a number of investigators, under the direction of a team leader who, like his colleagues, is not responsible to his normal superiors in the hierarchy for the job and whose reports escape normal hierarchical reviews and changes. GAO had with considerable success conducted a few studies on a team basis; a notable example was its study of the effectiveness of federal banking inspections.[13] Teams could be organized with appropriate skills to handle projects, as they had been considered and scheduled through a central planning system. They would be quicker, more efficient in use of specific talents, and more productive. But they could be enormously dangerous if not destructive for the morale and the status of the troops, particularly those in higher echelons who might lose their authority and their *raison d'être* to team leaders. Team management in GAO gave rise to many problems; its implementation was slow, uneven, subject to changes in the ground rules, and less

13. See Erasmus H. Kloman, *Cases in Accountability: The Work of the GAO* (Boulder, 1979), 73–81.

than total. By 1981, the approach had been generally abandoned as a mandatory way of doing business, although it is encouraged when appropriate.[14]

SERVICE FOR A RESURGENT CONGRESS

GAO's growing involvement in program evaluation and the many internal
changes that stemmed from it were related to, and in some degree derived
from, a growing interdependence with the Congress. For its first quarter century, GAO's relationships with the legislature had been loose, fragmentary,
and occasional; neither of the two wanted a continuing affair with the other.
The beginnings of closer ties started after World War II, partly because of the
mutual esteem of Comptroller General Warren and his former colleagues in
Congress. They were given some legal expression by the Reorganization Act
of 1945, which declared GAO "part of the legislative branch," and by the
Legislative Reorganization Act of 1946, which directed the office to "make
an expenditure analysis of each agency in the executive branch" and report its
findings to the appropriate committees of Congress (Public Law 79-601, section 206). But no additional staff were provided for the purpose, and it does
not appear that GAO ever paid much attention to the directive. Both houses
assigned individual committees to oversee GAO operations, now Governmental Affairs in the Senate and Government Operations in the House. But neither
established anything comparable to the British Committee on Public Accounts
to receive, hold hearings, and act on GAO reports.

On his arrival, Comptroller General Staats was dismayed to find how limited were GAO's relationships with Congress, and he determined at the outset
to make its work more timely, more relevant, and more responsive to congressional interests. Indeed, this became a basic theme of his entire term. He
apparently envisaged a role for GAO in its relationship to Congress quite
comparable to that of BoB/OMB in its relationship to the president: a source
of disinterested, objective, and professional information, analysis, and advice, and a reviewer, coordinator, and evaluator of federal programs. One of
the first moves was to establish and beef up a Congressional Relations Office
(which replaced a small legislative liaison group) to coordinate and monitor
GAO's congressional activities. Later that office organized a weekly meeting
of all the top officials in the agency's headquarters, which became in effect its

14. For those interested in managerial theory and practice, team management is in no significant sense different from what has elsewhere been labeled project management or matrix management. Its problems in GAO have been essentially comparable to those experienced in other
organizations.

regular staff meeting, a clear indication of Staats's view that GAO's work re-
volved around its relation with Congress.

Staats and, with his encouragement, other top GAO officials established
and maintained personal relationships with individual congressmen and leaders among their staffs. Congressional requests for studies were encouraged,
and a rising proportion of GAO's analyses were officially initiated by requests
of committee chairmen, minority leaders, and others. In fact, during Staats's
term, the proportion of GAO reports initiated by Congress grew from one-
tenth to more than one-third. Both the initiative and the details of many of
these requests were often worked out in joint GAO–congressional committee
staff meetings. A good many of the studies GAO initiated on its own were
anticipatory of problems that might later be of concern to Congress. These
were often discussed with congressmen and their staffs in the planning stages.
GAO was increasingly required to prepare reports on given subjects, either on
a one-time, continuing, or periodic basis. In addition, it was required to conduct any study that might be requested by any committee of the Congress, and
it also did studies sought by individual members of Congress, though here it
had some discretion.

The normal procedure for GAO reports begins with copies of drafts being
sent for review, criticism, and comment to the executive agencies concerned
and to the Office of Management and Budget. The agencies are given a limited period, usually thirty days, to review, criticize, take action, and respond
to GAO, and OMB, through its appropriate program division, is called upon
to monitor agency responses. The report is then modified if necessary, edited,
reproduced, and sent to Congress—to the leadership and all members if it is
highly significant or to interested committees and individual members if not.
Copies are also sent to the agencies involved and to OMB. The agencies are
required to report to Congress and OMB on the actions they take in response
to the GAO recommendations and if necessary on the reasons they do not accept certain recommendations.

Reports, addressed primarily to Congress, are still the main product of
GAO's efforts, but its other services to Congress have been growing. One is
the lending of staff to work directly with congressional committees. Others
include helping in the review and drafting of proposed legislation, developing
statements of legislative objectives and reporting requirements, holding informal briefings on studies under way, and producing questions and other materials in preparation for committee hearings. But probably its most important
and fastest-growing service is the provision of testimony at committee hearings by GAO officials from the comptroller general on down. The testimony
is sometimes on reports already issued, sometimes on work under way, and

sometimes on general issues and proposed legislation concerning which GAO is believed to have expert knowledge from previous work or wisdom growing out of its experience. On average, several GAO officials testify before a congressional committee or subcommittee every working day. The range of subjects on which they testify is about as broad as GAO's charter, which means nearly as broad as the federal government's work itself. The subjects on which GAO testimony was provided in the month of May, 1979, are illustrative.[15]

the Office of Federal Procurement Policy

emergency preparedness around nuclear power plants

the impact and validity of PACE, a federal employment examination

Indochina refugee assistance programs

the Presidential Transition Act of 1963

improving development coordination

two bills affecting small businesses

an urban development action grant program

congressional oversight reform legislation

interrelationships of the federal and Washington, D.C., retirement systems

enforcement of crude oil reseller price controls

uranium supply and demand estimates

repeal of the Davis-Bacon Act

implementation of time frames in the Speedy Trial Act of 1974

set-aside program for federal timber sales

Merit Systems Protection Board and Office of Special Counsel

the University and Small Business Procedures Act

a GAO report entitled *Conditions of Older People: National Information System Needed*

the National Cancer Institute's management of a contract

placement of foster care children with members of the People's Temple

It would be a mistake to assume that the shifts in GAO orientation during the last fifteen years—toward program evaluation and toward Congress—and the general rise in the organization's stature were due solely to its own initia-

15. Sperry *et al.*, *GAO 1966–1981*, p. 23.

tive and capabilities. That period, particularly the decade of the 1970s, witnessed a major resurgence in the influence and activities of the Congress as well as major changes in the nature and organization of its membership. No agency related to Congress could fail to be affected by the changes in Congress itself, and GAO was but one of the beneficiaries of those changes. The principal causes were a succession of events—mostly failures or disasters— that happened to American government and principally to the presidency. First were the upsetting domestic developments of the 1960s—the assassinations, the civil rights disturbances, the alleged failures and costs of the Great Society programs, the rebellion of youth against the "establishment." Second was Vietnam and related developments—the controversies over the Gulf of Tonkin resolution, the bombing of Cambodia, and the ignominious evacuation. Finally came the growing aggressiveness of the Nixon administration on a variety of foreign and domestic matters, which brought wiretaps, other alleged invasions of privacy, and impoundments of appropriated funds—all leading up to Watergate and the nastiness that accompanied it and culminating in the only resignations in history of a vice-president and a president.

These developments led to massive changes in the Congress and in presidential-congressional relationships, most of which occurred during the 1970s. These need not be detailed here, but the following were some of the main ones in terms of relevance to the GAO.[16]

> There was general growth in congressional aggressiveness and assertiveness, both in framing public policies and overseeing the performance of the executive branch. This was reflected in a variety of legislative enactments—the Legislative Reorganization Act (1970), the War Powers Resolution (1973), the Congressional Budget and Impoundment Control Act (1974), the strengthening of the Freedom of Information Act (1974), and others. It was further expressed in a number of other ways, such as increasing temporary authorizing legislation and establishing requirements for legislative vetoes.

> There were also changes in congressional organization in the directions of devolution of powers from committees and their chairmen to subcommittees and their chairmen and to individual members; democratization, so that most individual members have a voice on the floor on most measures and so that the majority are either chairmen or mi-

16. For a thorough analysis of these changes, see James L. Sundquist, *The Decline and Resurgence of Congress* (Washington, D.C., 1981). The same subjects and their influence on the GAO are discussed in Frederick C. Mosher, *The GAO: The Quest for Accountability in American Government* (Boulder, 1979), ch. 9.

nority leaders on at least one subcommittee; and fragmentation of interest and influence on bills among a great array of subcommittees and individual members.

Congressional resources, especially for gaining independent information, have been expanded, so that Congress in its deliberations need no longer rely exclusively upon materials and statements of officials in the executive branch and of interest groups. The enlarged resources have included the addition of new congressional support agencies and expansion of existing ones, tremendous proliferation of congressional staffs, (both of committees and of individual members), improvement of information technology, and increasing specialization of individual members on particular topics of congressional interest.

Oversight of the performance and effectiveness of executive agencies and programs has been given greater emphasis.

The characteristics of members of Congress have changed, particularly of the Democrats, who were the majority in both houses from 1955 to 1981. The new congressmen are more independent, individualistic, and assertive, and less reliant upon, and less disciplined by, the party leadership and senior members.

Most of these congressional changes worked in favor of a stronger and more influential GAO. In the first place, the expanding congressional assertiveness and concern about oversight were entirely congruent with GAO's own aspirations, especially as they were remolded by Staats. Congress and GAO were mutually reinforcing in these areas. As a result, GAO had greater confidence that its recommendations would be read, used, appreciated—and often mandated. The fact that this was so probably added to the executive branch's respect, concern, and even fear of GAO in its investigations. The increasing congressional knowledge, interest, and involvement in federal policy and administration brought with it a heightening of Congress' stature vis-à-vis the president and the executive branch generally, and some of this could hardly fail to brush off on the GAO. For Congress, GAO had unique advantages as a source of information: It had direct and immediate access to the operations of the executive agencies both in Washington and the field, and from long years of study in the many different fields of federal work, it had background data, personal acquaintance, and long memories, both institutional and individual. In return, Congress could help GAO by applying its powers and prestige to agencies that were reluctant or slow to provide GAO with information. Through both legislation and informal pressure during the 1970s, Congress extended GAO's access to data in domestic intelligence, banking regulation, taxation, unappropriated fund activities, energy, contractors' records, and many other areas.

The congressional resurgence produced some new potential institutional competitors for the GAO and rejuvenated the one existing one. One of the newcomers was the Office of Technology Assessment (OTA), established by law in 1972 to provide in-depth studies of technological developments now and in the future and anticipate warnings of their probable impact. The other was the Congressional Budget Office, established by the Congressional Budget and Impoundment Control Act of 1974 to aid in the conduct of the new congressional budget process, to "keep score" on budget decisions and actions in the Congress, and to provide projections and analyses of both a macro and micro nature on problems of budgetary policy and governmental programs. The Legislative Reorganization Act of 1970 changed the name of the old Legislative Reference Service, which predated the GAO, to Congressional Research Service (CRS) and greatly expanded its responsibilities. To its previous duties as a source of factual and legal information on request of the members and staff of Congress—itself an enormous workload, amounting to over 300,000 requests per year—were added responsibilities for analytical studies on policy issues. For the latter purpose, it greatly increased its professional and scholarly staff, which is largely made up of social scientists and other professionals. So GAO is not alone as a nonpolitical staff aid for the Congress. There is potential overlap and duplication among the four, and a fairly elaborate system has been installed so that each can keep up with, and perhaps work with, the others on common and related problems.

GAO has certain obvious advantages over the other support agencies that are in some cases quite comparable to those OMB has over other agencies in the Executive Office of the President. Its director is the only head of these support agencies who is a constitutional officer of the United States, appointed by the president with the advice and consent of the Senate. GAO is about four times the size of the other three combined. It is the only one with a field establishment in the United States and overseas and with site offices in the various agencies. It has more independence than the others in the choice of its projects—by far. It can and does make recommendations, which for the most part are verboten to the others. And it has a number of statutory powers with respect to the executive branch that, to the extent they are exercised, make its position unique.

There are accompanying disadvantages. It seems less quickly and psychologically responsive to Congress generally and more particularly, to those in Congress with whom it mostly deals. Its very size and scatteredness invite more formality and distance, as do its more bureaucratic procedures and processing requirements. Personal contacts with members of Congress and their staffs are restricted largely to GAO's upper-level officials in Washington. The majority of its professionals in the capital and the field have no or almost no contacts with Congress. This is less true of the other support agencies. Its services are often late, its reports long, technical, frequently dull, and sometimes not as well focused on the matters of interest to the few congressional members and staff who look at them. Finally, the professional credentials (and therefore the perceptions by many outsiders of their work) of many of GAO's personnel, particularly at upper levels, are in a field not well known or esteemed very highly in Congress—accounting. This association of GAO with accounting continues in many quarters even though its staff includes several hundred people with other fields of specialization—lawyers, economists, business and public administrators, and others. In CBO, the prevailing professionals are Ph.D.'s in economics; in CRS, they are Ph.D.'s in social sciences plus a scattering of other fields; in OTA, they are engineers and Ph.D.'s in the exact sciences.

GAO faces a different kind of problem in the staffs of the members and committees of Congress, which have grown in numbers and also probably in intellectual qualifications almost unbelievably in the 1970s. Members of Congress have little time to read (eleven minutes a day according to one study), study, and plan. They rely on their staffs to obtain and sift data, to organize and guide the conduct of hearings, to write their correspondence and reports, and to negotiate with organizations such as GAO on studies and investigations. The newer professionals on congressional staffs are young, bright, ambitious, little experienced in organizational problems, oriented to politics and policy but not management, temporary, seeking favorable publicity for their congressional superiors, and too often, arrogant. Many are trained in law, journalism, or the social sciences—or simply in winning elections. At the working level, it is the staff people with whom GAO mainly deals. And they present problems for GAO (and the other support agencies) quite comparable to those the OMB regulars have with White House political personnel, who are likewise typically young, bright, relatively inexperienced (except in winning elections), ambitious, political, and temporary. There is the danger in both situations that the institutional agency will be called upon to take positions on controversial issues, to make studies in support of partisan positions, to suppress potentially embarrassing findings, to publish extravagantly critical reports about agencies and programs that their sponsors do not like, and in toto to threaten the objectivity on which the credibility of the agency rests. This is a potent argument for GAO's centralization of planning and supervision over studies and for its careful and multiple reviews of reports before they are issued. Without the mechanics of central discipline, GAO personnel could easily become minions of the members and committees of Congress operating through their staffs to obtain data and provide recommendations to support political positions already taken.

One of the most important means GAO has to reach the Congress and the public is through the media—television, radio, and the press. Very probably, most members of Congress look at the Washington *Post* over their morning coffee or while riding to work. If there is a story about a governmental problem in which they have any interest and it is credited to a GAO report, especially if it is on the front page, they are likely to ask one of their staff to look into it. Virtually all unclassified GAO reports, which contain summary statements in the front, are released to the press. One GAO official has said that GAO is the most popular federal agency among media people in Washington, mainly because it provides more critical information about what is "really" going on than anyone else and also because it is reliable. Investigative reporters in pursuit of flashy stories are said to love the GAO, and Jack Anderson, widely syndicated purveyor of federal "inside" stories, has one of his reporters in the halls of the GAO Building almost constantly. In the spring of 1979, CBS's "Sixty Minutes" broadcast a segment about GAO, in which Dan Rather was the reporter and interviewer. Almost unique among "Sixty Minutes" productions (or any other TV presentation), the show was basically favorable to the government agency being described and pictured. Obviously, the media provide very important channels to the Congress, the rest of the government, and the general public—channels that were not sought by OMB, at least not before 1981.

Other GAO Activities and Powers

The General Accounting Office is not only a support agency for the Congress, and some of its officers object vociferously when it is so described. All of the comptrollers general have treasured and defended the independence of their office, not alone from the president but also from the Congress itself. Of course, independence is a relative term. Like the other institutions in the government, GAO depends upon Congress for its powers, its resources, and its general oversight. But it also possesses continuing legal powers, of both long and recent standing, that Congress has granted it and that it can exercise in a quite independent fashion. And the comptroller general, realistically speaking, is immune from removal during his fifteen-year term for anything short of a capital crime, a crippling illness, or insanity. Many of the older GAO powers, some of which date back to the Treasury Act of 1789, were inherited in 1921 by the comptroller general from the comptroller and auditors of the Treasury. Although they are still there, the use of many of them became rare after the postwar transformation and the Budget and Accounting Procedures Act of 1950. Examples include the countersigning of warrants, the settling of accounts of accountable officers, and the disallowance of payments that are judged by the GAO to be improper or illegal.[17]

Some of those old powers, however, are still very much alive and give rise to a significant segment of GAO's work, particularly in the office of its general counsel. For a century, the comptroller general or his predecessor has been required by law to render advance decisions on the legality of proposed payments when requested by any of the executive departments, and his decisions are binding upon the executive branch, though aggrieved private parties can appeal them to the courts. Decisions or advice are also requested by committees and members of Congress, by state and local governments, and even by the courts. The workload of interpreting statutes and answering questions on procurement, personnel, compensation, and other matters is almost unbelievable, running into the thousands every year. Most of these are on relatively small and technical matters, often occurring only once in history, but some have enduring significance. The major decisions of the comptroller general, which are published annually, are very nearly the Bible, verse, and footnotes on financial law in the national government.

A more recent activity that has grown to large proportions in the last three decades is the rendering of decisions on bids for procurement or other contracts when disappointed contractors appeal on the ground that adverse decisions violated a law or regulation or were unjust. GAO's procedure on such bids, which mount to hundreds every year, is relatively simple, inexpensive, and quick when compared to a court case. Agencies may appeal GAO's decisions, but they must bear in mind that payments made in contravention of a GAO decision after the rendering of the decision may be disallowed. The aggrieved contractors, for their part, may appeal to the courts.

The basic act of 1921 called upon GAO to investigate and settle financial claims both for and against the government. This service—both cheaper and

17. For example, warrants are now used almost solely to authorize expenditures when appropriations have not passed the Congress and continuing expenditures have been authorized by congressional resolutions. A most interesting recent example of a near disallowance of expenditures was the GAO's threat to disallow payments for Secret Service protection of Spiro Agnew after he had resigned from the vice-presidency—a threat addressed to the secretary of the treasury. A little known vestige of the settlement power is that every month the comptroller general issues a certificate of settlement to cover the salary and expense allowance of the president.

quicker than going to court—continues to help when the agencies themselves cannot negotiate or enforce proper settlements. GAO has also long been required to help agencies in the development of their accounting systems, and it is still required to review and approve or disapprove them, both in their design and after they have been installed.

More recently, Congress has legislated or informally required that GAO perform certain activities of a continuing nature that hardly fit within the usual gambit of auditing or evaluating. For example, since 1970 the GAO has produced annual or biennial reports on the acquisitions of major weapons systems—their progress, financial status, cost overruns, and so forth. Since 1975 it has also done this on civil acquisitions. The Congressional Budget and Impoundment Control Act in 1974 required GAO to develop information systems for financial management, including standard terminology, classifications, and definitions of program and budget data. That act also directed that GAO monitor, check on, and report to Congress on all presidential impoundments of appropriated funds (which are divided into two categories—recisions and deferrals), and that when the president violated congressional wishes (as expressed through procedures in the act), it should bring court action to enforce compliance. One court case has been initiated under this provision, *Staats* v. *Lynn et al.*, but it was dropped when the president released the funds in question.[18] It was a supreme irony that GAO, an agency set up to minimize federal expenditures, should bring suit against OMB (its sibling agency that had been established for much the same purpose) in an effort to force the president to spend money.

In addition, there have been a number of congressional acts that have required GAO to obtain, analyze, and report on particular problems. Among these, the Energy Policy and Conservation Act of 1975 called upon GAO to verify energy data submitted to the government by corporations in the energy field, and the Civil Service Reform Act of 1978 required it to monitor and report on the implementation of that act. One of the most interesting episodes in GAO's history grew out of the responsibilities Congress gave it, over the comptroller general's vigorous objections, in the Federal Election Campaign Act of 1971 (Public Law 92-225), which became effective April 7, 1972. GAO was called upon to prepare and issue regulations relevant to campaign contributions in presidential elections, to monitor, audit, and investigate all

18. The suit was initially filed on September 20, 1974, in the District of Columbia, as Civil Action No. 75-0051. The case was originally brought against President Ford, but the principal defendant later was changed to James T. Lynn, director of the budget. To my knowledge, this was the only court action that ever occurred between the director of the budget and the comptroller general.

presidential campaign financing, and to initiate legal proceedings where appropriate. Almost overnight it organized a substantial staff in a new Office of Federal Elections with parallel resources in the regional offices. Its reports began to flow within weeks of the passage of the act. In August, it reported that campaign contributions had been used to finance the Watergate break-in. Later reports disclosed the cash contributions of Robert L. Vesco, the financing of a college student to play "dirty tricks" on Democratic primary candidates, cash payments to Watergate defendants and their attorneys, and other matters. But the surveillance of campaign financing, which certainly overstepped GAO's original charter, proved temporary. In 1974, Congress, probably wary that GAO was more diligent than it wished, transferred all of GAO's responsibilities in this area to a Federal Election Commission (Public Law 93-443).

In spite of, and in addition to, the growing emphasis GAO placed upon program evaluation and other nonfinancial assignments after 1965, it applied renewed efforts to financial management and auditing. Unlike its earlier work in this field, which was largely operational in character, most of what it undertook in this more recent period was the development and publication of standards, technical assistance, review and criticism of proposals, and research. Some of this work was done through the Joint Financial Management Improvement Program (JFMIP) (discussed in Chapter 3), and in this area more than any other there was active collaboration with OMB. GAO organized both national and regional audit forums for auditors at all levels of government; published manuals for auditors of governmental activities, public and private; and worked with foreign officials through the International Organization of Supreme Audit Institutions. Following its first transformation in the late 1940s, it had yielded a large part of its audit responsibilities to internal auditors in the various agencies, and after that time it endeavored to strengthen internal auditing throughout the government. In the mid-1970s, when the proposal for semi-independent inspectors general in the various departments and agencies was being considered, GAO was a principal backer. But it urged that the title be changed to auditor general or auditor and inspector general, to lay more emphasis upon the preventive auditing function and less upon the punitive inspection. Congress has now required the establishment of inspectors general in most of the larger departments and agencies and may in the next few years prescribe them for all executive branch agencies.

In 1979, following the furor attending the disclosure of scandals, particularly in the General Services Agency, GAO set up a nationwide toll-free hotline through which federal employees or private citizens could telephone alleged instances of federal waste, fraud, or abuse. A small special staff was established to follow up, investigate, and where appropriate, initiate action on all such calls.

The Mix of GAO Roles: Is the Menu Digestible?

It was suggested in the Introduction that relatively few people know what GAO is. One reason may be that it is many different things, some of which may not coexist very comfortably: It is an agent of Congress, but it is also independent. Its head is appointed by the president but does not work for him; nor can he be removed by him. It is a legislative agency, but some of its work is executive, some, judicial. It is politically neutral but makes recommendations on many politically controversial matters.

The GAO has long been referred to as the watchdog of the United States Treasury, and this is the kind of role it tried to fill at first. If it tried today, every one of its auditors would have to observe and attest to expenditures and revenues of more than $200 million a year. It is rather a watcher of other watchers to some extent and, probably more important, a guide to others who set up and oversee systems that will diminish the need for watching. It would probably be more nearly accurate to use the metaphor of *bird dog*: it scents, points, searches, and retrieves its prey, which is useful information, and delivers it to the hunter (the Congress). It is many other things.

an evaluator and critic

an investigator

an adviser on policies and programs, both those already in place and those contemplated

a teacher, especially of financial management, auditing, and the methodology of program evaluation

a technical assistant and consultant on these same subjects and others

a rule maker on financial matters

a judge on questions of financial management and contract bidding among others

a financial auditor on certain kinds of operations and organizations, including government corporations

a researcher into a variety of matters of its own or of congressional interest

an ombudsman that looks into questions and complaints raised by members of Congress, federal employees, private contractors, and private citizens

This is a lengthy and elaborately varied menu, particularly for an organization that must carry on in a dynamic political environment. The difficulty is accentuated by the functional range of GAO's scope—virtually as broad as that of all American governments themselves. The time seems ripe for another thorough rethinking of GAO's most useful directions for the future, one that would accompany or shortly follow the rethinking currently under way for the government as a whole. GAO needs to be more selective in the kinds of programs it addresses as well as the types of individual projects it works on. Even with a simpler and shorter agenda, the agency would need a staff of the highest competence and unusual versatility, calling for a carefully designed program of staffing, training, assignments, and rewards—a possibility that now seems more attainable with its exemption from most civil service constraints. It needs also to rely more extensively than it has upon outside expertise in areas it cannot afford to staff itself on a continuing basis. But precedent to changes in such directions is a clearer understanding of role and mission, and this in turn will require a simpler definition of mission itself.

CHAPTER 6

Congressional
Agency–Presidential
Agency

The independence entailed in neutral
competence does not exist for its
own sake; it exists precisely in order
to serve the aims of elected partisan
leadership.

HUGH HECLO, 1975

It is clear that from the very beginning, the roles of the GAO and the BoB/ OMB have been different, joined in only the most general terms by a common intent to make the national government more efficient, economical, and effective. They were given distinctly different tools and modes of entrée into government operations, so that the nature of their work and their work products have also been different. Both changed drastically during the first sixty years of their existence. Yet, there is reason to believe that since World War II, their concerns and capacities have been moving toward each other. During that period, GAO evinced growing interest in general management, in the substance and effectiveness of programs. Although there remained much emphasis upon the financial aspects of programs, the earlier concentration on bookkeeping and auditing in its commercial sense declined. On the other hand, BoB/OMB seemed overall to move the weight of its efforts away from the managerial and in the direction of financial considerations. This movement was not steady and consistent. There was a vigorous effort in the late sixties in the direction of managerial reform, especially with regard to intergovernmental relations. Later, following the reports of the Ash council and the renaming of the Bureau of the Budget as the Office of Management and Budget, budget directors and their deputies under Nixon, Ford, and Carter repeatedly, though in different ways, sought to build momentum on the management side. But none of these efforts seems to have had lasting effect. Meanwhile, leadership on executive policy and program questions moved toward the political staffs in the White House. OMB's role became increasingly fiscal, financial, and usually conservative—much like that traditionally associated with the GAO and the early BoB.

In one other respect, the two "twins" seem to be moving toward each other—their perspective on time. Traditionally, government audit agencies have focused on the past, on deeds already done, and their purposes have been partially or heavily punitive in nature. This was never totally true of GAO, since it has long rendered advance decisions and conducted some preaudits, both of which were intended to be preventive of future errors or violations. The main thrust of BoB/OMB's work almost by definition has been toward the future: how much should be done and spent next year and in subsequent years? But this distinction, too, is losing its sharpness. A great deal of GAO's work today is directed to the future. In fact, the keynote of most of its reports is a statement of recommendations of what it thinks should be done. And though the bulk of the materials it examines is drawn from the present and past, this is true of most OMB work as well. Indeed, GAO is probably more interested in the long-range future today than is OMB. This is reflected in its studies of energy, of weapon systems, of industrial productivity, and of the implementation of metric systems, for example. In the development of its own program plans, it frequently conducts meetings and seminars with scholars and other experts from outside the agency to discuss future problems and emerging issues that it should or might begin studying. And GAO has been a regular participant in an informal group of the various congressional support agencies devoted to the subject of what the future holds.

Contiguity, Cooperation, and Confrontation

The nature of the relations between these two agencies over their first six decades has been so varied as to defy generalization. One may assert with some assurance that these relations have not been as close or as frequent or as sharing as one might have expected of twin siblings, particularly in view of the similarity of their scope (virtually all federal executive agencies), their interests (financial, managerial, and programmatic), and some of their objectives (economy, efficiency, effectiveness, legality, and integrity). Their contacts have generally been spasmodic in time and partial in terms of individuals or segments of the two organizations. One does not have the sense that they come together periodically to say grace and share the Thanksgiving turkey and mince pie. There has been an organizational and social distance between the two, like families living across the country from each other and lacking occupational or other common interests. There is a lingering feeling of superiority among OMB staff, who feel nearer the center of things, more influential, and better qualified. The GAO people are seen by some of them as book-keepers or dabblers who most of the time may safely be ignored, who lack power or responsibility for decision, but who occasionally annoy and obstruct. At the working level of GAO, there is a certain amount of jealousy and resentment of OMB because, they allege, it pays insufficient attention to GAO recommendations. But most GAO personnel have little contact with and little concern about OMB.

Yet, there have been some significant episodes of contact between the two organizations over the years, both friendly and hostile. Budget directors from the time of General Dawes until after World War II were critical of GAO's failure or slowness to improve federal accounting practices as well as of its obstructionism toward executive initiatives, particularly in the New Deal period. During World War II the two agencies worked closely together in devising means of better controlling government corporations, but this was a relatively minor matter at that time for both of them. After the war, with the leadership and close personal friendship of Comptroller General Lindsay Warren and Budget Director James E. Webb, they worked together in developing the cooperative relationship still carried on under the label of the Joint Financial Management Improvement Program and also in drafting the Budget and Accounting Procedures Act of 1950 and certain other legislation. Since that time they have been associated with each other in the development and implementation of many new policies: those set forth by the Commission on Budgetary Concepts, the Legislative Reorganization Act of 1970, the Procurement Commission and the act that followed it, the Congressional Budget and Impoundment Control Act of 1974, the Paperwork Commission and the subsequent Paperwork Reduction Act of 1980, and others. Their operating work has involved a degree of mutuality and collaboration in a number of different fields, such as federal-state-local relations, auditing of federal grants, program evaluation, productivity, improvement of accounting systems, personnel reform, cash management, debt management, the activities of inspectors general in the various federal agencies, and prevention of waste, fraud, and abuse. These joint undertakings were more frequent during the Carter administration than before.

There have been two direct confrontations between the two agencies concerning the functional jurisdiction of one with respect to the other. The Budget and Accounting Act of 1921 in its Section 306 provided, "All laws relating generally to the administration of the departments and establishments, shall, so far as applicable, govern the General Accounting Office." This meant that the GAO for many purposes would be subject to the procedures and controls of the executive branch.[1] Its budget would be subject to review and change by the Bureau of the Budget like that of all the agencies in the executive branch. GAO was considered, for budgetary purposes, an independent agency and not an agency of Congress for the first quarter century of its existence. After Congress in its Reorganization Act of 1945 for the first time declared GAO a "part of the legislative branch," GAO's budgets, like those of other congressional agencies, have not been subject to BoB/OMB review. But there appears to have been some misunderstanding on this matter in the late 1950s when Maurice Stans was budget director and Joseph Campbell was comptroller general. The two men were old friends, both certified public accountants and leaders in their profession. Stans is reported to have called Campbell by phone and asked him to come to his office to discuss certain problems in the GAO budget request. Campbell was dismayed that Stans did not appreciate that GAO's budget was outside of executive jurisdiction and so advised Stans. Since that time, to this writer's knowledge, there has been no discussion between the two agencies about GAO's budget. But it was not until the budget for fiscal year 1968 that the congressional status of GAO was recognized in the budget document itself and in the appropriations acts. Until then, it had been treated as an independent agency, not as part of the legislative branch.

There was probably not any connection, but at about the same time that the BoB was trying to "do its thing" with the GAO, the GAO was trying to "do its thing" with the BoB. In early 1959, the chairman of the House Government Operations Committee wrote the comptroller general to ask that GAO conduct a comprehensive audit of the Executive Office of the President, the largest part of which was of course the Bureau of the Budget. During the summer and fall of 1959, there was a variety of correspondence among the BoB, the House committee, and GAO about accessibility of BoB documents to GAO auditors. Although the BoB on several occasions expressed its desire to cooperate in the study, it was adamantly against revealing "various items which contain advice, opinions, suggestions, or recommendations by persons in the Executive Branch to each other or to their supervisors." A GAO team actually began explorations early in 1960. Its study was directed to three major activities: the management improvement program, the user-charge pro-

1. Thus GAO's personnel system was under the jurisdiction of the Civil Service Commission and its laws and rules until the passage of the GAO Personnel Act of 1980 (Public Law 96-191). Likewise, GAO had no control over the use of its own building until passage of the General Accounting Office Act of 1974 (Public Law 93-604), Title 5 of which authorized the comptroller general "to the use of such space [in that building] as he determines to be necessary."

gram (for private use of federal services and resources), and the formulation, review, and execution of the federal budget. On the first two of these, the GAO group conducted studies, though with some difficulties in gaining access to information, and issued a report to the Congress.[2] But on the third and by far the most important, it ultimately gave up because, it alleged, of denial or almost permanent delay of access to essential information on the familiar grounds of executive privilege. The issue carried over to the Kennedy administration and the new budget director, David Bell, who in effect continued the delay for his successor, Kermit Gordon, who assumed office in December, 1962. By that time, the project was dead and nearly forgotten. One student, who has studied and described this episode in much greater depth, characterized it as a "debacle" for the GAO.[3] Certainly it did not improve relations between the two agencies, and it probably represented in sharp focus the separation of executive and legislative powers, even as had the earlier exclusion of GAO's budget from BoB review. But those who took part on either side do not today look back on it with acrimony; it is even a source of mild amusement.[4]

Some Likenesses

At this point it may be useful to stress some comparisons and contrasts between GAO and BoB/OMB, primarily to suggest their less obvious implications. The two agencies are similar in origin. Not only did the same law create them, but the social and political pressures that brought them into being were similar, and they had a common purpose of economy and efficiency in federal expenditure. Despite deviations and modifications of that original ethos, there remains in both agencies a fundamental bent toward matters financial and toward saving money and eliminating extravagance, waste, and fraud. There have been significant shifts away from strict frugality under certain presi-

2. Maurice Stans to Joseph Campbell, January 4, 1960, in GAO Files, GAO Building, Washington, D.C.; U.S. General Accounting Office, *Report by the Comptroller General of the United States: Review of Selected Activities of the Bureau of the Budget, Executive Office of the President* (June, 1961).

3. Joseph Pois, *Watchdog on the Potomac: A Study of the Comptroller General of the United States* (Washington, D.C., 1979), 100.

4. There are some interesting personal aspects of this episode. A principal negotiator, spokesman, and leader on the OMB side is said to have been Deputy Budget Director Elmer B. Staats, who would a few years later become comptroller general. Staats hired Velma N. Baldwin to assist, accompany, and monitor the GAO's auditing team. She would later serve as director of administration of OMB. Leader of the GAO auditing group was Clerio P. Pin, who would later become GAO's director of administration and still later assistant comptroller general under Staats.

dents, Congresses, budget directors, and comptrollers general, but these have been temporary. The more usual stance of BoB/OMB has been financially conservative and skeptical about new and potentially expensive programs, and GAO staff normally give their preferred attention to areas where there is promise of dollar savings.

Except just before and during World War II, staff growth within both agencies has been inhibited by their identification with economy in government. Both strive to be models of what they preach—frugality. And when in the past they sought to veer from that standard, congressional appropriations committees put them back on course. Despite the gargantuan growth in the responsibilities, scope, and expenditures of the federal government, both agencies are today no larger than they were at the close of World War II. One consequence is that both have been occasionally, perhaps continuously, understaffed for what they have tried, or wanted to try, to do. Another consequence of this constraint has been to make possible, indeed to necessitate, tremendous changes in their responsibilities and modes of operating. Both have decentralized large parts of their functions to operating agencies while retaining central responsibility for making the rules, guiding and coordinating, checking results, and sampling. This has been as true, for example, of budgeting, management analysis, control of regulations, and program evaluation as for accounting and development of accounting systems, auditing, and the pursuit of financial integrity.

There have been conspicuous exceptions, but the characteristic stance of most staff members in both agencies is that of *reactor* and *counterpuncher*. From Congress and the White House and, mostly, from executive agencies, they receive regulations, ideas, proposals, budgets, and reports, and they make their own observations of behavior in American government and society. They review, consider, and study and then respond, negotiate, or report. There have been periods in BoB/OMB's history—during World War II and during the 1960s—when it was a most important initiator and contributor to new policies and programs. And, particularly during the decade of the 1970s, GAO submitted new proposals in a variety of areas. Yet, neither can be properly regarded, and neither regards itself, as a planning agency. My own observation is that in recent years GAO has done more planning work, though spotty and scattered, than has OMB.

The attitude of the auditors in GAO and the examiners in BoB/OMB toward new programs and policies, toward programs in operation, and toward the agencies that initiate and run them has been generally critical and negative. Part of the business of both is finding fault with the way things have been done, are being done, or are planned to be done. For agencies and operations that are not exempt from OMB budgetary review or GAO evaluation, both OMB and GAO are usually considered natural enemies to be feared and resisted with all the interest-group and political support they can muster. Therefore, neither is very popular with agency managers down the line, though they may be allies of the top leaders and their counterparts (budget officers and auditors) in the agencies. Both are criticized, especially by professionalized agencies, on the grounds that they do not really understand the problems of agency operations and that they seek and publicize only the bad, failing to praise or even acknowledge the good. Budget examiners are probably the more generally feared because of their decisive influence upon the next year's budget. But GAO reports can be embarrassing and can provide fodder for critical and politically hungry congressmen.

They are similar in other respects. Both are "generalist" organizations in the sense that they are concerned with just about any and every subject. No other agencies staffed largely with career personnel have so broad a jurisdiction, which in the case of GAO extends even to a few agencies in the legislative branch. Neither has any continuing interest-group constituency comparable to most of the other executive departments and bureaus, though there is some evidence in recent years of interest in OMB on the part of the banking and business communities. Both rely heavily upon permanent career personnel, and the influence of both depends upon a reputation for neutral competence. OMB's credibility as a neutral has declined in recent years because of an increase in noncareer positions. The GAO staff's reputation for competence as generalists is lessened by the continuing, though declining, majority of trained accountants among its personnel.

Despite the wide disparity in their sizes, both have the characteristics and problems of bureaucracies as they were described long ago by Max Weber, but these are considerably more pronounced in GAO than in OMB. There are a considerable number of layers of authority and responsibility in each. Professionals, except at the bottom and the top, are slotted in particular fields of specialization and find it difficult and uncongenial to move from one field—or office—to another. Appointment and advancement in both agencies are based upon merit and proficiency (as prescribed by Weber), but these are measured by different criteria between and within the two agencies. In general, the standards of proficiency in both, according to many observers, appear to be high. There is a good deal of compartmentalization in both organizations, and interpersonal contact and association crossing organizational and hierarchical lines are no longer as easy and frequent as they once were, especially as they were in the old Bureau of the Budget. Social and organizational distance is more pronounced in GAO than in OMB partly because of size, partly because of the geographic scattering of staff in site offices of federal agencies and in regional and overseas offices. Much of the work in both agencies is routinized, governed by rules, regulations, and custom, and a great part of it involves the use of written words—and numbers.

Over the last several decades, both agencies have lost their near-monopoly status in their respective spheres. GAO rocked along for nearly its first half century with virtually no competition in the legislative branch. True, the Legislative Reference Service (now the Congressional Research Service) antedated it, but the mission of that agency was restricted principally to the provision of factual information on request of congressmen, drawn largely from secondary sources. There were expenditure committees in both houses with minimal staffs and few activities. A few of the other committees, including particularly those on appropriations, had small yet effective staffs, but none had resources or independence in any way comparable to those of GAO. Changes in this situation began modestly with passage of the Legislative Reorganization Act of 1946 (Public Law 79-601), which mandated to congressional committees the duty of overseeing federal agencies and programs. But more competition, as well as collaboration, for GAO came during the 1970s with the conversion and expansion of the Legislative Reference Service into a real research and program-evaluation agency and the establishment of the Office of Technology Assessment and the Congressional Budget Office, the activities of either of which might have been placed in GAO. More important for GAO was the tremendous increase in the number and specialization of congressional subcommittees and staffs, capable themselves of conducting or commissioning studies, often with a political bias, and of initiating, receiving, and utilizing for their own purposes studies by the presumably neutral support agencies including, of course, GAO.

The Bureau of the Budget had a comparably monopolistic situation in its relationship to the president during its early years. Even when it was technically part of the Treasury Department, it was practically the only "neutral" agency reporting to the president on substantive matters. Later, when it became part of the Executive Office of the President, it was *primus inter pares* among the institutionalized units in that office, and it gained in that leadership when the National Resources Planning Board was abolished in 1943. Its powers were somewhat reduced with the growth of the Office of War Mobilization and, during and just after World War II, with the establishment of the Council of Economic Advisers in 1946, the National Security Council and its staff in 1947, and later by the creation of other institutionalized units in the EOP. More important for BoB/OMB was the growth in numbers, stature, and influence of noncareer staffs in the White House, beginning with President Roosevelt's six anonymous assistants and culminating in 1970 in the establishment of the Domestic Council (later renamed the Domestic Policy Staff) and the designation of a number of influential political officers in the White House.

And Some Differences

The most obvious differences between BoB/OMB and GAO are in size and geographic spread. As noted at the beginning of this study, the GAO staff (now about 5,100) is many times larger than that of OMB (now about 580). But OMB is closer to the central founts of government decisions. Its staff is more varied in education and background and includes a greater proportion of personnel in top executive grades; the grade average for its journeymen is also considerably higher. In the past fifteen years, new GAO personnel have come increasingly from fields other than accounting, but the majority, including almost all those near the top, were originally educated as accountants. OMB has long employed professionals from a wide variety of disciplines and professions and in this sense has a more cosmopolitan staff. The difference here is declining since most of GAO's work today does not call for accounting skills. Indeed, the nature of knowledge and aptitudes required in the two agencies is quite similar. Practically all of GAO's staff are career personnel who have spent most of their working lives in the organization and who expect to remain with it for many years in the future. The career people in OMB are generally more mobile. Many have had prior experience in other agencies, and many will leave before retirement for employment elsewhere in the government or in the private sector. Furthermore, as pointed out earlier, OMB has relied on noncareer appointees in about a dozen of its top positions. One effect of their presence is to provide one or two layers, organizational and psychological, between the director and deputy director of the budget and top career personnel.

GAO has a somewhat comparable problem resulting from its field organization. A very substantial part of its staff and its work are in offices in the headquarters of the various executive agencies in and around Washington, in regional offices located across the country, and in overseas offices spanning the continents of the world. This creates problems of supervision and coordination, of communications, of status and prestige, of standards, and perhaps most acutely, of perceptions of agency purpose.

The Bureau of the Budget established four field offices during World War II to provide and verify information for the Washington office and to coordinate field operations of the various federal agencies to the extent feasible. These were abolished for reasons of economy in the first year of the Eisenhower administration. On several occasions after that, BoB sought funds to renew them, but Congress never acceded. Since the regional councils were set up in 1969, BoB/OMB has assigned representatives to the federal regions to attend, coordinate, and service the various regional organizations of the departments, but these representatives were on travel status. The home base of all OMB personnel is Washington. While GAO's widely dispersed field offices make organizational synchronization more difficult, it enjoys substantial advantages from them. It is far less dependent upon the agencies and their channels for information. It can send people to see for themselves; it can conduct studies of national or worldwide dimensions simultaneously in various places; it can compare what it is told in Washington with what it can see out where the operations are actually conducted.

Much of the difference in operating style as well as in the products of the two agencies stems from the simple fact that the bulk of the work of BoB/OMB is disciplined and scheduled by the calendar, whereas most of GAO's is not. The budget process itself is the principal ringer of the school bell for OMB. The budget must be completed and sent to the printer by a certain date, and the many stages in preparation and execution in the process before and after that are dictated by law or by necessity to meet the requirements of the fiscal year and of the publication of the budget. Many years ago, budgeting was a spasmodic affair, requiring heavy work at certain periods—late summer and fall for review and hearings, early winter (right around Christmas) for final decisions and putting the document together.[5] Today, the budget process is more nearly a year-round proposition, with seasonal stages, punctuated by deadlines. In years of rapid and unexpected economic change, as in 1980, significant revisions may require special and additional budget processes. And in years of political transition, as in 1981, new presidents customarily prepare one or more revised budgets after their inauguration.

The budget is not the only bell ringer for OMB. It has long been involved in the development or review of items for the president's legislative program. Its legislative reference group is always under time constraints in its review and coordination of proposed legislation, enrolled bills, and departmental testimony. One has the impression of an organization frantically endeavoring to meet deadlines and under constant stress with insufficient time for contemplation, long-term thinking and planning, attention to personal and family matters, and sometimes even common courtesy.

5. A major argument for the BoB reorganization of 1952 was to balance out the workload for management and analytical studies during off-budget seasons.

The atmosphere has been quite different for GAO. Most of its work, though related to the budget and to legislation, has not been temporally tied to either. It can select, program, and schedule its projects internally and self-impose its deadlines. Comptrollers general, particularly Elmer Staats, have sought to make the agency's products more directly useful to Congress, and this has meant, among other things, relating them to the time of congressional consideration of appropriations and other legislation. The growing use of and emphasis upon testimony and correspondence (instead of or in addition to the formal reports) reflect a growing concern about making GAO's work more relevant to the ongoing processes of Congress. But in fact, the bulk of it continues to be carried on relatively independently and according to GAO's own program, pace, and convenience. One of the most frequent criticisms of the agency voiced by congressmen and their staffs is the lack of timeliness of its reports and its failure to respond quickly enough to congressional needs.[6] There are certainly exceptions, but one senses much less feeling of urgency and deadline pressure within GAO generally than within OMB. This condition has potential advantages. GAO has more time and more opportunity to look ahead, to anticipate long-term problems without the temporal demands of the fiscal year and the budget process and without the political constraints of a particular presidency.

The principal products of both of these agencies are communications, mostly written. They are testimony, proposed legislation, regulations, reports, memoranda, letters, and budgets. In both cases, they are *staff* products dealing with government, with what and how it performs, but they are not the stuff of governing—of fighting wars, training troops, delivering mail, making grants to state governments, inspecting meat, providing for education, and a thousand other matters. Both are critics, prodders, and restrainers. But their audiences were very different, at least until 1981. GAO writes for Congress, but its best channel to Congress is the media—the press and television. At least until the Reagan administration, OMB was authoritative but not newsworthy. It published the annual budget and accompanying documents, but the budget is the president's, not OMB's. It issues all sorts of regulations, orders (including executive orders of the president), circulars, and memoranda. But most of these latter are internal, however authoritative, to the government. They are little known and seldom seen by ordinary citizens.

6. This criticism was made in a number of reports in the 1970s by groups of both the House and the Senate: U.S. Congress, Senate, Commission on the Operation of the Senate, *Congressional Support Agencies: A Staff Study*, Ernest S. Griffith (ed.), 94th Cong., 2nd Sess. (1976); U.S. Congress, Senate, Commission on the Operation of the Senate, *Toward a Modern Senate*, Senate Document 278, 94th Cong., 2nd Sess. (1976); and U.S. Congress, House, Select Committee on Congressional Operations, *General Accounting Office Services to Congress: An Assessment*, 95th Cong., 2nd Sess. (1978).

The Leaders

The relative anonymity of the BoB/OMB outside the government itself was, until recently, matched by the low public profile of its leadership—its directors and deputy directors. Few were widely known as budget officers, though a good many won some fame in other capacities before and/or after they served in BoB/OMB, including Charles Dawes, James Webb, Maurice Stans, Kermit Gordon, Charles Schultze, George Shultz, James Schlesinger, and Caspar Weinberger.[7] Of course, a comparable anonymity attended most of the comptrollers general and their deputies. It is doubtful that more than a fraction of 1 percent of the American people outside of government itself could name the comptroller general today.

Yet, the incumbents of these offices have had great significance for the course of modern American government. First, though to varying degrees, they have been advisers to their principals—presidents and presidential intimates and congressional committee leaders and staff. Second, they have been administrators of sizable and influential professional organizations. In both capacities and in the joining of the two, the nature and the abilities of the incumbents are crucial. The leaders of these agencies have been significant in one other respect. The kinds of persons selected reveal much about the presidents who appointed or nominated them. How did the presidents perceive these posts? To what extent have there been trends or continuities?

Between July 1, 1921, when the Budget and Accounting Act took effect, and July 1, 1981, there were five comptrollers general and five assistant (later retitled as deputy) comptrollers general. In the same span of time there were twenty-five directors of the budget and twenty-four assistant (later retitled as deputy) directors of the budget. The comptrollers general and the budget directors have shared many characteristics.

All have been white males.

Virtually all have been regarded as intelligent and fair-minded persons, and some have been brilliant.

Most have had significant and responsible prior experience, though not necessarily in governmental budgeting or finance.

Few (perhaps only McCarl, the first comptroller general) can properly be regarded strictly as patronage appointees. Only four (Comptrollers General Brown and Warren and Budget Directors Douglas and Stockman) had previously served in Congress, and all of these were of the

7. Probably the most influential of all budget directors down to 1981 was, and remains, largely unknown outside of the government—Harold D. Smith. Probably the most widely known budget director won fame because of alleged scandal—Bert Lance.

same political party as the president who appointed them. With the exception of the first two incumbents, Dawes and McCarl, it is doubtful that any perceived their posts as stepping-stones to high elective political office.

No comptroller general was drawn from the career service of the GAO or had any prior experience in the agency. Only one budget director (Lawton) had been in BoB's career service, but a number were promoted from noncareer appointments as assistants or deputies (Pace, Lawton, Hughes, Brundage, Stans, Weinberger, and McIntyre).

There has been an even clearer pattern among the second-level officers in both agencies. The assistant (or deputy) comptrollers general and budget directors were likewise white male nonpoliticians. Of those in GAO, all but one (Elliott, a former congressman) had had long prior experience in the agency, and most were trained in law—usually regarded as essential when the comptroller general was not a lawyer because of the judicial character of some of the work. Most served all or the bulk of their fifteen-year terms, with the result that only five different persons filled the job, not counting the relatively few months over the sixty-year period when it was held on an acting basis.

Unlike their counterparts in the GAO, the assistant and deputy directors of the budget have provided no such continuously stabilizing force. A few served relatively long terms: Kloeber, 1922–1933; Appleby, 1941–1947; Staats, 1950–1953 and 1959–1966; and Hughes, 1966–1969. But most moved in and out within two or two and one-half years—as frequently as did their superiors and often at the same times. Between World War II and 1970, most came from BoB's own career staff, but since then all except one, Paul H. O'Neill (1975–1978), came from outside. Nonetheless, almost all appointees in the decade of the 1970s had prior governmental experience—in Washington or in Georgia. That experience was usually of a general managerial character, not necessarily budgetary, financial, or legal.

The development of the BoB/OMB over its first sixty years may usefully be described as a series of waves, each with its own thrusts and emphases, each with a somewhat distinctive type of leader in terms of background and orientation. To some extent the nature of the leadership was reflected in the orientations and performance of the staff, but the degree to which this was true varied. Most of the staff were career people who tended, without extensive prodding, to carry on much as before. The nature of the successive waves is described in Table 2.

Clearly, there was a pattern in what different presidents perceived to be the nature of, and qualifications for, the job of budget director, and the perceptions were generally different between the two parties. During the Republican

TABLE 2

The Development of BoB/OMB, 1921–1981

WAVE	APPROXIMATE PERIOD	BACKGROUNDS OF DIRECTORS	DIRECTORS	EMPHASES, DIRECTIONS, AIMS
1	1921–33	Military officers with experience in logistics in World War I	Dawes Lord Roop	Economy, business management (narrowly defined), detail
—	1933–39	Mixed, transitional	Douglas Daniel Bell	Economy; beginning of expanding activities in latter part of period
2	1939–53	Public administration	Smith Webb Pace Lawton	Administrative management, policy coordination, fiscal considerations, neutral competence, acting as general adviser to presidents
3	1953–61	Bankers, accountants	Dodge Hughes Brundage Stans	Accounting reform, regularity of business management, economy
4	1961–69	Economists (mainly micro-)	David Bell Gordon Schultze Zwick	Policy analysis, program evaluations, PPBS, policy development, declining concern with general management
5	1969–81	Varied; some emphasis on business; most had prior administrative experience in government	Mayo Shultz Weinberger Ash Lynn Lance McIntyre	Loyalty and responsiveness to president; distance from, and sometimes hostility to, Congress; deregulation
6	1981–	Political	Stockman	Drastic economy, deregulation

regime of the 1920s, the preference was clearly for hardheaded, economy-minded financial and logistical officers of the army, though it should be noted that two of the three (Dawes and Roop) had also had extensive experience in private business. After some uncertainty during the New Deal period, Roosevelt and Truman turned to a growing public administration fraternity, though two of Truman's appointees also had extensive experience in private business. Eisenhower appointed bankers, then accountants, clearly seeing the job as primarily a financial one. Kennedy and Johnson saw economics as a sine qua non. All four of their appointees had advanced degrees in economics, three of them Ph.D.'s and all of them some teaching experience. Dominant among the nominees of Nixon and Ford were men with business experience, but almost all had occupied high governmental posts before their budget posts. Under Carter, Lance was a banker but had been a department head in Georgia, and McIntyre, a lawyer, had been Carter's budget director in Georgia.

In evaluating this table, it must be borne in mind that it depicts only the top of the stream, the crest of the waves. Some of these were transitory in duration, and some had little influence on the steady, main currents flowing several feet below. One has the sense that throughout all of these six decades, the dominating drives and ethos of BoB/OMB have been the severe rhythms of the budget process and the pressures for regularity, economy, and routine. Presidents and directors may come and go, as may those many frills like performance budgeting, PPBS, MBO, ZBB, and others sure to come. But that strong, steady, deep current for meeting deadlines and saving the taxpayers' money continues to flow as it has since General Dawes first propelled it—regardless of the turbulence of the waves up on top.

A comparable chart for the GAO (see Table 3) is much simpler, if only because there have been many fewer wavemakers and despite the fact that the deep-flowing current has undergone a greater change in its direction. Until Eisenhower's nomination of Campbell, all the comptrollers general were trained in law and had experience in, or in close association with, Congress—a background similar to that of most of the comptrollers of the treasury before them. Eisenhower abandoned that precedent, turning to a professional accountant in 1954, as did Reagan in 1981. Both of the two, Campbell and Bowsher, had prior federal experience in the executive, not the legislative, branch. The Johnson nominee, Staats, was sui generis with his training and long experience in public administration, including many years near the top of the Bureau of the Budget.

However, the same caveats about the waves and the underlying currents also apply to the GAO leaders as well as to those in BoB/OMB, though perhaps to a lesser extent. There is still some of the detailed fault-finding, finan-

TABLE 3

The Development of GAO, 1921–1981

WAVE	PERIOD	BACKGROUNDS OF COMPTROLLERS GENERAL	COMPTROLLERS GENERAL	EMPHASES, DIRECTIONS, AIMS
1	1921–45	Lawyers, politicians	McCarl Brown Warren	Strict legal compliance, detail, punitive investigation
2	1945–54	Lawyer, politician	Warren	Professionalizing of accounting; cooperation with executive and Congress; financial systems and management
3	1954–66	Professional accountant	Campbell	Professionalizing of accounting; strict segregation of auditors from those audited; punitive and publicizing searches of government contractors
4	1966–81	Public administrator	Staats	Program evaluation, service to Congress, professionalization in many fields in addition to accounting.
5	1981–	Professional accountant	Bowsher	?

cial nit-picking, and suspicion of the executive branch that so permeated the McCarl regime. And despite the important changes during the fifteen years of Staats's leadership, the orientation of much of GAO's work remains significantly financial with some of the style, methods, and attitudes characteristic of public accounting firms in the private sector.

Another observation about the heads of GAO and BoB/OMB is of interest because it constitutes one aspect in which their postures are opposite to each other. Budget directors (and to a lesser extent, their deputies) are and always have been almost completely dependent upon the president for their effectiveness and even their survival in office. Congress has tried in various ways to modify that dependence—such as legislating certain powers directly to the budget director or making his appointment subject to senatorial confirmation, as it did in 1974. But the director remains the president's man, who can be removed at any time or who will find it wise to remove himself if he finds himself or his views in disfavor with his boss. The surest strategy to relieve the pressure of such dependency is to make the president increasingly dependent upon his budget chief, and this means maximizing the utilization of budget personnel and other resources in support of presidential interests. But such a strategy may threaten the credibility of the institution for the next president. The budget directorship has become a short-term job, in many cases leading to more lucrative posts in the private sector or sometimes to more prestigious ones in government.

In contrast, comptrollers general, once appointed, are completely independent of the president or anyone else in the executive branch. They are dependent upon various elements of Congress for their appropriations and other kinds of support. The leadership and the membership of both houses of Congress of course change, and the maintenance of congressional support is a more complicated and subtler problem than for an officer with a single superior. But every comptroller general has maintained his independence even of Congress in certain areas and with respect to certain powers. Thus, in some ways he can and must maintain a posture that is above current political parties, politics, and ideologies.

A closing observation about the incumbents of these positions is that, with very few and very recent exceptions (principally Carter appointees Bert Lance and James McIntyre), none was an intimate friend or in the inner circle of the president who appointed him. Most were appointed on their merits, usually with due regard to their political and ideological sympathy, but often with no prior personal acquaintance whatever. It speaks well for both the budget directors and their presidents that most of them saw the boss frequently and were apparently among the most influential of his advisers as well as the most respected if not feared by other executive officials. Somewhat similarly, none of the comptrollers general was on intimate terms with the president who appointed him, and only one, Lindsay Warren, had close personal ties with leaders of Congress.

Finally, two problems concerning these two agencies need to be addressed. These problems have permeated the past of both agencies, though in somewhat different ways, and they are certain to condition their future. The first is that of maintaining credibility through competence and political neutrality while at the same time serving highly political masters. The crucial problem of the top leadership of each agency in its respective sphere is to provide a bridge between truth and power, that is, between facts, knowledge, understanding, and objective recommendation on the one hand and the purely political on the other.[8] It is not an easy stance and is probably more difficult in OMB than in GAO. At any given time, there is a single president, a single party, and a single administration for OMB to serve. And that president may not be receptive to ideas based on the experience of his predecessor; he may not be concerned about what kind of institution he leaves for his successor. In that hazy zone between what is purely political and what is purely administrative, the temptation and the pressure to please the boss are great, even when dangerous to the long-range effectiveness of the institution. It may very possibly prove that the interposition of a sizable political White House staff and of a number of political officers near the top of OMB is a necessary protection to the neutrality of the career staff.

In contrast, GAO always must work for two different parties in two different houses and for many blocs and subdivisions of them. Naturally, there is pressure for studies and for findings and recommendations that will be useful to individuals or groups or parties, and there are indeed occasional charges of partiality against GAO. This is one reason for the caution, the reliance on figures and provable facts, and the repeated internal reviews that characterize much of GAO's work. The planning and selection of GAO projects require a large amount of political astuteness. Yet, by and large, congressmen and many congressional staff have come to recognize the necessity for partisan neutrality in GAO, and the pressures are less immediate than in OMB.

The second problem concerns the mission and scope of the two agencies. Should OMB be primarily or solely a numbers agency, bringing together and reviewing and recommending the estimates of the agencies and overseeing their outlays? Or should it be the general staff of the president, focusing not alone on the budget but also on his policies and programs and their management? Much the same question applies to the GAO. Should it revert to being the principal auditor of the government's finances? Or should it continue in the directions it has been moving to study and advise the Congress—as well as the executive agencies—on all sorts of questions concerning their policies and their operations? In short, should it emulate a pure auditing agency or a general staff for the Congress?

The two problems are not unconnected. The functions of financial budgeting and auditing, are safer, less politically vulnerable, than the general-staff types of activity. We shall see what happens.

8. I am indebted to the title and, to some extent, a theme of the book by Aaron Wildavsky, *Speaking Truth to Power: The Art and Craft of Policy Analysis* (Boston, 1979).

The First Reagan Year

Reversion and Reversal

It was the best of times, it was the
worst of times, it was the age of
wisdom, it was the age of foolish-
ness, it was the epoch of belief, it
was the epoch of incredulity, it was
the season of light, it was the season
of darkness, it was the spring of
hope, it was the winter of despair,
we had everything before us, we
were all going direct to Heaven, we
were all going direct the other
way—

CHARLES DICKENS,
A Tale of Two Cities

On January 21, 1981, the day after the inauguration of President Ronald
Reagan, Comptroller General Staats addressed a letter to Caspar Weinberger,
the new secretary of defense, to call his attention to possible economies in the
defense budget that had been discovered in earlier GAO studies and that had
not been fully acted upon. To the letter was attached a twenty-three-page paper,
listing and summarizing some fifteen major "cost reduction opportunities"
that, according to Staats, would amount to "*several billion dollars a year of
savings*" (emphasis in original).

This was one of Staats's last official actions, since his fifteen-year, non-
renewable term would end within seven weeks, and it was ironic in several
ways. First, the message was of a kind one might have expected from the
president's budget office, the OMB, rather than from the congressional auditor. Second, although the new president had leaned heavily on the promise of
reduced federal spending in his election campaign, he had made it clear that
he intended to greatly increase, not economize on, defense spending. Third,
Weinberger's position itself was highly ironic. In a previous incarnation, he
had served as director of OMB—where he won the nickname of Cap the
Knife for his budget-cutting proclivities—and his deputy in Defense, Frank
Carlucci, had also been his deputy at OMB. But saving money in Defense,
which many observers consider the most profligate government agency in the
country, was not, and has not become, a prime interest of Weinberger and

Carlucci. Weinberger extended Staats a courteous reply, saying that the suggestions would be carefully considered. But most of what emanated from the Defense Department after that was new and expanded ways of spending money, not saving it. And except for a few important decisions in the defense area, including the approval of some new strategic weaponry, most of the president's attention during his first year in office was directed to his program for economic recovery, principally to sharp cuts in taxes and domestic spending. The Defense Department was specifically and emphatically exempted from the spending reductions; indeed, it was encouraged to move as fast or faster in the opposite direction.

It is not within the purview of this study to describe in any depth the economic program of the Reagan administration. But it would be remiss if it failed to sketch at least in general terms the impact upon the OMB of that program and of the way it was given momentum in the president's first year. For that impact—upon its influence, posture, relationships, and functioning—was simply enormous. When President Reagan took office in January, 1981, President Carter had already submitted his budget for fiscal year 1982. Reagan, like most of his recent predecessors, undertook immediate changes in the 1982 budget and commitments for future budgets that would carry through to 1985. His basic plan involved several points.

cuts each year in the domestic outlays in the budget; these would include discretionary items as well as entitlement programs and grants to state and local governments; but enough would be left to assure a "safety net" for the poor

consolidation of many categorical grants to state and local governments into a relatively small number of block grants in broad functional fields with substantial discretion granted to state governments as to how they would be spent

sharp annual reductions in taxation of corporations and individuals; these would make possible greater savings and investment in plant and other capital, thus increasing productivity in the future; this in turn would increase income in the private sector and lead to greater revenues from taxation, even with declining tax rates

elimination of federal deficits by 1984

monetary controls to decrease inflation until growth in productivity made them less necessary

large annual increases (after inflation) in the defense budget

drastic reductions in federal regulation of the private sector "to get the government off our backs" and encourage productivity growing reliance upon voluntarism in the private sector to take care of the poor and otherwise disadvantaged

To these were added in the 1982 state of the union message a proposal to exchange grant programs between the states and the federal government whereby the latter would assume full responsibility for Medicaid and the states would take over several of the others, assisted financially and temporarily by a special fund to be provided from federal revenues.

The earliest and in many ways the hardest of these proposals to formulate and get accepted was the first one—the cross-the-board reductions in domestic spending. From the standpoint of administration objectives it was also, in 1981, one of the most successful, resulting in some of the most drastic changes in budgetary directions and totals in modern peacetime history. Its achievement, like several of the other items on the Reagan agenda, was largely the product of a refashioned OMB and particularly of its new director, David Stockman.

Stockman was a maverick among the twenty-five OMB budget directors who have served to the time of this writing.[1] He had been a divinity student at Harvard, where he had also taken some graduate courses in the Kennedy Graduate School of Government and had lived in the home of Professor (later Senator) Daniel Patrick Moynihan. He had been an assistant to Congressman John Anderson well before Anderson ran as a candidate for president in 1980. Stockman had then served two terms as Republican representative from Michigan. He was young, smart, articulate, persuasive, knowledgeable, aggressive, and self-confident. As a congressman and with his staff assistants, he had studied and obtained a thorough knowledge of the domestic side of the budget and of the congressional role in the budget process. His ideas about government and its proper role in American society had obviously been in flux for years, but by the time of the Reagan candidacy he had become convinced that the federal role and expenditures should be drastically reduced, that responsibilities for the society should be shifted preferably to the private sector or at least to state and local governments. He had not studied the defense problem in depth and was hopeful but, it later appeared, not altogether convinced about supply-side economics (the basic rationale for tax reduction).

President Reagan indicated that Stockman would be his budget director well before his inauguration, and by that time Stockman had a plan of action, which included a number of new appointments, well under way. Thencefor-

---

1. He was only the second who had previous congressional experience. The first, Lewis W. Douglas, who had been a Democratic representative from Arizona, was Franklin D. Roosevelt's first budget director. He left because of disagreement with Roosevelt's fiscal policies at the end of August, 1934.

ward, for most of a year, OMB Director Stockman would be the administration's leading policy and political spokesman on domestic matters, except for the president himself. Reagan made his economic program his focal program, and he made Stockman its principal advocate—in the administration, before the Congress, and in public speeches. The anonymity of the budget director was completely lost, as was that of the organization he headed. Except in the fields of foreign affairs and national defense, statements and releases from OMB seemed more authoritative than those emanating from the heads of departments and major agencies—or indeed from the White House itself. This was true for the public, for the press, for the Congress, and for the rest of the administration. For a considerable period in 1981, OMB was *the* voice of the executive branch of the government; its word was *the* policy.

Whether or not as a designed administrative strategy, OMB made administrative decisions on agency policies and programs during the spring of 1981 with little reference to the departments and agencies concerned. While the president, like most of his predecessors, was extolling cabinet government with maximum delegation of policy and administrative discretion to line subordinates and while he was providing them offices near the White House, he was separating them from the agencies they were charged with running. He was also leaving vacant the many intermediate political positions that provide the channels between the professional bureaucrats who could interpret the real significance and probable effects of budgetary changes or could provide the arguments against them. The result was that in that first round, OMB made the decisions with little input from the operating agencies. The possible arguments against them were not understood by newly appointed political appointees at the top and were never effectively expressed within the administration. The cuts were made within a month of the inauguration when the president conveyed them to Congress; they amounted to about $41 billion under the 1982 Carter budget of about $730 billion.

A comparable result was achieved in the Congress, though with quite different tools.[2] As noted earlier, Congress had in 1974 passed the Congressional Budget and Impoundment Control Act, mainly to reestablish more congressional influence and control over the budget. That act provided a procedure

2. It is not feasible in these few paragraphs to describe the congressional organization and procedures for handling the federal budget and how they were modified by the reconciliation process as it was used in 1981. Indeed, I doubt that more than a very few, even among those directly involved, fully understand what happened in 1981 or would predict what may happen in the future. It is unlikely that more than a handful of people had fully read and understood the Reconciliation Act of 1981 when it passed—and few have done so since. The act contains twenty-seven titles and covers 576 printed pages, each of which contains myriad references to other acts that it modifies or supersedes. In this brief description I have drawn upon a number of articles, including several published in *PS*, XIV (Fall, 1981), and "Reconciliation Roundup," *Congressional Quarterly*, XXXIX (August 15, 1981), 1461–1516.

whereby the two houses could direct their legislative committees to reduce entitlement programs to meet targeted outlays approved by the houses in their second concurrent budget resolutions, which would be adopted in September of each year. This process, known as "reconciliation," had not been used until 1980 because the second resolution was too late in September—about two weeks before the beginning of the fiscal year—to allow the committees to act. In 1980, the congressional budget committees working with officials of the Carter administration, sought a way to reduce the budget quickly by about $15 billion. Using a little-known provision of the act to institute "any other procedure which is considered appropriate" [section 301(b)(2)], they applied the reconciliation procedure to the first concurrent budget resolution, which is adopted every May. Furthermore, they applied the procedure not alone to entitlement programs for which reconciliation was originally designed but also to authorizations for discretionary spending.

With the guidance of Reagan and Stockman, the Congress adapted this precedent to its proposed budget cuts in 1981, and it extended the process to the changing of substantive provisions of acts previously passed, to the outright elimination of many programs, to the substitution of block grants, and to the fixing of spending limits not alone for 1982 but for 1983 and 1984 as well. What followed in all the committees of both houses, in a mass of meetings of conference subcommittees, and in floor actions was several weeks of almost utter confusion. The Republicans stood with the president with almost perfect discipline. Their majority in the Senate won every vote without difficulty. In the House, nominally under Democratic control, enough southern Democrats ("boll weevils") defected for the Republicans to win every major vote. The "Omnibus Budget Reconciliation Act of 1981" (Public Law 97-35) was signed by President Reagan on August 13. Its principal architects were David Stockman and his OMB staff, who worked with each of the committees involved and in fact drafted the bulk of the bill. The act itself was a monstrous document, modifying, cutting, sometimes eliminating more than 250 domestic programs and representing savings of more than $35 billion in 1982 and even greater cuts in future years.

Perversely, the Congressional Budget and Impoundment Control Act of 1974, designed to enhance the power of Congress and limit that of the president, provided the machinery to do just the opposite. With the backing of Reagan, Stockman and the OMB had not alone dominated the top officials in the executive branch; they had impressed their will upon the decisions of Congress. In the process, they had at least temporarily broken the influence of a myriad of the proverbial "iron triangles" consisting of sympathetic federal administrators, congressmen, and interest groups. The interest groups had little access to the decision processes in either the administration or the Congress. Finally and not least, they had assumed leadership for the entire Reagan administration on most aspects of domestic policy and of his economic program, Reagan's announced *pièce de résistance* in the first year of his presidency. Little was heard during that year from the Domestic Policy Staff. Indeed, few even knew who its director was until he resigned in February, 1982, and it is probably significant that he was replaced by Stockman's deputy director of OMB, Edwin L. Harper. The trend of the previous several decades was thus substantially reversed. No longer did the budget follow major policy initiatives or changes. Policy followed the budget or, perhaps more accurately, was made through the budget.

During 1981, too, Stockman and the OMB's other political officers became the principal public spokesmen for the president's domestic budget and the program it embodied. Such anonymity and political immunity as had once shielded OMB and its leaders from the public spotlight had disappeared, and the extent to which even the career budget staff can in the future claim political neutrality and objective professional expertise is at least questionable. By the fall of 1981, OMB and its director had assumed a primacy in American politics and policy, in relation to the Congress and the executive branch, and indeed in the Executive Office of the President that had never before been realized or even envisioned by the most ambitious founders and developers of the agency.

But before one jumps to conclusions about OMB and its prospects, some other factors must be considered. In the first place, 1981 was an unusual if not unique political year, and what happened then may provide little precedent for the future. There was a new president whose communicative abilities and popularity were enhanced by a nearly fatal assassination attempt that he survived with courage and cheer. With his election came a swing of votes that gave his party a majority in the Senate and, on many substantive issues, a majority in the House. Like most of his predecessors, he chose to construe his election as a mandate for the programs he espoused in his campaign. He had an unusually happy honeymoon, and he made the most of it. He turned to Congressman David Stockman, a supporter and an unusually informed and astute student of the federal budget, and to the only organization in the executive branch, the OMB, that could claim a presidential perspective as well as an institutional memory of what had happened before.

Not all of these conditions will pertain again for Reagan—or for OMB. As these lines are written, Reagan's personal popularity is declining and the Reagan program appears to be in trouble because of the recession, rising unemployment, increasing federal deficits, high interest rates, and what seems to be a general failure of the supply-side predictions on which it was partly based. Budget Director Stockman has damaged his credibility because of the tape recordings of his luncheon conversations in which he expressed his own doubts about the Reagan economic program.[3] Stockman's congressional presentation and defense of the 1983 budget in early 1982, which called for still more drastic expenditure cuts and admitted an unprecedented peacetime deficit—anathema to most conservatives—demonstrated a remarkable resiliency to charges that others might have found annihilating. His proposals were received in the Congress with less than overwhelming enthusiasm on either side of the aisle. Whether there will be any such deference to OMB decisions or any substantial reconciliation process as in 1981 is at least doubtful. We may have witnessed a one-time phenomenon but still one that may have a lasting effect upon the nature, influence, and credibility of the institution known as OMB.

A second factor is that, more than in any other presidency in the last half century, decisions about budgets and the programs they support were made on the basis of a firm and basically very simple ideology about what government should and should not do and, more specifically, what the federal government should and should not do. These were givens: federal expenditures for national defense must be greatly increased; such domestic government as is necessary should be delegated to governments "closer to the people," that is, the states; but most activity and initiative should be left or returned to the private sector and voluntarism. Certain concessions might have to be made, such as a "safety net" to prevent the destitution of some citizens and continuing federal activity to meet intractable problems that cross state lines, such as drug traffic.

Given such firm guidelines, the problems of policy making and budget examining were far different than in any previous year. Most domestic programs had to go; the only questions were how far and how fast, given the political climate then and in the future. There was little need, even had there been time, to analyze policies and programs, to assess their costs against benefits, to evaluate their results, or to consider alternative means of achieving their objectives. The only real problems were how much traffic the political highways would bear and what were the best means of steering and maneuvering the traffic along those highways. Substantive program analysis and evaluation, which over the previous fifteen years had become the meat and drink of budgeting and the centerpiece of most training programs for public admin-

3. William Greider, "The Education of David Stockman," *Atlantic Monthly*, CCXLVIII (December, 1981), 27–54.

istrators, gave place to political footwork. The goals of minimal domestic government answered the substantive questions, and they were fixed in the concrete of ideology.

One further observation about OMB's greatly enlarged influence in the budget field in 1981 is that it was basically *negative*. It was not called upon to develop, or to help other agencies develop, new programs. Rather it sought to reduce or eliminate old ones, a kind of exercise in which its examiners had long and often frustrating experience. In 1981, they had vigorous, nearly invincible political backing to do what in many cases they had wanted to do for many years. Some of the career budget people in OMB were unhappy because they felt that the decisions were made above them and that they were called upon merely to fill in the figures and run errands. But others probably enjoyed doing what the founders and early leaders of the Bureau of the Budget intended for it to do—reduce the activities and costs of government. Many of the utterances of president Reagan and Budget Director Stockman are virtual paraphrases of statements of Charles Dawes and Presidents Harding and Coolidge.

In addition to its vigorous pursuit of budgetary reductions, the Stockman OMB renewed its efforts in two other fields of activity. One was the review and reduction of federal regulations applying to the private sector. Within a month of taking office President Reagan signed Executive Order No. 12291, which in effect made OMB the clearinghouse for all proposed regulations under consideration by executive agencies. Independent agencies were exempted, as they were under President Carter's order, not on the grounds that the president lacked authority to include them, but to avoid unnecessary conflict with Congress. OMB was called upon to review proposed rules, analyze their costs and benefits, return them to the initiating agency for change when necessary, and, where disagreement persisted, refer them to the newly established Task Force on Regulatory Relief, chaired by the vice-president. OMB could not rewrite the regulations but could recommend changes or deletions or hold them up if they were not modified to its satisfaction. In form the order preserved the legal notion that final decisons rest with the heads of departments and agencies to whom Congress has given authority under the various regulatory laws. The practical effect, however, may have been to give OMB the final say on proposed rules that it deemed highly important, at least when an agency head was unwilling to appeal to the task force or the president. A regulatory reform bill, first supported by President Carter in 1978, imposed a general cost-benefit requirement on new regulations. Revised versions of it are still under consideration in both houses of Congress as these lines are written.

The other area of vigorous OMB activity in 1981 was leadership in the effort to reduce "fraud, waste, and abuse," another pursuit that the president, like practically all of his predecessors, had promised in his campaign to carry forward energetically. He formed a President's Council on Integrity and Efficiency, chaired by the deputy director of the budget, to superintend the efforts in the departments and agencies. The council included all of the inspectors general as well as representatives of other departments and agencies (including, on invitation, the comptroller general). It was a successor to President Carter's Executive Group to Combat Financial Waste in Government. Reagan fired all of the inspectors general who had been set up in the various departments primarily for the same purpose, then rehired most of them (though sometimes in different departments), apparently in a tactic to assure loyalty to the new administration. OMB had been cool to the establishment of those offices a few years before, and among their principal proponents had been the GAO. Paradoxically, OMB became an advocate, collaborator, and user of the inspectors general in 1981. Its deputy director met periodically with the council and called the inspectors general frequently on questions pertinent to their agencies. All of them had networks in the field that became, in effect, a partial substitute for an OMB field service.

OMB continued to review, modify, and approve or disapprove requests for information and forms proposed by the various agencies under the terms of the Paperwork Reduction Act of 1980 (Public Law 96-511), and it made studies and introduced changes in a number of practices common to most federal agencies, such as travel. But it actually did little in the general area of federal management. The Carter reorganization act had expired and President Reagan sought no extension of it. He pressed, as he had in his campaign, for the elimination of the Education and Energy departments, but these efforts were essentially for political reasons and public relations rather than managerial purposes. In the first Reagan year at least, management improvement ran a poor fourth in OMB to the budget, to regulatory change, and to the waste, fraud, and abuse program.

While the OMB was assuming its dominant role on both the executive and legislative sides of the government in 1981, the GAO continued essentially as usual, issuing reports, testifying and otherwise advising committees and staffs of Congress, and getting a fair share of newspaper space in the nationwide press. Unlike the transitions between presidents, the transitions between comptrollers general occupy little newspaper space aside from reports, mainly in the society columns, about parties for the retiring comptroller general. Elmer Staats retired from the position in early March. The former deputy comptroller general, Robert Keller, had retired and later died, and Staats named as acting comptroller general the general counsel, Milton J. Socolar. Later, in accordance with a new law, the president nominated Charles A. Bowsher to be the next comptroller general.[4] Bowsher was unanimously endorsed in the Senate and assumed office on October 1, 1981. He was the second professional accountant to be named comptroller general. He was a senior partner of one of the largest of the "big eight" firms in public accounting, Arthur Andersen and Company, for which he had been principal Washington representative for many years. He had had experience with a number of federal agencies and for about four years had served as assistant secretary of the navy (for financial management). For reasons discussed earlier, there is no need or reason for a comptroller to move as fast or as far as a director of the budget. To the end of President Reagan's first year—which means Bowsher's fourth month—GAO continued to issue reports, many of which were summarized in metropolitan newspapers. It apparently had little if any impress upon the Reagan budget proposals or upon congressional consideration of them. The directions it may move in the future remain problematical.

4. General Accounting Office Act, Public Law 96-226, April 3, 1980.

The Golden Days

We shall never forget thee
Thou golden college days.

TOM LEHRER,
"Bright College Days"

It seems to be a common human foible to look back at certain periods of our lives with particular sentiment and cheer as the days of keen happiness and association. Thus do many of us consecrate our childhood, our adolescence, our college days, our first days of marriage or parenthood, or even our lives that began at forty. (Notwithstanding that those days may have been filled with gloom and despair.) The same is true of organizations and our associations with them. We tend, I think, to glorify organizations when we were associated with them at their beginning or at their reincarnations or when our own work was most important in them, and we have a tendency to believe that the organizations have been going downhill ever since.

So it is, I think, with the GAO and the BoB/OMB—and probably with a great many other private and public agencies. The dating of the golden age depends heavily upon *who* was there *when*. Among the senior GAO staff and many of the alumni, the finest days were in the postwar era when true auditing was imposed on the executive branch. Some of them, particularly those with field experience, associate the gold with the auditing of defense contracts, and for many of them the Holifield hearings and their aftermath in 1965–1966 were the beginning of the decline of GAO. It is quite probable that some who worked in GAO in the 1920s and 1930s would look back upon the McCarl era of voucher-checking as golden for GAO. But none of those veterans—few are still alive—spoke to me in these terms.

There is a good deal of disagreement today about the golden age in the BoB/OMB. Many of the old-timers associate it with the Roosevelt-Truman years after 1939, when its Division of Administrative Management not only developed structures and strategies for war and postwar agencies but also served as the eyes and ears of the president and his small staff on policy and managerial problems. It was capable, creative, analytical, nonpolitical, and justifiably proud. It may well have been, for its time, the finest staff of management analysts ever assembled, and its reputation far surpassed that of the budget examiners of the time.

For some, the Eisenhower days were golden. It was an orderly, structured, regularized administration, whose new programs were relatively few and well

worked out through BoB machinery. The renewed stress on the goal of economy no doubt appealed to those budget examiners who shared such sympa-
thies. In sharp contrast were those who sought an active domestic role for the
government and particularly those many with Keynesian or post-Keynesian
economic training. For them, the Eisenhower years had been bleak, but the
early and mid-1960s, the era of the New Frontier, the Great Society, PPBS,
and creative federalism, were surely golden. But that era ended with a series
of thuds—the Vietnam War, economic stagflation, the Domestic Council, a
rebellious Congress, and finally Watergate.

There were those in OMB during the Ford and Carter administrations who
assert with confidence that the "golden years" idea is a myth, that the agency
was never stronger, more influential, and more capable than it was in the 1970s.
And many in OMB today are even more confident of the same thing—and
probably with greater reason. Had they the age and the memories, they would
no doubt hold that the real golden age of the Bureau of the Budget was the
1920s, when its mission in government was economy. It was then truly the
president's general staff, since his mission was also economy. In this sense,
OMB is now enjoying a second golden age, quite comparable to the first one
fifty to sixty years ago.

Principal Officers and Basic Organizational Patterns of BoB/OMB and GAO

TABLE 4
Principal Officers, BoB/OMB and GAO, 1921–1982

		BoB/OMB		GAO	
YEAR	PRESIDENT	DIRECTOR	ASSISTANT OR DEPUTY DIRECTOR	COMPTROLLER GENERAL	ASSISTANT OR DEPUTY COMPTROLLER GENERAL
1921	Warren G. Harding	Charles G. Dawes	William T. Abbott J. C. Roop	J. Raymond McCarl	Lurtin R. Ginn
1922		Herbert L. Lord	Royall O. Kloeber		
1923	Calvin Coolidge				
1924					
1925					
1926					
1927					
1928					
1929	Herbert C. Hoover	J. Clawson Roop			
1930					
1931					Richard N. Elliott
1932					
1933	Franklin D. Roosevelt	Lewis W. Douglas	F. W. Lowery		
1934		Daniel W. Bell (acting)			
1935			John N. Edy		
1936				Richard N. Elliott (acting)	
1937			Fred Bailey (Executive Asst.)		
1938					

Year	President	Director, Bureau of the Budget	Deputy Director	Comptroller General	Assistant Comptroller General
1939		Harold D. Smith	John B. Blandford, Jr.	Fred H. Brown	
1940				Lindsay C. Warren	
1941					
1942					
1943					Frank L. Yates
1944					
1945	Harry S. Truman		Paul H. Appleby		
1946		James E. Webb			
1947					
1948					
1949		Frank Pace, Jr.	Frederick J. Lawton (acting)		
1950		Frederick J. Lawton	Elmer B. Staats		
1951					
1952					
1953	Dwight D. Eisenhower	Joseph M. Dodge	Rowland R. Hughes		Frank H. Weitzel
1954		Rowland R. Hughes	Percival F. Brundage	Frank H. Weitzel (acting)	
1955			Arnold R. Jones	Joseph Campbell	
1956		Percival F. Brundage			
1957					
1958		Maurice H. Stans	Robert E. Merriam / Roger W. Jones / Elmer B. Staats		
1959					
1960					
1961	John F. Kennedy	David E. Bell			
1962		Kermit Gordon			

| | | BoB/OMB | | GAO | |
YEAR	PRESIDENT	DIRECTOR	ASSISTANT OR DEPUTY DIRECTOR	COMPTROLLER GENERAL	ASSISTANT OR DEPUTY COMPTROLLER GENERAL
1963	Lyndon B. Johnson				
1964					
1965		Charles L. Schultze		Frank H. Weitzel (acting)	vacant
1966			Phillip S. Hughes	Elmer B. Staats	Frank H. Weitzel
1967					
1968		Charles J. Zwick			
1969	Richard M. Nixon	Robert P. Mayo			Robert F. Keller
1970		George P. Shultz	James R. Schlesinger (acting) Caspar W. Weinberger		
1971					
1972		Caspar W. Weinberger			
1973		Roy L. Ash	Frank C. Carlucci		
1974	Gerald R. Ford		Frederic V. Malek		
1975		James T. Lynn	Paul H. O'Neill		
1976					
1977	James E. Carter	Thomas B. Lance James T. McIntyre (acting)	James T. McIntyre		
1978		James T. McIntyre	John P. White		
1979					
1980					Milton J. Socolar* (acting)
1981	Ronald W. Reagan	David A. Stockman	Edwin L. Harper	Charles A. Bowsher	
1982					

*Socolar acted as comptroller general for the months between Staats's departure and Bowsher's arrival and then returned to the post of acting deputy comptroller general.

TABLE 5
Basic Organizational Patterns of BoB/OMB and GAO at Different Periods[a]

	BoB (1951)	GAO (1970)
OFFICES	—	General Counsel Policy and Special Studies Program Planning

DIVISIONS	Administrative Management
	Estimates
	Fiscal Analysis
	Legislative Reference
	Statistical Standards
		Civil Accounting and
		  Auditing
		Defense Accounting and
		  Auditing
		International
		Claims
		Transportation

	Field Service	Field Operations
	BoB (1953)	**GAO (1972)**
OFFICES	Budget Review Legislative Reference Management and Organization Statistical Standards	General Counsel Policy Internal Review Program Planning

DIVISIONS	Military
	Resources and Civil Works
	Commerce and Finance
	Labor and Welfare
	International
		General Government
		Resources and Economic
		  Development
		Logistics and
		  Communications
		Procurement and Systems
		  Acquisition
		Manpower and Welfare
		International
		Financial and General
		  Management Studies
		Federal Personnel and
		  Compensation
		Transportation and Claims
		
		Field Operations

TABLE 5 (*continued*)

	OMB (1981)	GAO (1981)
OFFICES[b]	Budget Review (Division) Legislative Reference (Division) Information and Regulatory Affairs Management Federal Procurement Policy	General Counsel Policy Program Planning Program Analysis (Division) Institute for Program Evaluation Defense Programs Planning and Analysis Staff
DIVISIONS[c]	International Affairs National Security Health and Income Maintenance Labor, Veterans, and Education Transportation, Commerce, and Housing Justice, Treasury, and General Management Natural Resources Energy and Science	International Procurement, Logistics, and Readiness Mission Analysis and Systems Acquisition Human Resources Community and Economic Development Federal Personnel and Compensation General Government Energy and Minerals Accounting and Financial Management Claims Field Operations

a. Offices and activities common to most organizations are omitted: directors, deputies, associates, and assistants; administrative services and support; budgeting and finance, information or public affairs, congressional relations, etc. The GAO general counsel is included since he provides a particular service government-wide.
b. The first two OMB units listed here as offices, along with the Program Analysis unit listed with the GAO offices, are now called divisions. Under the other three OMB offices listed, there are a number of smaller units, some of which are also called divisions. These divisions are distinct from those listed in the following section of this chart.
c. Each pair of OMB divisions is headed by an associate director, and each associate director also has a third division referred to as Special Studies.

Selected Bibliography

Public Documents

(Sources in this section are listed chronologically under each heading.)

I. General

A. STATUTES AND CASES (SEE ALSO RELEVANT HEARINGS, COMMITTEE REPORTS, FLOOR DEBATES, AND VETO MESSAGES)

Treasury Act of 1789. Public Law 1-12. September 2, 1789.
Prompt Settlement of Public Accounts Act. Public Law 14-45. March 3, 1817.
Dockery Act. Public Law 53-174. July 31, 1894.
Deficiency Act. Public Law 33-217, Sec. 3679. March 3, 1905.
Urgent Deficiencies Appropriation Act (Antideficiency Act). Public Law 34-28. February 27, 1906.
Budget and Accounting Act of 1921. Public Law 67-13. June 10, 1921.
Myers v. *United States*. 272 U.S. 52 (1926).
Humphrey's Executor v. *United States*. 295 U.S. 602 (1935).
Reorganization Act of 1939. Public Law 76-19. April 3, 1939.
George Act. Public Law 79-4. February 24, 1945.
Government Corporation Control Act of 1945. Public Law 79-248. December 6, 1945.
Reorganization Act of 1945. Public Law 79-263. December 20, 1945.
Employment Act of 1946. Public Law 79-304. February 20, 1946.
Legislative Reorganization Act of 1946. Public Law 79-601. August 2, 1946.
Federal Property and Administrative Services Act. Public Law 81-151. June 30, 1949.
National Security Act Amendments. Public Law 81-216. August 10, 1949.
Post Office Department Financial Control Act. Public Law 81-712. August 17, 1950.
Budget and Accounting Procedures Act of 1950. Public Law 81-874. September 12, 1950.
Improve Governmental Budgeting and Accounting Methods Act. Public Law 84-863. August 1, 1956.
Truth-in-Negotiations Act. Public Law 87-653. September 10, 1962.
Hewlett-Packard Co. v. *United States*. 385 F. (2d) 1013 (1967).
Legislative Reorganization Act of 1970. Public Law 91-510. October 26, 1970.
Budget and Accounting—Appointments—Offices. Public Law 93-250. March 2, 1974.
Congressional Budget and Impoundment Control Act. Public Law 93-344. July 12, 1974.
Office of Federal Procurement Policy Act. Public Law 93-400. August 30, 1974.
General Accounting Office Act of 1974. Public Law 93-604. January 2, 1975.

Inspector General Act of 1978. Public Law 95-452. October 12, 1978.
General Accounting Office Personnel Act of 1980. Public Law 96-191. February 15, 1980.
General Accounting Office Act of 1980. Public Law 96-226. April 3, 1980.
Paperwork Reduction Act of 1980. Public Law 96-511. December 11, 1980.

B. BUDGETS

U.S. Bureau of the Budget/Office of Management and Budget. *The Budget of the United States Government.* 1922–1983. Including budget appendices, budgets in brief, and special analyses.

C. EXECUTIVE ORDERS

U.S. President. Executive Order No. 3550. "The Budget—Revision of the Estimates." September 21, 1921. Presidential Executive Orders Serial Set. Ann Arbor: University Microforms.
———. Executive Order No. 3567. "Uniform Efficiency Ratings." October 24, 1921. Presidential Executive Orders Serial Set. Ann Arbor: University Microforms.
———. Executive Order No. 6166. "Organization of Executive Agencies." June 10, 1933. Presidential Executive Orders Serial Set. Ann Arbor: University Microforms.
———. Executive Order No. 8248. "Organization of the Executive Office of the President." *Federal Register*, September 12, 1939, p. 3864.
———. Executive Order No. 11541. "Prescribing the Duties of the Office of Management and Budget and the Domestic Council in the Executive Office of the President." *Federal Register*, July 2, 1970, p. 10737.
———. Executive Order No. 11821. "Inflation Impact Statements." *Federal Register*, November 29, 1974, p. 41502.
———. Executive Order No. 12044. "Improving Government Regulations." *Federal Register*, March 23, 1978, p. 12661.
———. Executive Order No. 12291. "Federal Regulation." *Federal Register*, February 17, 1981, p. 13193.

D. PRESIDENTIAL REPORTS AND MESSAGES

U.S. President. *Message of the President of the United States on Economy and Efficiency in the Government Service.* 62nd Cong., 2nd Sess., January 17, 1912.
U.S. Congress. House. Economy and Efficiency Commission. *The Need for a National Budget: Message from President of the United States Transmitting Report.* House Document 854. 62nd Cong., 2nd Sess., June 27, 1912.
U.S. President. *Message Submitting for Consideration of Congress Budget with Supporting Memoranda and Reports.* Senate Document 1113. 62nd Cong., 3rd Sess., February 26, 1913.
U.S. Congress. House. Select Committee on the Budget. *Veto Relating to a National Budget System.* House Document 805. 66th Cong., 2nd Sess., June 4, 1920.

U.S. President. *Addresses of the President and Director of the Bureau of the Budget at the Seminannual Meeting of the Business Organization of the Government.* Semiannual. June, 1921–December, 1928.

U.S. Executive Office of the President. Council of Economic Advisers. *Economic Report of the President.* Annual. 1947–1983.

E. REORGANIZATION PLANS (SEE ALSO ACCOMPANYING MESSAGES, HEARINGS AND REPORTS, AND FLOOR DEBATES)

Reorganization Plan No. 1. *Statutes at Large,* LIII, 1423–30. July 1, 1939.

Reorganization Plan No. 2 of 1970. *Statutes at Large,* LXXXIV, 2085. July 1, 1970.

Reorganization Plan No. 1 of 1977. *Statutes at Large,* XCI, 1633–35. October 20, 1977.

F. SPECIAL REPORTS AND HEARINGS

U.S. Congress. House. *Plan for a National Budget System: Submitted by Hon. Medill McCormick.* House Document 1006. 65th Cong., 2nd Sess., 1918.

U.S. Congress. House. Select Committee on the Budget. *Hearings on the Establishment of a National Budget System.* 66th Cong., 1st Sess., September–October, 1919.

U.S. President. President's Committee on Administrative Management. *Report of the Committee with Studies of Administrative Management in the Federal Government.* January, 1937.

U.S. Congress. Commission on Organization of the Executive Branch of the Government. *Report on Budgeting and Accounting.* 81st Cong., 1st Sess., February, 1949.

———. *Concluding Report.* 81st Cong., 1st Sess., May, 1949.

U.S. Congress. Commission on Organization of the Executive Branch of Government, 1953–1955. *Budget and Accounting.* 83rd Cong., 1st Sess., June, 1954.

———. *Final Report to the Congress.* 84th Cong., 1st Sess., May 1955.

U.S. Congress. House. Committee on Government Operations. *The General Accounting Office: A Study of Its Organization and Administration with Recommendations for Increasing Its Effectiveness.* House Report 2264. 84th Cong., 2nd. Sess., November, 1956.

U.S. General Services Administration. *Pension Building.* Historical Studies Series No. 1. January, 1964.

U.S. President. President's Commission on Budget Concepts. *Report.* October, 1967.

U.S. Congress. Senate. Committee on Government Operations. *Capability of GAO to Analyze and Audit Defense Expenditures: Hearings.* 91st Cong., 1st Sess., September, 1969.

U.S. General Services Administration. *Executive Office Building.* Historical Studies Series No. 3. Revised. September, 1970.

U.S. Congress. Senate. Committee on Government Operations. *Financial Manage-*

ment in the Federal Government. Senate Report 50. 2 vols. 92nd Cong., 1st Sess., December, 1971.

U.S. Office of Management and Budget. *Papers Relating to the President's Departmental Reorganization Program: A Reference Compilation* (Ash Report). Revised. February, 1972.

U.S. Commission on Government Procurement. *Report.* 4 vols. December, 1972.

U.S. Congress. House. Committee on Government Operations. Subcommittee on Legislative and Military Operations. *Hearings Concerning Confirmation of the Director and Deputy Director, Office of Management and Budget.* 93rd Cong., 1st Sess., March, 1973.

U.S. Congress. Senate. Committee on Government Operations. Ad hoc Subcommittee on Federal Procurement. *Establishing Office of Federal Procurement Policy: Hearing on S. 2198 and S. 2510.* 93rd Cong., 1st Sess., October–November, 1973.

U.S. Office of Management and Budget. *Actions on Recommendations of the President's Advisory Council on Management Improvement: Communication from the Deputy Director.* May, 1975.

U.S. Congress. Senate. Committee on Government Operations. *GAO Legislation: Hearings.* 94th Cong., 1st Sess., October, 1975.

U.S. Congress. Senate. Commission on the Operation of the Senate. *Congressional Support Agencies: A Staff Study.* Ernest S. Griffith, 94th Cong., 2nd Sess., 1976.

———. Committee on Government Operations. *The Accounting Establishment: A Staff Study.* 94th Cong., 2nd Sess., December, 1976.

U.S. Commission on Federal Paperwork. *Final Summary Report.* October, 1977.

U.S. Privacy Protection Study Commission. *Personal Privacy in an Information Society.* July, 1977.

U.S. Congress. House. Select Committee on Congressional Operations. *General Accounting Office Services to Congress: An Assessment.* House Report 1317. 95th Cong., 2nd Sess., June, 1978.

G. REFERENCE WORKS

U.S. Congress. *Congressional Directory.* 1915–1983.

U.S. General Services Administration. Office of the Federal Register. *U.S. Government Manual (U.S. Government Organization Manual).* 1935–1983.

———. *Federal Register.* 1936–1983.

II. BoB/OMB

A. ANNUAL REPORTS

U.S. Department of Treasury. *Annual Report of the Secretary of the Treasury on the State of the Finances.* For the Fiscal Years Ended June 30, 1908–June 30, 1921.

U.S. Bureau of the Budget. *Annual Report of the Director of the Bureau of the Budget.* 1922–1931.

B. REGULATIONS ON BUDGET ESTIMATES

U.S. Bureau of the Budget. *Circular A-11: Preparation and Submission of Budget Estimates.* Various years, 1921–1983.

C. SELF-STUDIES AND OTHER REPORTS ON INTERNAL ORGANIZATION

U.S. Bureau of the Budget. Committee on Records of War Administration. "The United States at War." 1946.
U.S. Bureau of the Budget. "Review of the Organization of the Bureau of the Budget." January, 1952.
————. "A Self Survey of the Bureau of the Budget: Report to the Director by a Staff Study Group." May, 1959.
U.S. President. "Outside 1966 Task Force on Government Organization Report" (Heineman Report). June, 1967.
U.S. Bureau of the Budget. "The Work of the Steering Group on Evaluation of the Bureau of the Budget." 3 vols. July , 1967.
U.S. Office of Management and Budget. "Task Force Analysis of Bureau Workload." March, 1973.
————. "Office Memorandum No. 73–39: Plans for Reorganization." March, 1973.
————. "OMB Reorganization." May, 1973.
————. "Framework for the Future: A Study of the Organization of the Office of Management and Budget." June, 1979.

III. GAO

A. ANNUAL REPORTS

U.S. Comptroller General. *Annual Reports of the Comptroller General of the United States.* 1922–1982.

B. OTHER REPORTS AND AUDITS

U.S. General Accounting Office. *Report by the Comptroller General of the United States: Review of Selected Activities of the Bureau of the Budget, Executive Office of the President.* June, 1961.
————. *Review of the Impoundment Control Act of 1974 After Two Years: Report to the Congress by the Comptroller General of the United States.* 1977.

C. COMPTROLLER GENERAL'S DECISIONS

U.S. Comptroller General. *Decisions of the Comptroller General of the United States.* Annual. Volumes 1–60 (July 1, 1921–November 30, 1981).

D. MANUALS AND OTHER ISSUANCES

U.S. General Accounting Office. *Comprehensive Audit Manual.* 1952, with periodic
   revisions since.
———. *Report Manual.* 1958, with periodic revisions since.
GAO Review. Quarterly. 1966–1982. See especially the Summer, 1971, issue, which
   is devoted to the fiftieth anniversary of the GAO.
U.S. General Accounting Office. *Improving Management for More Effective Govern-
   ment.* 1971.
———. *Standards for Audit of Governmental Organizations, Programs, Activities,
   and Functions.* 2nd ed. 1974.
———. *Evaluating Governmental Performance: Changes and Challenges for GAO.*
   1975.
———. *Intergovernmental Administration and Grants Management.* Donald C.
   Stone, ed. 1977.

Books

Agger, Eugene E. *The Budget in the American Commonwealths.* Columbia Univer-
   sity Studies in History, Economics and Public Law, XXV, No. 2. New York,
   1907.
Bailey, Stephen Kemp. *Congress Makes a Law: The Story Behind the Employment
   Act of 1946.* New York, 1964.
Benveniste, Guy. *The Politics of Expertise.* San Francisco, 1977.
Berman, Larry. *The Office of Management and Budget and the Presidency,
   1921–1979.* Princeton, 1979.
Bolles, Albert S. *The Financial History of the United States, from 1861 to 1885.*
   New York, 1886.
Broesamle, John J. *William Gibbs McAdoo: A Passion for Change, 1863–1917.* Port
   Washington, N.Y., 1973.
Brown, Richard E. *The GAO: Untapped Source of Congressional Power.* Knoxville,
   1970.
Browne, Vincent J. *The Control of the Public Budget.* Washington, D.C., 1949.
Brownlow, Louis. *The President and the Presidency.* Chicago, 1949.
———. *A Passion for Anonymity.* Chicago, 1958. Vol. II of *The Autobiography of
   Louis Brownlow.* 2 vols.
Brundage, Percival Flack. *The Bureau of the Budget.* New York, 1970.
Bullock, Charles J. *The Finances of the United States from 1775–1789, with Espe-
   cial Reference to the Budget.* Madison, 1895.
Burkhead, Jesse. *Government Budgeting.* New York, 1956.
Carey, John L. *The Rise of the Accounting Profession: From Technician to Profes-
   sional.* 2 vols. New York, 1969.
Cleveland, Frederick A., and Arthur Eugene Buck. *The Budget and Responsible
   Government.* New York, 1920.

Collins, Charles Wallace. *The National Budget System and American Finance.* New York, 1917.

Congressional Quarterly, Inc. *Budgeting for America: The Politics and Process of Federal Spending.* Washington, D.C., 1982.

Cooper, William W., and Yaji Ijiri, eds. *Eric Louis Kohler—Accounting's Man of Principles.* Reston, Va., 1978.

Cronin, Thomas E., and Sanford B. Greenberg, eds. *The Presidential Advisory System.* New York, 1969.

Dawes, Charles G. *The First Year of the Budget of the United States.* New York, 1923.

Diamond, Robert A., ed. *Origins and Development of Congress.* Washington, D.C., Press, 1976.

Dodd, Lawrence C., and Bruce I. Oppenheimer, eds. *Congress Reconsidered.* New York, 1977.

Emmerich, Herbert. *Federal Organization and Administrative Management.* University, Ala., 1971.

Fesler, James W. *Area and Administration.* University, Ala., 1949.

————. *Public Administration: Theory and Practice.* Englewood Cliffs, N.J., 1980.

Fisher, Louis. *Presidential Spending Power.* Princeton, 1975.

Fitzpatrick, Edward A. *Budget Making in a Democracy: A New View of the Budget.* New York, 1918.

Griffith, Ernest S. *The American Presidency: The Dilemmas of Shared Power and Divided Government.* New York, 1976.

Harris, Joseph P. *Congressional Control of Administration.* Washington, D.C., 1964.

Heclo, Hugh, and Lester M. Salamon, eds. *The Illusion of Presidential Government.* Boulder, 1981.

Hobbs, Edward H. *Behind the President: A Study of Executive Office Agencies.* Washington, D.C., 1954.

Karl, Barry Dean. *Executive Reorganization and Reform in the New Deal: The Genesis of Administrative Management, 1900–1939.* Cambridge, Mass., 1963.

Kaufman, Richard F. *The War Profiteers.* New York, 1970.

Kloman, Erasmus H. *Cases in Accountability: The Work of the GAO.* Boulder, 1979.

Langeluttig, Albert. *The Department of Justice in the United States.* Baltimore, 1927.

Leloup, Lance T. *Budgetary Politics.* Brunswick, Ohio, 1977.

Maclay, Edgar S., ed. *Journal of William Maclay, United States Senator from Pennsylvania: 1789–1791.* New York, 1890.

Mansfield, Harvey C. *The Comptroller General: A Study in the Law and Practice of Financial Administration.* New Haven, 1939.

————, ed. *Congress Against the President.* New York, 1975.

Marx, Fritz Morstein. *The President and His Staff Services.* Chicago, 1947.

Moran, Phillip, ed. *Warren G. Harding.* Dobbs Ferry, N.Y., 1970.

Mosher, Frederick C. *The GAO: The Quest for Accountability in American Government.* Boulder, 1979.

————. *Program Budgeting: Theory and Practice.* Chicago, 1954.

———, ed. *Basic Documents of American Public Administration, 1776–1950.* New York, 1976.

Mosher, Frederick C., et al. *Watergate: Implications for Responsible Government.* New York, 1974.

Murray, Robert K. *The Harding Era: Warren G. Harding and his Administration.* Minneapolis, 1969.

Myers, William Starr, and Walter H. Newton. *The Hoover Administration: A Documented Narrative.* New York, 1936.

Nash, Bradley D. *Staffing the Presidency.* Washington, D.C., 1952.

Nathan, Richard P. *The Plot that Failed: Nixon and the Administrative Presidency.* New York, 1975.

Naylor, Estill E. *Federal Government Accounting.* Washington, D.C., 1943.

———. *The Federal Budget System in Operation.* Washington, D.C., 1941.

Neustadt, Richard E. *Presidential Power: The Politics of Leadership from FDR to Carter.* Rev. ed. New York, 1980.

Normanton, E. L. *The Accountability and Audit of Governments.* New York, 1966.

Pfiffner, James P. *The President, the Budget, and Congress: Impoundment and the 1974 Budget Act.* Boulder, 1979.

Pois, Joseph. *Watchdog on the Potomac: A Study of the Comptroller General of the United States.* Washington, D.C., 1979.

Polenberg, Richard. *Reorganizing Roosevelt's Government 1936–1939.* Cambridge, Mass., 1966.

Rossiter, Clinton, ed. *The Federalist Papers.* New York, 1961.

Schick, Allen. *Congress and Money: Budgeting, Spending and Taxing.* Washington, D.C., 1980.

———, ed. *Perspectives on Budgeting.* Washington, D.C., 1980.

Schlesinger, Arthur M., Jr. *The Coming of the New Deal.* Boston, 1959.

———. *The Politics of Upheaval.* Boston, 1960.

Schnitzer, Paul A. *Government Contract Bidding.* Washington, D.C., 1976.

Schultze, Charles L., et al. *Setting National Priorities: The 1971 Budget.* Washington, D.C., Brookings Institution, 1970. See also succeeding years to 1982.

Seckler-Hudson, Catheryn, ed. *Budgeting: An Instrument of Planning and Management.* 6 vols. Washington, D.C., 1944–45.

Seidman, Harold. *Politics, Position, and Power: The Dynamics of Federal Organization.* 3rd ed. New York, 1979.

Seligman, Lester G., and Elmer E. Cornwell, Jr., eds. *New Deal Mosaic: Roosevelt Confers with His National Emergency Council.* Eugene, 1965.

Selko, Daniel T. *The Federal Financial System.* Washington, D.C., 1940.

Sherwood, Robert E. *Roosevelt and Hopkins: An Intimate History.* New York, 1948.

Smith, Bruce L. R., ed. *The New Political Economy: Public Use of the Private Sector.* New York, 1975.

———, and D. C. Hague, eds. *The Dilemma of Accountability in Modern Government: Independence Versus Control.* New York, 1971.

Smith, Bruce L. R., and James D. Carroll, eds. *Improving the Accountability and Performance of Government.* Washington, D.C., 1982.

Smith, Darrell H. *The General Accounting Office: Its History, Activities, and Organization.* Baltimore, 1927.

Smith, Harold D. *The Management of Your Government.* New York, 1945.
Somers, Herman. *Presidential Agency: OWMR—The Office of War Mobilization and Reconversion.* 1950; rpr. New York, 1969.
Sperry, Roger L., *et al. GAO 1966–1981: An Administrative History.* Washington, D.C., 1981.
Stein, Herbert. *The Fiscal Revolution in America.* Chicago, 1969.
Stourm, René. *The Budget.* New York, 1917.
Sundquist, James L. *The Decline and Resurgence of Congress.* Washington, D.C., 1981.
Timmons, Bascom N. *Portrait of an American: Charles G. Dawes.* New York, 1953.
Waldo, Dwight. *The Enterprise of Public Administration: A Summary View.* Novato, Calif., 1980.
White, Leonard D. *The Federalists: A Study in Administrative History.* New York, 1948.
———. *The Jacksonians, 1829–1861: A Study in Administrative History.* New York, 1954.
———. *The Jeffersonians, 1801–1829: A Study in Administrative History.* New York, 1951.
———. *The Republican Era, 1869–1901: A Study in Administrative History.* New York, 1958.
Wildavsky, Aaron. *The Politics of the Budgetary Process.* 3rd ed. Boston, 1979.
Willoughby, William F. *The Problem of a National Budget.* New York, 1918.
———. *The Legal System and Functions of the General Accounting Office of the National Government.* Baltimore, 1927.
———. *The National Budget System, with Suggestions for Its Improvement.* Baltimore, 1927.
Wilmerding, Lucius. *The Spending Power.* New Haven, 1943.

Articles and Other Materials

Alexander, Charles Beatty. "The Need for a National Budget System." *Annals of the American Academy of Political and Social Science*, LXXVIII (July, 1918), 144–48.
American Political Science Association. "The Reagan Budget: Redistribution of Power and Responsibilities." *PS*, XIV (Fall, 1981). A symposium of articles by several authors.
Appleby, Paul. "Harold D. Smith—Public Administrator." *Public Administration Review*, VII, (Spring, 1947), 77–81.
———. *The Reminiscences of Paul H. Appleby.* New York *Times* Oral History Program, Columbia University Collection, Part 1. New York, 1972.
———. "The Role of the Budget Division." *Public Administration Review*, XVII (Summer, 1957), 156–58.
Barth, James R. "The Reagan Program for Economic Recovery: A Historical Per-

spective." *Federal Reserve Bank of Atlanta Monthly Review*, LXVI (October, 1981), 14–25.

Berman, Lawrence S. "The Evolution of a Presidential Staff Agency: Variations in How the Bureau of the Budget–Office of Management and Budget Has Responded to Presidential Needs." Ph.D. dissertation, University of Michigan, 1977.

———. "The Office of Management and Budget That Almost Wasn't." *Political Science Quarterly*, XCII (Summer, 1977), 281–303.

———. "OMB and the Hazards of Presidential Staff Work." *Public Administration Review*, XXXVIII (November–December, 1978), 520–24.

Bernstein, Marver H. "The Presidency and Management Improvement." *Journal of Law and Contemporary Problems*, XXXV (Summer, 1970), 505–18.

Bombardier, Gary. "The Managerial Function of OMB: Intergovernmental Relations as a Test Case." *Public Policy*, XXIII (Summer, 1975), 317–54.

Bonafede, Dom. "The Making of the President's Budget: Politics and Influence in a New Manner." *National Journal*, III (1971), 151–65.

———. "White House Report/White House Reorganization—Separating Smoke from Substance." *National Journal*, IX (1977), 1307–11.

———. "Lobbying Brings Last-Minute Victory for Nixon's Reorganization Plan." *National Journal*, II (1970), 1018–19.

———, and Jonathan Coffin. "Nixon, in Reorganization Plan, Seeks Tighter Rein on Bureaucracy." *National Journal*, II (1970), 620–26.

Brownlow, Louis, ed. "The Executive Office of the President: A Symposium." *Public Administration Review*, I (Winter, 1941), 101–40.

Brownlow, Louis. "Reconversion of the Federal Administrative Machinery from War to Peace." *Public Administration Review*, IV (Autumn, 1944), 309–26.

Campbell, Joseph. "Recruiting, Training, and Professional Development in the General Accounting Office." *USA GAO Staff Bulletin*, II (August, 1957), 33.

Cannon, Joseph G. "The National Budget." *Harper's*, CXXXIX (October, 1919), 617–28.

Carey, William D. "Presidential Staffing in the Sixties and Seventies." *Public Administration Review*, XXIX (September–October, 1969), 450–58.

———. "Reorganization Plan No. 2." *Public Administration Review*, XXX (November–December, 1970), 631–34.

———. "Roles of the Bureau of the Budget." *Science*, CLVI (April 14, 1967), 206–208.

———. "Control and Supervision of Field Offices." *Public Administration Review*, VI (Winter, 1946), 20–24.

———. "Leadership and Management in the Federal Government." *Public Administration Review*, XXXIII (September–October, 1973), 456–59.

Clark, Timothy B. "OMB to Keep Its Regulatory Powers in Reserve in Case Agencies Lag." *National Journal*, XIII (1981), 424–29.

Cleveland, Frederick A. "Evolution of the Budget Idea in the United States." *Annals of the American Academy of Political and Social Science*, LXII (November, 1915), 15–35.

Colm, Gerhard. "The Executive Office and Fiscal Economic Policy." *Journal of Law and Contemporary Problems*, XXI (Autumn, 1956), 710–24.

Cohn, Samuel M. "Economic Policy and the Federal Budget." *Federal Accountant*, IX (September, 1959), 19–30.

Corey, Herbert. "A Conscience in Black." *Collier's*, November 29, 1924, pp. 26, 42.

Crecine, John P., and Phillip Bromley. "Budget Development in OMB: Aggregate Influences of the Problem and Information Environment." *Journal of Politics*, XLII (November, 1980), 1031–64.

Egger, Rowland. "The United States Bureau of the Budget." *Parliamentary Affairs*, (Winter, 1949), 39–54.

Finley, James J. "The 1974 Congressional Initiative in Budget-Making." *Public Administration Review*, XXXV (May–June, 1975), 270–78.

Fisher, Louis. "Congress, the Executive, and the Budget." *Annals of the American Academy of Political and Social Science*, CDXI (January, 1974), 102–13.

Ford, Henry Jones. "Budget Making and the Work of Government." *Annals of the American Academy of Political and Social Science*, LXII (November, 1915), 1–14.

Frese, Walter F. "Early History of the Joint Financial Management Improvement Program." Unpublished recollections, 1974–76.

Garfield, James A. "National Appropriations and Misappropriations." *North American Review*, CXXVIII (June, 1879), 572–87.

Gaus, John M. "The Presidency and the Hoover Commission." *American Political Science Review*, XLIII (October, 1949), 952–58.

Gilmour, R. S. "Central Legislative Clearance: A Revised Perspective." *Public Administration Review*, XXXI (March–April, 1971), 150–58.

Gladieux, Bernard L. "Management Planning in the Federal Government." *Advanced Management*, V (1940), 77–85.

———. *The Reminiscences of Bernard L. Gladieux*. New York *Times* Oral History Program, Columbia University Collection, Part 2. New York, 1972.

Gordon, George, Jr., "Office of Management and Budget Circular A-95: Perspective and Implications." *Publius*, IV (1974), 45–68.

Graham, George A. "The Presidency and the Executive Office of the President." *Journal of Politics*, XII (November, 1959), 599–621.

Greider, William. "The Education of David Stockman." *Atlantic Monthly*, CCXLVIII (December, 1981), 27–54.

Gulick, Luther. "War Organization of the Federal Government." *American Political Science Review*, XXXVIII (December, 1944), 1166–79.

Haider, Donald. "Presidential Management Initiatives: A Ford Legacy to Executive Management Improvement." *Public Administration Review*, XXXIX (May–June, 1979), 248–59.

Harris, Joseph P. "Needed Reforms in the Budget System." *Public Administration Review*, XII (Autumn, 1952), 242–50.

Havemann, Joel. "OMB's Legislative Role Is Growing More Powerful and More Political." *National Journal*, XLIII (1973), 1589–98.

Heclo, Hugh. "OMB and the Presidency: The Problem of Neutral Competence." *Public Interest*, XXXVIII (Winter, 1975), 80–98.

Ink, Dwight A. "The President as Manager." *Public Administration Review*, XXXVI (September–October, 1976), 508–15.

"J. R. McCarl Dead." New York *Times*, August 3, 1940, p. 15.

Jones, Roger W. *The Reminiscences of Roger W. Jones*. New York *Times* Oral History Program, Columbia University Collection, Part 3. New York, 1976.

————. "The Role of the Bureau of the Budget in the Federal Legislative Process." *American Bar Association Journal*, XL (November, 1954), 995–98.

Kraft, Joseph. "Washington Insight: The Remarkable Mr. Gordon and His Quiet Power Center." *Harpers*, (May, 1965), 40–50.

Kraines, Oscar. "The President Versus Congress: The Keep Commission, 1905–1909: First Comprehensive Presidential Inquiry into Administration." *Western Political Quarterly*, XXIII (March, 1970), 5–24.

Latham, Earl. "Executive Management and the Federal Field Service." *Public Administration Review*, V (Winter, 1945), 16–27.

Lewis, Frank L., and Frank G. Zarb. "Federal Program Evaluation from the OMB Perspective." *Public Administration Review*, XXXIV (July–August, 1974), 308–17.

McCarl, John R. "Government-Run Everything." *Saturday Evening Post*, October 3, 1936, pp. 8–9, 52, and October 17, 1936, pp. 8–9, 70–74.

Mansfield, Harvey C. "Reorganizing the Federal Executive Branch: The Limits of Institutionalization." *Journal of Law and Contemporary Problems*, XXXV (Summer, 1970), 461–95.

Marx, Fritz Morstein. "The Bureau of the Budget: Its Evolution and Present Role." *The American Political Science Review*, XXXIX (August and October, 1945), 653–84, 869–98.

McOmber, Dale. "An OMB Retrospective." *Public Budgeting and Finance*, I (Spring, 1981), 78–84.

MacMahon, A. W. "The Future Organizational Pattern of the Executive Branch." *American Political Science Review*, XXXVIII (December, 1944), 1179–91.

————. "Congressional Oversight of Administration: The Power of the Purse." *Political Science Quarterly*, LVIII (June–September, 1943), 407–14.

Merriam, R. E. "The Bureau of the Budget as Part of the President's Staff." *Annals of the American Academy of Political and Social Science*, CCCVII (September, 1956), 15–23.

Moe, Gustave A. "The Bureau of the Budget and Governmental Budgeting in Wartime." *National Association of Cost Accountants Bulletin*, XXV (1943), 48.

Morgan, Thomas D. "The General Accounting Office: One Hope for Congress to Regain Parity of Power With the President," *North Carolina Law Review*, LI (October, 1973), 1279–1368.

Morse, Ellsworth H., Jr. "Report of the President's Commission on Budget Concepts in Retrospect." *Public Administration Review*, XXXI (July–August, 1971), 443–50.

Mosher, Frederick C. "The Executive Budget, Empire State Style." *Public Administration Review*, XII (Spring, 1952), 73–84.

Natchez, Peter B., and Irvin C. Bupp. "Policy and Priority in the Budgetary Process." *American Political Science Review*, LXVII (September, 1973), 951–63.

Nathan, Richard P. "The Administrative Presidency." *Public Interest*, XLIV (Summer, 1976), 40–54.

National Academy of Public Administration. *A Presidency for the 1980s: A Report by a Panel of the National Academy of Public Administration*. Washington, D.C., 1980.

————. *Strengthening OMB's Role in Improving the Management of the Federal Government*. Washington, D.C., 1981.

Neustadt, Richard E. "The Presidency and Legislation: The Growth of Central Clearance." *American Political Science Review*, XLVIII (September, 1954), 641–71.

————. "The Presidency and Legislation: The Growth of Central Clearance." *American Political Science Review*, XLIX (December, 1955), 980–1021.

Niskanen, William A. "Why New Methods of Budgetary Choices? Administrative Aspects." *Public Administration Review*, XXXII (March–April, 1972), 155–61.

"The OMB Recovers Some Clout." *Business Week*, February 5, 1979, pp. 55–56.

O'Neill, Paul H. "OMB's Role in Planning and Coordinating Federal Statistics." *Statistical Reporter*, LXXVI (May, 1976), 205–209.

Pearson, Norman M. "The Budget Bureau: From Wartime Bureau to General Staff." *Public Administration Review*, III (Spring, 1943), 126–47.

————. "A General Administrative Staff to Aid the President." *Public Administration Review*, IV (Spring, 1944), 127–47.

Peters, Carol. "Reconciliation: What Happened?" *PS*, XIV (January, 1982), 732–36.

Price, Don K. "Staffing the Presidency." *American Political Science Review*, XL (December, 1946), 1154–68.

————. "General Dawes and Executive Staff Work." *Public Administration Review*, XI (Summer, 1951), 167–72.

Rappaport, P. "The Bureau of the Budget: A View from the Inside." *Journal of Accountancy*, CI (March, 1956), 31–37.

Reed, Leonard. "The Budget Game and How to Win It." *Washington Monthly*, X (January, 1979), 24–33.

Reese, John H. "The Role of the Bureau of the Budget in the Legislative Process." *Journal of Public Law*, XV (January, 1961), 63–93.

Ripley, Randall B., and J. W. Davis. "The Bureau of the Budget and Executive Branch Agencies: Notes on Their Interaction." *Journal of Politics*, XXIX (November, 1967), 749–69.

Rourke, John T. "The GAO: An Evolving Role." *Public Administration Review*, XXXVIII (September–October, 1978), 453–57.

————. "The GAO: Auditor, Analyst, Advocate." *Bureaucrat*, X (Spring, 1981), 43–49.

Samuelson, R. J. "The People Everyone Loves to Hate." *Washingtonian*, XI (November, 1975), 62–90.

Schick, Alan. "The Budget Bureau That Was: Thoughts on the Rise, Decline, and Future of a Presidential Agency." *Journal of Law and Contemporary Problems*, XXXV (Summer, 1970), 519–39.

————. "Budget Reform Legislation: Reorganizing Congressional Centers of Fiscal Power." *Harvard Journal on Legislation*, II (1974), 303–60.

————. "The Road to PPB: The Stages of Budget Reform." *Public Administration Review*, XXVI (December, 1966), 243–58.

Shipman, George A. "Current Developments in Public Administration: Bureau of the Budget and Federal Agencies." *Public Administration Review*, XXVII (September–October, 1968), 466.

Smith, Harold D. "The Budget as an Instrument of Legislative Control and Executive Management." *Public Administration Review*, IV (Summer, 1944), 181–88.
———. "The Bureau of the Budget." *Public Administration Review*, II (Winter, 1941), 106–15.
Staats, Elmer B. *The Reminiscences of Elmer B. Staats*. New York *Times* Oral History Program, Columbia University Collection, Part 3. New York, 1976.
Stans, Maurice. "The President's Budget and the Role of the BoB." *Federal Accountant*, IX (September, 1959), 5–16.
Steelman, J. R., and H. D. Kreager. "The Executive Office as Administrative Coordinator." *Journal of Law and Contemporary Problems*, XXI (Autumn, 1956), 688–709.
Stockman, David A. "The Social Pork Barrel." *Public Interest*, XXXIX (Spring, 1975), 3–30.
Wade, L. L. "The U.S. Bureau of the Budget as Agency Evaluator: Orientation to Action." *American Journal of Economics and Sociology*, XVII (January, 1968), 55–62.
Waldo, Dwight, and William Pincus. "The Statutory Obligations of the President: Executive Necessity and Administrative Burden." *Public Administration Review*, VI (Autumn, 1946), 339–47.
Wann, A. J. "Franklin D. Roosevelt and the Bureau of the Budget." *Business and Government Review*, IX (March–April, 1968), 32–41.
Weitzel, Frank H. "Lindsay Carter Warren: Comptroller General of the United States, 1940–1954." *GAO Review*, (Spring, 1977), 1–30.

Index